ENTERTAINING
— WITH —
KATIE STEWART

ENTERTAINING
— WITH —
KATIE STEWART

IN ASSOCIATION WITH
WOMAN'S JOURNAL

PAVILION

First published in 1990 by
PAVILION BOOKS LIMITED
196 Shaftesbury Avenue, London WC2H 8JL

Designed by Lisa Tai

A CIP catalogue record for this book is available
from the British Library.

ISBN 1 85145 216 8

10 9 8 7 6 5 4 3 2 1

Printed and bound in Spain
by Graficas Estella

CONTENTS

INTRODUCTION

We all want to give marvellous parties. The question is how to organize things in such a way that we can enjoy them too. There is no secret formula or perfect plan for party-giving because parties are personal, and the situation is always different, but there are sensible ways of going about things that cut out unnecessary effort and lost time. And, while recipes are always interchangeable, some suit particular occasions better than others. The trick is to pick the right ones.

For many years now I've worked as food editor on *Woman's Journal* magazine, a job that I greatly enjoy. Those of you who are readers of the magazine may recognize some of the recipes in this book (although they have been revised to make them particularly suitable for entertaining) and the colour photographs that accompany them. Preparing food for photography is no different from setting it before your friends – the aim is to make the food look so appetizing and irresistible that you really want to eat it. All the little tricks I've picked up over the years, the ideas for prettying-up and presenting dishes and how to combine the right colours and textures, I share with you here in this book. Remember that first impressions count for a lot.

I like to think I'm a practical cook, so you won't find complicated or elaborate recipes in this book. In fact, I know from experience that coming up with the right mix of dishes for a menu and getting the timing right are the parts we all find the most difficult when entertaining.

I get inspiration for party menus mainly from discussing food with friends. I would have found it much more difficult to write this book if I hadn't worked with a very talented and artistic colleague, Caroline Young. We spent many hours discussing recipes over my kitchen table and then cooking up the ideas. The result is this varied collection of dishes for you to choose from, with preparation guidelines and lots of useful hints and tips.

Whatever kind of party you are planning, I hope this book contributes to its success and that you get as much enjoyment out of using it as I have writing it.

Katie Stewart

SIMPLE STRATEGIES

The moment of decision comes when you sit down with pen and paper to plan a menu. There are a number of considerations to take into account which all narrow down your choice – like your time available for preparation, the season of the year and the sort of occasion you are thinking about. It really is worth taking time over this most important part – planning the right menu for a party is half the battle.

Don't be afraid to keep things simple – done with style, simplicity is very elegant. Food that is simply cooked and presented requires just as much skill in the preparation as more elaborate dishes, and it makes the most of first-rate ingredients: it's the kind of approach to take when there is some new delicacy available – fresh sea trout, or the new season's lamb. I like a dish that is simply cooked because you can clearly see what it is; it's comforting for guests too – no question of trying to figure out what the food is and whether they will like it or not.

Consider the season and make full use of seasonal foods, especially salad greens, vegetables and fruits – it shows you've taken some extra care. Best of all, it means that you will be buying ingredients that are at their freshest and best for flavour and quality, so you won't have to work so hard at making them taste good. Even little touches will bring your menus very much up to the minute – a few asparagus tips included in a green salad or a dessert of fresh raspberries, for instance.

Do look around for home-produced goods. We have so much to be proud of – our wonderful smoked fish, naturally produced meats, farmhouse cheeses, organic vegetables and fruits. If you have a good find it will interest guests too. And do offer the occasional traditional dish. I find homemade soups and hot old-fashioned puddings are particularly popular with men – so few people cook them any more.

On the other hand, no cook needs to feel obliged to prepare every course in a menu when there are so many good-quality ready-prepared products to buy. Getting the right balance between the amount of work required and the time you have to cope with it is very important. Consider buying in a course if it makes things easier and lets you spend time on other details.

Buying prepared foods – anything from smoked salmon to a delicious sorbet – and then presenting it in your own way will be just as much appreciated and it's a lot less hassle.

When you've considered all the possibilities and are making the final decision, remember that a menu should have a good balance. Consider your choice of dishes in relation to each other and visualize how the food will look. This will help you avoid a sequence of rich sauces, or similar colours, or textures that are all smooth, for instance. Dishes should present contrasts of colour, flavour and texture through the courses of the menu.

GETTING ON WITH THE JOB

● When there is extra cooking to be done, take a moment to organize yourself. Make lists – they are very helpful and serve as reminders; there's also a great feeling of satisfaction when you cross items off.

● Go over the recipes and party details thoroughly. Plan to spread the work over more than one day – shopping for non-perishable foods can be done in advance, leaving the purchase of perishable items and the cooking until last.

● Work out what you can cook beforehand. It's surprising how many dishes actually benefit from being made in advance, and almost every recipe has a stage up to which it can be prepared. Recipes indicate this with the symbol **P**, and give footnotes where required.

● Go over the dishes you will need for serving. There are all kinds of alternatives for dishing up food and showing it off to best advantage (see page 13).

● Sort out the refrigerator before you start, removing items that don't have to be there; refrigerator space is one thing you need a lot of – summer or winter, it makes no difference.

● Make sure you have a good supply of clear film wrap and rolls of large and small tear-off polythene bags. Food that's prepared ahead and chilled must be covered – throw-away wrappings are better than containers that need washing-up.

● Cover the surface of everything to be refrigerated with clear film or kitchen foil, or place in polythene bags – without protection, food dries out and both the texture and flavour will suffer.

● Cooking for friends can put pressure on your mixing bowls and there's nothing more frustrating than trying to mix ingredients in a bowl that's too small or, worse still, running out of them altogether. I have a spare set of large plastic mixing bowls that are easily stored and not heavy to handle.

● Allow yourself plenty of time – cooking for more people than usual takes much more <u>preparation</u> time than normal, and it's the one thing nobody ever takes into consideration.

● Find a box into which you can tip all the trimmings and rubbish – just one visit to the supermarket and your own kitchen bin will quickly overflow with just the wrappings.

● Get out ingredients, weigh them, and sort out baking dishes or tins required – this is very important when it's a new recipe. Then when you start it's a 'straight through' procedure.

● Let prepared, cooked dishes cool before chilling them in the refrigerator. You can hurry some things along by setting bowls or containers in iced water.

● Perishable foods like homemade soups, cooked meats, poultry or fish dishes, mousses and pâtés should get priority in the refrigerator. Don't leave cooked food lying around at room temperature.

● Salad greens will crisp up beautifully in the refrigerator and you can get them ready ahead. Separate and wash leaves, then shake dry to remove all water droplets. Enclose leaves in a polythene bag and tie closed – they will crisp up nicely and can be kept for 24 hours. Fresh herbs also take well to this treatment – chill them in a closed polythene bag and they'll keep fresh and flavoursome.

● Rubbed-in ingredients for pastry or scones are improved by chilling – the fat firms up, making the mixture easier to handle. Pastry can be made 24 hours ahead, but be sure to let it come back to room temperature again when you try to roll it out.

NEARER SERVING TIME

● Chilling masks delicate flavours, so remove foods at least 1 hour before serving – this applies equally to cold cooked meats, sweet or savoury mousses and prepared vegetable and pasta salads. Fresh fruits like strawberries and raspberries also need to be at room temperature to reach their full summery flavour.

● A cooked main dish that is cold from the refrigerator will take 20-30 minutes longer to heat up than one at room temperature. Take dishes for reheating out of the refrigerator about 1 hour beforehand and you will find it easier to judge the reheating times.

● A long, slow reheating is better than a short time at a high temperature – after all, you are only heating food through, not cooking it. The best oven temperature for reheating is 150°C (300°F or gas no. 2).

● Starting from room temperature, an average-sized casserole will take 40-60 minutes to become bubbling hot; if you stir the contents occasionally it will speed things up. More closely packed dishes like lasagne will take about 1½ hours.

● Reheating time will also depend on the size of the dish and the number of dishes in the oven at one time. Several dishes absorb a lot of oven heat and will take longer than a single dish; deep dishes take longer to heat through than shallow ones. Always extend the heating time rather than raise the oven temperature.

● Check heated dishes by testing them in the centre – a knife tip or spoon pushed into the middle should feel hot. Bubbling around the edges can be deceptive; the centre is always the last part to heat through.

● Cover dishes that are to be reheated (or kept hot), using the container lid or kitchen foil, to prevent sauces drying out – unless, of course, the recipe specifies otherwise, such as dishes with a crisp crumb or pastry topping.

● Once dishes are hot, serve them as soon as possible. If you have to keep them warm, reduce the oven temperature to very low.

● A double boiler, that is a saucepan which holds simmering water with a second pan fitting snugly on top, is useful for keeping sauces hot. Sometimes I just set a smaller pan or bowl with its contents in a large pan of hot water – off the heat.

● Don't get caught out with cold serving plates for hot foods. If there is no oven space left to warm them, plunge the whole lot into a washing-up bowl of piping hot, clean water. It takes only a moment to dry them.

Looking Good

Presenting food in a party mood is something that anyone can do. It certainly doesn't involve any complicated culinary skills, nor should it take up too much time since these days food presentation has more to do with the shape, colour and style of the ingredients you choose in the first place than the garnishes you might add when the dish is finished.

Simple things can add tremendous style – like the way an ingredient is cut. For example, it's fashionable to leave new young vegetables in their natural state – whole if they are small, or barely trimmed: leave short green stalks on carrots and new potatoes with their skins on, for instance. On the other hand, cutting vegetables in different ways – on the slant, in slices or sprigs – makes them interesting. Clever cutting techniques also apply to fruits as it offers the chance to show off their wonderful colours – kiwi fruits cut in sticks (instead of slices) or slices cut across a star fruit. A strawberry sliced (but not right through) then fanned out makes a pretty garnish, as do the seeds scooped from inside a passion fruit and pomegranate seeds shaken from their storage containers – crunchy and bright red.

Leaves can give a lift to foods. Herbs are useful for this (see page 41): a single spray of fresh coriander leaves on a plate is more unusual than parsley sprigs. Larger strawberry or blackcurrant leaves arranged beneath fruits or cheese add a cool touch. There is also a vogue for using whole flowers or flower petals as decoration – purple chive flowers, red or yellow nasturtiums or golden petals of marigolds are pretty. Sometimes guests find flower heads daunting, but the petals are nearly always acceptable.

Subtle changes of the same coloured ingredients are often more striking than direct contrasts. Try mixing the various greens of different salad varieties. Or use fruits of coordinating colours in fruit salads – a red, yellow or green fruit mixture, for instance. Equally, grouping colours of ingredients can have more impact than mixing them up. The roasted pepper salad (page 96) is a good example: the vibrant red and yellow colours are much stronger when grouped down either side of the serving plate – mix them up, and the impact is lost. Large platters are a better choice for this kind of idea than deep bowls because you have more room to set out the arrangement just the way you want it.

A sprinkling of exactly the right garnish is an excellent way of dressing up a simple dish. Plain food looks particularly good when sprinkled because this adds texture. Freshly milled pepper breaks up a pale mayonnaise topping; toasted sesame seeds look good on white cauliflower sprigs; a dusting of paprika or chopped chives on a cucumber mousse provide the right contrast. For desserts consider dusting icing sugar over sweet filo pastries, crushing amaretti or macaroons and sprinkling the crumbs on a whipped cream topping, or dusting cocoa powder on a white chocolate mousse. If the plate used for serving is plain coloured, sometimes letting the 'sprinkle' fall on the plate too is effective – it breaks up the plain surface.

Don't put decoration on food that you can't eat – it only has to be picked off again. And don't decorate too generously before considering the other dishes to be served, particularly if the spread is for a buffet – some dishes might be best left plain.

CONSIDERING THE SERVING PLATES

Serving plates are important, they make all the difference to the way food looks. Generous, large platters – like the old-fashioned ashets or modern french white porcelain – make it easier to arrange food attractively and are more convenient for guests to help themselves. Space rather than depth is the key to setting out food nicely.

Heavily patterned serving plates tend to draw the eye away from the food, and recipes that have a variety of colourful ingredients do stand out better on plain plates. Absolutely plain white china has been popular with the nouvelle cuisine style of cooking because the presentation tends to be so elaborate. Such white dishes are not essential: muted shades that are plain or with faded patterns provide good backgrounds too.

Consider big plates for serving a selection of hot cooked vegetables instead of putting them in separate bowls – vegetables look extremely pretty arranged to show off their colours and shapes. Most of the pasta, bean and vegetable salads in this book will look infinitely better arranged on plates in preference to deep bowls – the colourful ingredients have much more impact. Fashionable platters of fresh prepared fruits, often with fromage

frais for dipping, or platters of mixed smoked fish for a first course, all rely on roomy plates. You can't have enough of them – mine are never out of circulation.

Plates provide a frame for food. Setting a plate on a plate is a restaurant trick that works – underplates (as they are called) make dishes of food look more important. Bear this in mind and remember that small dishes like ramekins, soup or dessert bowls and stemmed glasses look much smarter when served with a plate underneath – it also gives guests somewhere to rest the spoon or fork. Have you noticed that restaurants tend to serve desserts on a 'plate' rather than individual bowls or glasses – it's a good idea. Fruit compotes, sorbets and slices of tart or gâteau look elegant on dessert plates where there is also room for a sauce or garnish.

Trays of a good size are indispensable and come in for a multitude of uses. I like the modern painted tin trays, in rounds or squares and in plain colours – cream, navy blue or black are very complementary to food. Use them for cocktail snippets, teatime sandwiches, bread selections and even dessert cakes.

Improvise whenever you have to – chopping boards or pizza trays can be covered with foil and used as platters and baskets for bread and small coffee cups with saucers can also make attractive serving dishes for chocolate mousse, for instance.

ON TABLE COVERINGS

For inspiration, nothing beats taking a good look at the table settings in china and glass departments of big stores – the designers are very clever and you can often pick up good ideas. I think the choice of a table covering is even more important than the cutlery and glasses. The tablecloth will be the most dominating colour that you are adding; it covers a large area and it will provide the background for everything else.

Tablecloths that are plain-coloured show up table setting and the dishes of food better than patterned coverings. Strong colours like navy, mustard yellow or deep rose are all very flattering. Take your cue from the wallpaper or curtains in your rooms or from your china and choose a shade that ties in attractively. White damask is very formal – I like to break the severity of it by putting an open stitched Victorian tablecloth over the top and letting the corners drop at the sides. White on white is very elegant.

A smaller tablecloth laid on top of a larger one is an attractive idea – something plain underneath that drops to the floor (like a skirt) with a coordinated patterned cloth that just covers the table top and drops partly down the sides. Paisley designs are pretty; the pattern is so small they give the effect of a dense colour. Some have navy backgrounds and others terracotta and it's lovely to mix them. Try combining stripes with plain, spots with checks – anything you like. The side of the top cloth can be drawn up in flounces and fixed with a ribbon bow if you like.

A buffet table looks imposing if the covering cloth drops to the ground. Compromise with sheets for the skirt underneath and put a single colour or simple patterned cloth over the top. If the occasion demands it, there are a lot of pretty things you can do with yards of inexpensive ribbon in swathes and a staple gun.

A thin blanket of felt under any tablecloth will protect the surface of the table from heat and it deadens the 'clunk' of dishes

too. A thin plastic undercovering can save a valuable wood surface from taking water marks from spilt wine.

Don't underestimate the charm of a beautiful polished table, if you have a good one, show it off and use place mats instead.

FLOWER POWER

Flowers need to be arranged carefully but without trying too hard. Like food, the simpler the better is how I feel about them. Expensive arrangements are by no means the best.

One colour, or at the most two shades, in a single vase has the most impact – all white tulips, pink roses or blue irises, for instance, will stand out better than mixed colours especially when they are in big bunches. I don't like 'arranged' flowers. Flowers are pretty just as they are – bunches set naturally in vases have an elegant simplicity about them.

Plain vases of clear glass are my preference because I like to see the flower stalks. Vases of different heights, tall and short, make pretty patterns especially if the flowers are grouped together in one area – on a side table or dresser. Or set a single bunch in front of a mirror, over a mantelpiece – it extends them by reflection.

Wild flower arrangements are more unusual and are becoming fashionable. No endangered species, of course, just simple country flowers picked from the cabbage patch or along the hedgerow. With wild flowers, the more you mix them the prettier they are since the shades are much more subtle than those of cultivated flowers.

On the whole I don't like flowers on the dining or buffet table because they compete with the food. If you do put flowers on the table, make sure the arrangements are low. Potted plants are an alternative choice for a dinner party table – small ones are about the right height. Bunches of herbs are nice too and smell lovely when you brush the leaves. Choose herbs that don't wilt too quickly – good ones are sage, mint or thyme. Parsley is pretty especially when the flower heads have gone to seed.

Some dried flower arrangements are ravishingly pretty but very expensive – I wish I was clever enough to do them myself. Instead, you could have a delicious time looking through the selection of individually dried flowers in a good shop. Avoid 'ready mixed' bunches and select colour and flower heads that suit your own scheme, then group them together. Several bunches in a big bowl (rather than a vase) will look stunning on a side table.

An alternative to flowers could be a centrepiece of fruits – polished apples on leaves, big bunches of grapes or an exotic fruit such as lychees – with nuts, that could be eaten with the cheese.

BRUNCHES

Hot sugared grapefruit

Spiced peaches with blueberries

Mixed red fruits in syrup

Winter fruit compote

Golden granola

.

Scrambled eggs in brioche

Baked eggs in cheese tartlets

Omelette Arnold Bennett

Smoked haddock kedgeree

Grated potato cake with oven-fried bacon

Cold meats with bubble and squeak

Prawn and rice jambalaya

Fresh salmon cakes with lemon

Gruyère and spinach crêpes

Blinis with smoked salmon

Chicory and apple salad

.

Bran muffins

Fruit muffins

Traditional soda bread

Lemon bubble bread

Cinnamon streusel cake

Apricot coffee cake

BRUNCHES

Brunches are not only easy, they are a change of party pace and a great opportunity to get busy friends together. Weekends are the best time for this essentially unhurried and relaxed meal.

Numbers for brunch can vary from a few friends staying over a holiday weekend to the planned party with invited guests. The time is flexible too, although it's a good idea to aim for around 11.30 in the morning. Set the mood with the perfect mid-morning drink, Buck's Fizz, a blend of fresh orange juice and champagne – keep juice and champagne separate and serve on demand.

You can set up the table anywhere – in the dining room, the kitchen if yours is large and roomy, or some sheltered corner of the patio – but not too far away from where you're cooking, as you're likely to be carrying out hot brunch dishes, breads and coffee. Arrange a pretty table with colours that glow – rose, blue or mustard yellow – and with textures, rather than patterns, in the table coverings and napkins. Nothing dainty or too fussy – strong colours make guests feel welcome. Keep flowers simple – big bunches of daffodils or scented stocks – and put them in the kitchen too if people are likely to be in and out. Set essentials on the brunch table – butter, preserves, honey or marmalade, mills of sea salt and peppercorns, and jugs of chilled fruit juice.

Brunch foods need to appeal to mid-morning appetites, which can range from light to the substantial. Fruits are a must – fresh or lightly cooked mixtures. A platter of fresh fruits prepared for eating straight, with knife, fork or spoon, and in an attractive selection, can be set directly on the table as a centrepiece for everyone to help themselves. Deeply coloured, fresh-tasting mixtures of red fruits in syrup or subtle dried fruits in a compote are perfect for serving with thick Greek-style yogurt or your own homemade granola which is deliciously crunchy. In winter offer grilled grapefruits – the warmth accentuates the fruit flavour. Let guests help themselves to these bright beginnings from a sideboard. Have fruit mixtures and yogurt in glass bowls; use wooden bowls for muesli or granola – wood has a nice feel about it. Add tall jugs of chilled milk – there should be no cartons or containers in sight. Take people's diet considerations into account, and offer a choice of semi-skimmed milk, low-fat yogurt and sugar substitutes. Set up hot dishes on heated trays, or keep cooked foods warm in a very low oven on big platters. Include such

Previous pages: Omelette Arnold Bennett

irresistibles as grilled kippers and scrambled eggs as well as the more sophisticated dishes.

Offer hot breads in a napkin-lined basket to keep them warm – fresh scones, soda bread or American bran or fruit muffins. And along with jugs of piping hot coffee, pass specially made sweet breads, or coffee cakes as they are called in the States. These are simple cake or yeast mixtures prepared with fruit or a crunchy streusel topping and are best eaten warm, cut from the baking tin. They are not so complicated as you might think for most can be weighed out the night before and, if the oven is ready heated, quickly mixed and baked – then you just take them straight to the table.

Have plenty of hot coffee and brisk Indian teas, plus all the morning newspapers. Draw the party to a close with a trip to the local pub – changing the location is a subtle way to do this – then guests can feel free to leave when it suits them.

A Fresh Start

A selection of exotic fruits makes a stunning brunch platter. Prepare each fruit ready for eating, then arrange attractively on one big plate and let everybody choose for themselves. Select fully ripe fruits for the best flavour – a choice of three or five fruits is nice.

● Luscious wedges of pink-fleshed *watermelon* are juicy and refreshing – make sure the melon is well chilled. Incidentally, watermelons are sold ripe and ready for eating. A *Galia melon* in wedges or smaller *Ogen melons* cut horizontally in half will probably be more popular – serve these melons at room temperature.

● *Papaya* is ready for eating when the skin turns yellow; the inside will be soft and juicy and orange or pinky in colour. Slice the fruit in half lengthways and scoop out the seeds. Offer wedges of fresh lime for squeezing over. This fruit can be scooped from the shell with a spoon.

● *Nectarines* are from the peach family – offer whole to be sliced for eating. If *peaches*

are your choice, buy them a day ahead and keep at room temperature for 24 hours to make sure they are ripe and fragrant.

● A new variety of grapefruit called *Sweetie* is seedless and has a bright green skin. Slice off the top and bottom through to the fruit, then cut down into eight sections. Best to bite into sections – it's tangy and pleasant, but not sour.

● A ripe *pineapple* has a wonderful aroma. Prepare wedges by cutting the fruit in half (from top to base), then cut halves into wedges. Loosen the flesh from the skin and cut across into pieces that can be speared with a fork – in the same way as you would prepare a melon.

● Serve *pink grapefruit* halves

– loosen segments for eating with a spoon. No sugar will be needed.

● Exotic *mangoes* can be served in halves. Place the fruit on a board and it will roll until the stone is parallel with the surface. Cut horizontally through the fruit, keeping the blade of the knife closely in line with the stone. Turn over and repeat the cut on the other side of the stone. Serve both halves – the flesh can be eaten directly from the skin with a spoon, or slice flesh into serving bowls and cover with orange juice.

● *Sharon fruits* resemble large orange-coloured tomatoes and have a sweet delicate taste without the astringency of the traditional persimmon. Just slice in half for eating – there are no pips or seeds.

WHO'S FOR COFFEE

Coffee flavours vary from mild to strong, aromatic or bitter. Continental or dark roasted beans are always stronger, while medium or light roasts are milder. For after dinner a strong roast is usually more appropriate, but during the day it's better to go for something milder. I personally like a mixed roast which is a combination of medium and dark roasted beans – it's a compromise that works well, with a good flavour. Decaffeinated coffee beans and fresh ground coffee are also widely available; some have a better flavour than others. Experiment – it's the only way to find the ones you like.

Morning revivers: Start the day with something smooth and full bodied – a Columbian blend, Costa Rica medium roast or any Breakfast blend.

Any timers: With full, rounded flavours for mid-morning or after lunch – a Brazilian blend, Blue Mountain Jamaican or any of the delicious Dutch blend medium roast coffees.

Late nighters: Go for darker roasted beans with pronounced flavours – any Continental blend, French blend dark roast or an After dinner blend; Italian Espresso (quite strong), a Kenya blend, has a pleasant acidity as has Mysore, a mountain-grown coffee from India. Or, choose pure Moka.

Coffee has a limited shelf life, so buy little and often. Beans will keep fresher if they are stored in the freezer (but not indefinitely). Keep fresh ground coffee in an airtight container somewhere cool or at the bottom of the refrigerator.

Coffee principles

● Coffee is ground to suit the method of making. Fine ground coffee gives up its flavour more quickly than medium ground coffee, so is used in equipment where the contact between coffee and water is relatively short. For ex-ample, filter and espresso coffee should be made with a finely ground blend, while the jug, cafetière and percolator require medium ground coffee.

● Use the right amount of ground coffee: generally 2 heaped tablespoons or 40-50 g (1½-2 oz) per 500 ml (1 pint) water is a good guide. Your equipment or coffee blend may carry specific instructions on amounts so follow these, at least until you establish your personal preference.

● Freshly boiled water that has been allowed to go just off the boil, poured over or dripped through the coffee grounds, will extract the full flavour. Chemically softened water should never be used as it will alter the flavour of the coffee.

● Serve coffee as soon after brewing as possible – this is when it tastes best. Do not reheat coffee or let it boil. If you must keep coffee hot, the latest vacuum jugs are very good. Strain in the freshly brewed coffee and it will keep well for an hour or so.

Coffee-making methods

In a jug: Measure medium ground coffee into a warmed jug and pour on freshly boiled water. Stir well and leave to stand for 3 minutes in a warm place. Draw a spoon across the surface to settle the coffee grounds, then serve by pouring gently (preferably through a strainer) into the cups or into a warm coffee pot.

Filter coffee: Measure finely ground coffee into the cone-shaped filter (lined with a filter paper) and set over the warmed jug base. Pour in freshly boiled water to dampen the grounds and then top up to the level required. Once the coffee has dripped through into the jug below it is ready to serve.

The cafetière: Measure medium ground coffee into the warmed jug. Pour over freshly boiled water. Stir well and place on the lid with plunger withdrawn. Allow to stand for 3 minutes, then gently, without forcing, push the plunger down to the bottom of the jug to gather the grounds at the base and serve.

Espresso coffee: There are electric machines on the market that make the real thing and there are cheaper espresso percolators that can be set directly on the electric hob. Fill the base with water up to the safety valve mark. Pack the percolator basket with finely ground coffee and set in the base section. Screw on the top tightly. Set over medium heat and, when you hear the coffee boiling up, draw off the heat and serve.

HOT SUGARED GRAPEFRUIT

SERVES 6

3 grapefruits

15 g (½ oz) butter

3-4 tablespoons demerara sugar

Take the time and trouble to loosen each grapefruit segment properly because it makes these so much nicer to eat. Put the fruits to heat through at the last moment and serve straight away – hot sugared grapefruits are deliciously juicy.

Cut a sliver off the top and base of each fruit so the grapefruits will stand steady, then cut them in half through the middle. Using a grapefruit knife, cut around the segments to loosen them. Turn the prepared fruits upside down on a large plate to drain as you are preparing them. Then arrange the grapefruit halves right way up in a baking dish or roasting tin. Reserve the grapefruit juices. **P**

To grill: melt the butter and use it to dab over the surface of each fruit. Sprinkle with the sugar. Set the dish of grapefruit about 7.5 cm (3 inches) from the heat and grill until the sugar is melted and bubbling hot – about 5 minutes. Spoon over the reserved juices and serve hot.

To bake: sprinkle the fruit with the sugar and dot with flakes of the butter. Set the dish in a heated 200°C (400°F or gas no. 6) oven and bake for 10-15 minutes or until bubbling hot. Spoon over the reserved juices and serve hot.

P Can be prepared ahead: cover and keep in a cool place for several hours, no longer than overnight. Let come to room temperature before cooking.

SPICED PEACHES WITH BLUEBERRIES

SERVES 6

175 g (6 oz) castor sugar

300 ml (½ pint) water

pared zest and juice 1 lemon

1 × 5 cm (2 inch) piece stick cinnamon

6 fresh peaches

225 g (8 oz) blueberries

Poached peaches are very tender and delicious. This is a good way to deal with slightly underripe fruits. Add blueberries and the mixture looks wonderfully exotic.

Measure the sugar and water into a large saucepan. Stir over low heat until the sugar has dissolved, then bring to the boil. Draw off the heat and add the pared lemon zest (use a vegetable peeler) and the cinnamon.

Cut into the peaches following the natural line around the fruit from the stalk end. Then twist halves in opposite directions to separate and remove the centre stone. Put the peach halves in a mixing bowl and pour over boiling water to cover them. Let stand 30 seconds, then drain and peel away the skins. As each fruit is prepared, add to the syrup in the pan. Replace the saucepan of fruits over the heat, bring to a simmer

P Can be prepared ahead: keep refrigerated no longer than overnight.

and cook gently for 5 minutes or until the peaches are tender. Using a perforated spoon transfer the peaches to a serving bowl. Add the blueberries to the peaches. Remove the cinnamon and lemon zest from the syrup.

Return the pan of syrup to the heat and boil rapidly for 2-3 minutes to reduce and concentrate the flavour. Add the lemon juice and pour over the fruits. Cool, then refrigerate for 6-8 hours. **P**

MIXED RED FRUITS IN SYRUP

SERVES 6-8

900 g (2 lb) prepared red fruits – choose from redcurrants, raspberries and strawberries

175 g (6 oz) granulated sugar

400 ml (¾ pint) water

1 level tablespoon cornflour

2 tablespoons cold water

This works just as well with frozen fruits from the freezer so you can make it all year round – just add frozen fruits to the hot syrup. The mixture comes up a wonderful bright red, especially if you include redcurrants.

Prepare the fruits according to kind – strip redcurrants from the stems, pick over raspberries, and hull strawberries. Measure the sugar and water into a large saucepan and stir over low heat to dissolve the sugar. Bring to a simmer and add the fruits. When the mixture comes back to a simmer, draw the pan off the heat.

Using a perforated spoon lift the fruits from the saucepan to a serving bowl. Return the pan of fruit syrup to the heat. Blend the cornflour with the cold water in a small bowl. Stir into the fruit syrup and bring to the boil, stirring all the time. When the syrup is clear, pour it over the fruits in the bowl – because syrup is slightly thickened, the mixture shines and the fruits float. Leave for several hours until cold. Do not refrigerate. **P**

P Can be prepared ahead: best after 24 hours.

Serve at room temperature with thick natural yogurt.

WINTER FRUIT COMPOTE

SERVES 6

100 g (4 oz) dried apricots

100 g (4 oz) dried figs

100 g (4 oz) prunes

75 g (3 oz) castor sugar

300 ml (½ pint) water

pared zest and juice 1 lemon

1 × 2.5 cm (1 inch) piece stick cinnamon

An old-fashioned method of cooking is used here, but I think it produces the best result and the nicest syrup. Start with the light coloured fruits, leaving the dark fruit and spices to the end. This way fruits come up juicy and plump and full of flavour.

Soak the fruits overnight in cold water in separate bowls. Drain.

Put 25 g (1 oz) of the castor sugar and the water in a saucepan and stir over low heat to dissolve the sugar. Add a

24

few strips of pared lemon zest (use a vegetable peeler) and the squeezed lemon juice. Put in the apricots, cover with the pan lid and cook gently until tender – about 10 minutes. Remove the fruit with a perforated spoon and place in a serving bowl.

Add the figs to the syrup, cover and cook gently until tender – about 20 minutes. Remove the figs with a perforated spoon and add to the apricots.

Add the prunes and the piece of stick cinnamon to the syrup, cover and cook until tender – about 10 minutes. Add the prunes to the other fruits, and strain the syrup to remove the lemon zest and cinnamon.

Make the syrup back up to 300 ml (½ pint) with water. Add the remaining sugar and stir over low heat to dissolve the sugar. Bring to the boil. Simmer for 1 minute, then pour over the fruits. Cool, then refrigerate to chill well before serving. **P**

GOLDEN GRANOLA

SERVES 6-8

50 g (2 oz) blanched almonds, shelled cashews or Brazil nuts

225 g (8 oz) mixed cereal grains such as oat, barley or wheat flakes

50 g (2 oz) wheat germ

2 level tablespoons sesame seeds

2 level tablespoons sunflower seeds

2 tablespoons sunflower oil

4 tablespoons clear honey

100 g (4 oz) seedless raisins

P Can be prepared ahead: will keep up to 1 month.

Deliciously crunchy. If you like this you can easily double the quantities. Serve with a compote of dried fruits or seasonal stewed fruit such as plums or damsons. In summer, sprinkle, fresh strawberries or raspberries over the granola, or cut in fresh peaches. Add cold milk and natural yogurt.

Chop the nuts. Combine the cereal flakes, wheat germ, chopped nuts, sesame seeds and sunflower seeds in a big mixing bowl. Heat the sunflower oil and honey in a saucepan until warm and runny. Add to the cereal mixture and turn the ingredients until everything is well mixed.

Heat the oven to 180°C (350°F or gas no. 4). Turn the granola on to an ungreased baking tin or a roasting tin and spread out. Set in the heated oven and bake for 25-30 minutes or until golden. Stir once or twice so the mixture colours evenly. Remove from the oven and stir in the raisins. Let cool completely before storing in an airtight container. **P**

SCRAMBLED EGGS IN BRIOCHE

SERVES 6

6 individual brioches or small
  soft rolls

75 g (3 oz) butter

9 eggs (size 2)

150 ml (¼ pint) single cream

salt and freshly milled pepper

75 g (3 oz) soft cheese with
  herbs

chopped fresh chives, to
  garnish

A large, heavy-based frying pan set on gentle heat is the best choice for making scrambled egg in quantity – it allows more room to stir the mixture and the cooking is even. Flakes of soft herb cheese added at the last moment keep the eggs moist and add a subtle flavour.

Heat the oven to 160°C (325°F or gas no. 3).

Cut a slice from the top of each brioche, then scoop out the soft crumbs to make a container. Melt 25 g (1 oz) of the butter and brush inside the brioche containers. Set on a baking tray and warm through in the heated oven for 6-8 minutes.

Meanwhile, crack the eggs into a mixing bowl. Add the cream and a seasoning of salt and pepper and mix with a fork. Heat the remaining butter in a 25 cm (10 inch) frying pan and when the butter is hot and frothing, pour in the egg mixture. Cook over moderate heat, using a metal spoon to draw up the mixture in folds as the eggs begin to thicken.

When the egg mixture is just set, draw off the heat and add the herb cheese in flakes to flavour and moisten – it will melt into the warm egg mixture.

Spoon the scrambled egg into the warmed brioche to fill them. Sprinkle with chopped chives, replace the tops and serve hot.

BAKED EGGS IN CHEESE TARTLETS

SERVES 6

15 g (½ oz) butter, melted

4 level tablespoons dry white
  breadcrumbs

6 eggs (size 2)

salt and freshly milled pepper

6 teaspoons single cream

For the cheese shortcrust

100 g (4 oz) plain flour

pinch salt

65 g (2½ oz) butter

2 level tablespoons grated
  Parmesan or mature Cheddar
  cheese

Instead of traditional cocotte dishes, cheese pastry tartlets will hold eggs perfectly. Prepared this way, eggs can be sprinkled with chopped herbs or grated cheese, and diced fried bacon or lightly cooked mushrooms could be spooned into the tartlets underneath.

First make the cheese shortcrust: sift the flour and salt into a mixing bowl. Add the butter cut in pieces and rub in with the fingertips. Stir in the cheese. Combine the egg yolk, water and vinegar, add all at once to the dry ingredients and stir with a table knife to form a rough dough in the bowl.

With floured fingers, draw the dough into a ball and turn on to a floured work surface. Knead two or three times just to smooth the surface. Place in a polythene bag and refrigerate for at least 30 minutes (or overnight).

1 egg yolk (size 2)

1 tablespoon cold water

1 teaspoon white wine vinegar

P Can be prepared ahead: keep the pastry shells in an airtight container.

Heat the oven to 190°C (375°F or gas no. 5).

Roll out the pastry and cut out six 7.5 cm (3 inch) rounds. Press the pastry rounds over the outside of upturned fluted brioche moulds. Or cut out 10 cm (4 inch) pastry rounds and use to line small individual quiche tins. Set in the heated oven and bake for about 15 minutes until the pastry is golden. Let the shells cool. **P**

Turn the oven heat to 180°C (350°F or gas no. 4). Arrange the baked tartlet shells on an oven tray.

Combine the melted butter and breadcrumbs with a fork; set aside. Crack one egg into each pastry shell and season with salt and pepper. Set in the heated oven and bake for 8 minutes or until the whites of the eggs are almost set, then spoon over the cream and sprinkle over the buttered crumbs. Replace in the oven to bake for a further 5 minutes or until the eggs are set.

OMELETTE ARNOLD BENNETT

SERVES 6

450 g (1 lb) smoked haddock fillet

milk (see recipe)

75 g (3 oz) butter

9 eggs (size 2)

salt and freshly milled pepper

150 ml (¼ pint) single cream

3 level tablespoons grated Parmesan cheese

There's nothing difficult about making an open omelette like this one, but you do need a large frying pan. A flexible spatula is the best tool for getting the servings out: loosen around the sides first and then slide it underneath.

Poach the smoked haddock in milk to cover for about 10 minutes, then drain and allow to cool. Separate the flesh into flakes, discarding skin and any bones. Put the fish to warm through gently in half the butter.

Meanwhile, separate the eggs, cracking the yolks into a large mixing bowl and the whites into a second bowl. Add a seasoning of salt and pepper and half the cream to the egg yolks and mix with a fork. Add the warmed smoked haddock and 2 tablespoons of the grated cheese. Stiffly whisk the egg whites and fold into the mixture.

Heat the remaining butter in a 25 cm (10 inch) frying pan. When hot and frothing, pour in the omelette mixture. Cook over moderate heat, lifting the base of the mixture as it sets to let the uncooked egg flow on to the hot pan surface.

When the underside of the omelette is brown and the top centre set but still moist, pour over the remaining cream and sprinkle with the rest of the cheese. Pass the omelette under a hot grill for about 1 minute to brown the surface. Serve from the pan, cutting the omelette into wedges, straight on to hot plates.

SMOKED HADDOCK KEDGEREE

SERVES 8

2 large smoked haddock on the
  bone, or about 900 g (2 lb)
  smoked haddock fillet

few parsley stalks

1 bay leaf

½ lemon

salt and freshly milled pepper

1 medium onion

100 g (4 oz) butter

1 tablespoon grapeseed or
  other mild oil

½ level teaspoon curry paste

450 g (1 lb) long-grain rice

3 hard-boiled eggs (size 2)

50 g (2 oz) seedless raisins

100 g (4 oz) shelled cashew
  nuts

4 tablespoons chopped fresh
  parsley

lemon wedges, for serving

The secret of the special taste of this kedgeree is the way the rice is cooked – in the water used for poaching the smoked haddock. This is a particularly flavoursome recipe.

Rinse the fish and cut into pieces that will fit in a medium saucepan. Cover with 1.1 litres (2 pints) water. Add the parsley stalks (save the curly tops for garnish), bay leaf and a slice from the lemon half. Bring to a simmer and poach until the fish is tender – about 6 minutes. Remove the haddock pieces with a perforated spoon, then strain the poaching liquid and reserve for cooking the rice. Check the seasoning with salt and freshly milled pepper. When the haddock is cool, discard the skin and bones and break the flesh into loose flakes.

Peel and finely chop the onion. Heat half the butter and the oil in a saucepan, add the onion and fry gently to soften – about 5 minutes. Add the curry paste and the rice and stir to mix with the butter and onion for a moment. Stir in the reserved poaching liquid. Bring to a simmer, stirring once or twice, then cover with the pan lid and cook gently until the rice is tender and all the liquid has been absorbed – 20-30 minutes.

Shell and chop the hard-boiled eggs. Using a fork, fold the eggs, flaked haddock, remaining butter, seedless raisins, cashew nuts, chopped parsley and the juice squeezed from the remaining lemon half into the cooked rice. Heat again until thoroughly hot, and serve at once with lemon wedges.

GRATED POTATO CAKE WITH OVEN-FRIED BACON

SERVES 6

900 g (2 lb) large potatoes

50 g (2 oz) butter

1 tablespoon grapeseed or
  other mild oil

salt and freshly milled pepper

12 rashers lean back bacon

This crisp-cooked potato mixture that cuts in portions for serving is not unlike the swiss rösti. Add grilled tomatoes, sausages or kidney along with the bacon rashers, if you like.

Peel and grate the potatoes (using a food processor is the quickest way). Turn the grated potato into a bowl of cold water and rinse thoroughly, then lift out the potato in handfuls, squeezing them to remove excess moisture.

Heat the oven to 190°C (375°F or gas no. 5). Heat half the butter and the oil in a 25 cm (10 inch) frying pan. When hot and foaming, add the potato shreds, spreading them evenly, and press down all over with a spatula to form a thick pancake. Season with salt and pepper, cover with the pan lid and fry gently for 20 minutes.

Meanwhile, arrange the bacon rashers on a rack in a roasting tin – do not overlap the slices. Set in the heated oven and bake, without turning, for 15-20 minutes.

When the underside of the potato cake is crisp and brown, loosen the edges with a spatula, cover the frying pan with a dinner plate and turn the potato cake on to it. Add the rest of the butter to the hot pan and slide the potato cake back in. Fry uncovered for a further 15 minutes.

Serve the potato cake, seasoned with salt and pepper, cut in wedges, with the crisp bacon rashers.

COLD MEATS WITH BUBBLE AND SQUEAK

SERVES 6

450-700 g (1-1½ lb) cold rare roast beef, cooked ham or cold roast turkey

1 medium green cabbage

salt and freshly milled pepper

grated nutmeg

700 g (1½ lb) potatoes

50-75 g (2-3 oz) beef drippings or butter

P Can be prepared ahead: cover and refrigerate for several hours; no longer than overnight. Allow a little extra cooking time to heat thoroughly.

It's the crispy bits that make bubble and squeak so attractive, and it has a homely appeal – something hot with cold meats is a nice combination. You can get the mixture ready ahead, and an extra frying pan (electric is ideal) is a help with the final cooking.

Have the cold meat sliced thinly, and arrange on a large serving platter. Cover with clear film and refrigerate if prepared ahead.

Remove the outer damaged leaves from the cabbage, then cut in quarters and slice away the core. Cut cabbage into shreds. Add to a pan of boiling salted water and cook for 15 minutes. Drain well, pressing to remove excess moisture. Turn into a mixing bowl and season with salt and freshly milled pepper and a little grated nutmeg. Set aside.

Peel the potatoes and boil in salted water until tender, then drain. Return the potatoes to the pan over the heat for a moment to dry them. Mash the potatoes, season with salt and pepper and add to the cooked cabbage. Mix the ingredients together with a wooden spoon. **P**

Heat the drippings or butter in two frying pans (or cook in batches). When hot, add the cabbage and potato mixture, smooth over and flatten with a palette knife. Fry until the mixture is beginning to brown underneath. Turn over portions of the mixture (a slice is handy) and brown the second side. When the mixture is thoroughly heated through – 8-10 minutes – spoon the bubble and squeak on to a hot platter and serve with the cold meats.

PRAWN AND RICE JAMBALAYA

SERVES 6

3 medium onions
2 cloves garlic
3 stalks celery
1 red sweet pepper
3 tablespoons grapeseed or other mild oil
½ level teaspoon mild chilli powder
225 g (8 oz) long-grain rice
1 × approx. 400 g can chopped tomatoes
1 level tablespoon concentrated tomato purée
1 level teaspoon dried oregano
salt and freshly milled pepper
400 ml (¾ pint) hot chicken stock or boiling water
450 g (1 lb) peeled, cooked prawns
2 tablespoons chopped fresh parsley

A lovely combination, this has rice and shellfish as the basic ingredients. Serve with hot French bread and a leafy green salad for an eye-catching brunch dish.

Peel and finely chop the onion and the garlic. Scrub and string, then shred the celery. Deseed and chop the sweet pepper. Heat the oil in a large saucepan. Add the onion and red pepper and fry gently until the onion is soft and golden – about 10 minutes. Stir in the celery, garlic, chilli powder and rice and cook, stirring, for 1-2 minutes.

Add the contents of the can of tomatoes (do not drain), the tomato purée, oregano, a good seasoning of salt and pepper and the stock or water. Bring to a simmer, then cover with the pan lid and cook gently for about 20-30 minutes or until the rice grains are tender.

Fork the prawns through the mixture and sprinkle with the chopped parsley. Heat gently until everything is thoroughly hot, and serve.

FRESH SALMON CAKES WITH LEMON

SERVES 6

1 tail end piece salmon, about
  700 g (1½ lb)

450 g (1 lb) floury potatoes

salt and freshly milled pepper

1 medium onion

50 g (2 oz) butter

grated nutmeg

2 tablespoons chopped fresh
  chives

2 eggs (size 2)

75-100 g (3-4 oz) uncoloured
  dry breadcrumbs

2 tablespoons grapeseed or
  other mild oil

3 lemons, for serving

P Can be prepared ahead: keep
refrigerated for no longer than
overnight.

My first taste of these was at a breakfast party in London's fish market, Billingsgate. They are made with flakes of fresh salmon, and it really is worth cooking a piece of fish specially for them.

Heat the oven to 180°C (350°F or gas no. 4). Enclose the salmon piece in oiled kitchen foil to make a baggy parcel. Place on a baking tray, set in the heated oven and bake for 25 minutes. Let cool completely in the unopened parcel. When cold, lift away the skin, discard the bones and flake the salmon flesh.

Peel the potatoes and cut up. Add to a pan of boiling salted water and cook until tender. Meanwhile, peel and finely chop the onion. Melt half the butter in a saucepan, add the onion and fry gently to soften – about 5 minutes.

Drain the potatoes, return them to the hot pan and dry over the heat for a few minutes, then mash or pass them through a vegetable mouli. Turn the potatoes into a mixing bowl.

Add the fried onion, flaked salmon, a good seasoning of salt and pepper, a grating of nutmeg and the chives. Separate the eggs, cracking the whites on to a plate and adding the yolks to the salmon mixture. Blend the ingredients for the salmon cakes together with a fork.

Lightly beat the egg whites with a fork to break them up. Spread the dry breadcrumbs on a sheet of greaseproof paper. Divide the salmon mixture into 12 equal portions and, with floured fingers and a flat-bladed knife, shape each one into a neat fish cake. Dip, one at a time, first into the beaten whites, then in the bed of dry crumbs. Transfer to a plate or tray. Cover and refrigerate for at least 1 hour. **P**

Heat the remaining butter with the oil in a roomy frying pan. When the fat is hot, add the salmon cakes (in batches) and fry gently to heat through, turning to brown both sides. They should be golden and crisp. Transfer to a hot platter and serve with lemon wedges for squeezing over.

GRUYÈRE AND SPINACH CRÊPES

SERVES 6

12 prepared crêpes (see page 104)

450 g (1 lb) fresh spinach, or 1 × approx 225 g packet frozen chopped spinach, thawed

40 g (1½ oz) butter

40 g (1½ oz) plain flour

400 ml (¾ pint) milk

salt and freshly milled pepper

grated nutmeg

100 g (4 oz) Gruyère cheese

P Can be prepared ahead: cover and refrigerate no longer than overnight. Let come to room temperature before baking, or allow extra baking time.

Spinach is my favourite 'green' filling for these crêpes, but I also make them with blanched florets of broccoli, and very good they are too.

Have the crêpes prepared and stacked – there is no need to heat them at this stage.

Wash the fresh spinach in several changes of cold water and remove the centre rib from the leaves. Lift the spinach straight from the rinsing water to a saucepan. Cover and cook over moderate heat for a few minutes or until the leaves have wilted. Drain in a colander and press well to remove excess moisture, then chop the spinach finely. Reheat frozen spinach following packet directions.

Melt the butter in a saucepan over low heat. Stir in the flour and cook for 1 minute. Gradually add 300 ml (½ pint) of the milk, beating well all the time to make a smooth thick sauce. Bring to the boil and simmer for 2 minutes. Season with salt and pepper and add a grating of nutmeg. Draw off the heat. Grate the cheese and stir all but 25 g (1 oz) of it into the sauce – it will melt in the heat of the sauce.

Heat the oven to 180°C (350°F or gas no. 4).

Stir half the sauce into the spinach purée. Fill the crêpes with the mixture, roll them up and place them in a buttered baking dish in one layer. Thin down the sauce that remains with the rest of the milk to make a coating consistency. Check the seasoning and pour over the filled crêpes. Sprinkle with the remaining cheese. **P**

Set the crêpes in the heated oven and bake for 20-25 minutes or until they are thoroughly hot and browned before serving.

BLINIS WITH SMOKED SALMON

SERVES 6-8

300 ml (½ pint) milk

150 ml (¼ pint) water

1 level teaspoon castor sugar

25 g (1 oz) butter

275 g (10 oz) plain flour

50 g (2 oz) wholemeal flour

½ level teaspoon salt

2 eggs (size 2)

oil for frying

300 ml (½ pint) soured cream

225-450 g (½-1 lb) smoked salmon – slices or off-cuts (or smoked mackerel, pickled herrings with chopped onion, lumpfish caviar or taramosalata)

P Can be prepared ahead: cool, then wrap in a baggy foil parcel. Reheat in a heated 160°C (325°F or gas no. 3) oven for 10-15 minutes before serving.

The size of blinis is determined by the spoonfuls of batter – smaller two-bite size or larger for eating with a knife and fork. Blinis take any kind of fish topping.

Put the milk, water, sugar and butter into a saucepan and warm until the butter melts (do not overheat). Pour into a food processor bowl. Add the plain flour, wholemeal flour and salt. Separate the eggs, putting the whites into a mixing bowl and adding the yolks to the food processor. Cover and blend to a smooth batter.

Alternatively, sift the dry ingredients into a mixing bowl, add the warm liquid ingredients and egg yolks and mix to a smooth batter.

Cover the batter and leave in a warm place for 1-1½ hours or until frothy and well aerated. Whisk the egg whites until stiff and fold into the batter.

Heat a heavy frying pan or griddle until thoroughly hot. Grease the surface with oil, using a pad of absorbent kitchen paper dipped in a saucer of oil. Drop the batter by dessertspoonfuls on to the hot surface. When the underside is brown, flip the blinis over and cook the second side. Keep the cooked blinis warm and soft in a folded cloth while you use up the rest of the batter to make about 30 blinis. Rub the hot pan surface with oil frequently. **P**

Serve the blinis warm with separate bowls of soured cream and cut-up smoked salmon (or flaked smoked mackerel, pickled herring with chopped onion, lumpfish caviar or taramosalata), and let guests help themselves.

CHICORY AND APPLE SALAD

SERVES 6

3 heads chicory

3 medium carrots

1 bunch (6-8) spring onions

2 green-skinned tart dessert apples

1 level teaspoon castor sugar

4-5 tablespoons oil and vinegar dressing (see page 185)

salt and freshly milled pepper

2 tablespoons chopped fresh parsley

A particularly fresh-tasting, crunchy salad, this is easy to prepare in quantity. Adding apple to a chicory salad takes away the bitter flavour.

Trim a slice from the base of each head of chicory and with a pointed knife scoop out the core from the stalk end. Shred the chicory finely across the leaves and put the shreds into a serving bowl.

Peel and grate the carrots. Trim the spring onions, then chop all the white and some of the green stems. Finally, peel, core and grate the apples. Add apples, carrots and spring onions to the chicory along with a sprinkling of sugar (to draw juices from the apple). Add the oil and vinegar dressing, a seasoning of salt and pepper and the parsley, and fork everything together.

BRAN MUFFINS

MAKES 12

225 g (8 oz) wholemeal flour

½ level teaspoon salt

1 level tablespoon baking powder

100 g (4 oz) bran flakes

100 g (4 oz) light muscovado sugar

1 egg (size 2)

150 ml (¼ pint) natural yogurt

150 ml (¼ pint) water

75 ml (3 fl oz) grapeseed or other mild oil

Speed is the great plus for these American muffins. Get the dry ingredients ready, combine liquid ones, then mix and bake when required: you can make muffins from scratch in no time at all.

Heat the oven to 225°C (425°F or gas no. 7). Well oil a tray of 12 deep bun tins.

Sift the flour, salt and baking powder into a large mixing bowl, then tip in any coarse flour remaining in the sieve. Add the bran flakes and sugar and mix. Crack the egg into a second bowl and break up with a fork. Stir in the yogurt, water and oil and mix well. **P**

Add the liquid mixture to the dry ingredients all at once. Stir just until the flour is moistened – do not overmix. Spoon into the prepared bun tins, filling each one two-thirds full. Set at once in the heated oven and bake for 15-20 minutes or until well risen. Let the muffins cool in the baking tin for 2 minutes, then loosen the sides and turn on to a wire cooling tray. Serve warm.

FRUIT MUFFINS

MAKES 12

175 g (6 oz) plain flour

½ level teaspoon salt

1 level tablespoon baking
  powder

75 g (3 oz) rolled oats

75 g (3 oz) light muscovado
  sugar

1 egg (size 2)

225 ml (8 fl oz) milk

3 tablespoons grapeseed or
  other mild oil

100 g (4 oz) fresh or thawed
  frozen blueberries,
  blackcurrants or cranberries,
  or 50 g (2 oz) seedless raisins

Freshly baked muffins are delicious served with butter and preserves, and they are nice for coffee mornings too. The muffins can be frozen, then thawed and popped into the oven to warm through when required.

Heat the oven to 225°C (425°F or gas no. 7). Well oil a tray of 12 deep bun tins.

Sift the flour, salt and baking powder into a large mixing bowl. Add the rolled oats and sugar and mix well. Crack the egg into a second bowl and break up with a fork. Stir in the milk and oil and mix well. **P**

Add the liquid mixture to the dry ingredients all at once and stir until the flour is moistened – the mixture will be lumpy. Stir in the fruit. Spoon into the prepared tins, filling each one two-thirds full. Set at once in the heated oven and bake for 15-20 minutes or until well risen.

Let the muffins cool in the baking tin for 2 minutes, then loosen the sides and turn on to a wire cooling tray. Serve warm.

TRADITIONAL SODA BREAD

MAKES 1 LARGE LOAF

225 g (8 oz) plain flour
225 g (8 oz) wholemeal flour
1 level tablespoon baking powder
1 level teaspoon bicarbonate of soda
1 level teaspoon salt
50 g (2 oz) butter
150 ml (¼ pint) natural yogurt
300 ml (½ pint) water

This is the easiest and quickest of hot breads to make. You can mix it with the traditional soured liquid by blending natural yogurt with water.

Heat the oven to 200°C (400°F or gas no. 6).

Sift the white and wholemeal flours, baking powder, bicarbonate of soda and salt into a large mixing bowl, and tip in any coarse bran particles remaining in the sieve. Add the butter cut in pieces and rub in with the fingertips.

Dilute the yogurt with the water. Pour the liquid into the dry ingredients all at once and, using a table knife, mix to a soft dough. Flour a clean work surface and turn the dough on to it. With floured hands, knead about three times just to remove the cracks, then flatten to a round about 4 cm (1½ inches) thick.

Place on a floured baking tray and, with a knife, cut a deep cross in the top of the round, to encourage even baking. Set in the heated oven and bake for 25-30 minutes or until well risen and a tap on the base produces a hollow sound.

Transfer to a wire cooling rack. For a soft crust, cover with a cloth. Cool slightly, then break into four quarters and serve warm cut in slices.

LEMON BUBBLE BREAD

MAKES 1 LOAF

450 g (1 lb) strong white flour
½ level teaspoon salt
50 g (2 oz) butter
1 × 7 g sachet easy blend dried yeast
25 g (1 oz) castor sugar
1 egg (size 2)
225 g (8 fl oz) mixed equal parts milk and water, hand hot

For the coating

50 g (2 oz) butter, melted
grated zest 2 lemons
75 g (3 oz) granulated sugar

You get a pretty result when this sweet dough is rolled in balls and tucked together in the baking tin. Each dough ball is butter-coated so it's easy to pull the baked bread apart for serving.

Sift the flour and salt into a mixing bowl. Add the butter and rub in with the fingertips. Add the dried yeast and mix through. Combine the castor sugar and egg in a bowl and mix with a fork. Stir in the warmed milk and water, pour into the dry ingredients and mix to a rough dough in the bowl.

Turn the dough on to a clean work surface and knead very thoroughly for 8-10 minutes or until smooth. Shape into a ball and replace in the mixing bowl. Cover and leave at room temperature to rise until the dough has doubled in size.

Thoroughly butter a 22.5 cm (9 inch) spring clip tin. Have the melted butter for the coating, and the grated lemon zest

P Can be prepared ahead: prove overnight in the refrigerator.

mixed with the granulated sugar to hand. Turn the risen dough out on to a work surface and press all over with the knuckles to flatten.

Divide the dough in half, then divide each portion into 12 equal pieces and shape them into balls.

Roll each dough ball first in melted butter and then in the mixed sugar and lemon zest. Arrange about three quarters of the balls in one layer over the base of the tin. Set the remainder in a second layer over the centre of the loaf – so the bread will rise in bubbles. Cover and leave to prove at room temperature until risen and puffy.

Heat the oven to 200°C (400°F or gas no. 6). Set the risen loaf in the heated oven and bake for 25-30 minutes or until golden brown. Serve warm – pull the pieces of loaf apart with two forks for serving.

CINNAMON STREUSEL CAKE

CUTS INTO 12 PIECES

225 g (8 oz) self-raising flour

1 level teaspoon baking powder

100 g (4 oz) butter

100 g (4 oz) castor sugar

grated zest ½ lemon

1 egg (size 2)

150 ml (¼ pint) milk

For the streusel topping

3 level tablespoons plain flour

1 level teaspoon ground
   cinnamon

25 g (1 oz) butter, at room
   temperature

50 g (2 oz) light muscovado
   sugar

25 g (1 oz) shelled walnuts

This is best served slightly warm – straight from the baking tin. With a lemony-flavoured soft cake base and a crunchy cinnamon top, it's a favourite of mine.

Start with the streusel topping. Sift the flour and ground cinnamon into a bowl. Add the butter and sugar and mash with a fork until the mixture is crumbly. Finely chop the walnuts, add to the crumb mixture and set aside.

Heat the oven to 190°C (375°F or gas no. 5). Well butter a 22.5 cm (9 inch) spring clip tin.

Sift the flour and baking powder for the cake base into a mixing bowl. Add the butter cut in pieces and rub in with the fingertips. Stir in the sugar and grated lemon zest. Lightly mix the egg and milk together and add all at once to the dry ingredients. Stir with a wooden spoon until the ingredients are blended, then beat until smooth.

Turn the mixture into the prepared tin and spread level. Sprinkle with the streusel topping. Set in the heated oven and bake for 30-35 minutes. Let cool 5 minutes, then remove the side of the tin and serve the cake warm, cut in slices.

APRICOT COFFEE CAKE

CUTS INTO 12 PIECES

175 g (6 oz) self-raising flour

pinch salt

100 g (4 oz) butter, at room
   temperature

100 g (4 oz) castor sugar

2 eggs (size 2)

½ teaspoon vanilla essence

1-2 tablespoons milk

For the topping

1 × approx 400 g can apricot
   halves, in fruit juice

150 ml (¼ pint) soured cream

1 egg yolk (size 2)

50 g (2 oz) blanched, toasted
   almonds (see page 210)

Fruits feature regularly in cakes for serving with hot coffee: they keep the mixture moist and provide a pretty finish. There's no need for an icing here – this cake looks good just as it comes from the oven.

Heat the oven to 180°C (350°F for gas no. 4). Grease a 30 × 20 cm (12 × 8 inch) baking tin or small roasting tin.

Sift the flour and salt on to a plate. In a mixing bowl, cream the butter with the sugar until soft and light. Lightly mix the eggs and vanilla essence together. Add to the creamed mixture a little at a time, beating well after each addition. Gently fold in half the sifted flour, then add the remaining flour with the milk and mix until blended.

Spread the mixture over the base of the prepared tin and spread level. Arrange the well-drained apricot halves over the surface, distributing them evenly so that each baked portion will contain one apricot half. Combine the soured cream and egg yolk and drizzle over the cake top around the fruit. Chop the almonds and sprinkle over.

Place in the heated oven and bake for 30-35 minutes or until the cake is baked and the topping is set. Cut in portions and serve warm from the baking tin.

LUNCH PARTIES

Fresh salmon mousse

Mushroom pâté

Swiss cheese tart

Courgette moulds with basil vinaigrette

Pasta and smoked chicken salad with yogurt dressing

Mixed leaf salad with bacon and white stilton

Lemon chicken with sweet red peppers

Spiced coconut lamb

Pilau rice

Marinated yellow peppers with bulgar wheat salad

.

Herb-crumbed chicken with mustard dipping sauce

Chicken breasts stuffed with apple and sage

Baked parcels of salmon with herb butter

Beef casserole with parsley dumplings

Marinated beef with a spiced crust

Onion marmalade

Cranberry crown roast of pork

Honey roast leg of lamb with honey mint sauce

.

Ambrosia fruit bowl

Creamed rice with candied fruits

Chilled lemon soufflé

Apple streusel pie

Queen of puddings

Trifle with syllabub

Trifle sponge layer

LUNCH
PARTIES

Lunch parties appeal to me; they are my favourite entertaining occasion – light-hearted, relaxed and often predominantly female affairs. Lunch parties are useful because you can ask new acquaintances along with others you know well, and mix the age groups – young and old will always blend into one happy group.

For weekday lunch parties, your friends will probably arrive on time and they will leave promptly too – there isn't the leeway in the middle of the day – so you need to be well organized. A small group which can be seated at the dining table is no problem. For a larger number, the dining table can be used as a buffet and small tables arranged at convenient spots in the sitting room. If the weather predictions are favourable, lunch can spill out into the patio or garden. I keep a supply of folding directors chairs and can easily produce them for indoors or outside – it's important to make sure everyone is comfortable.

Your choice of food should be light but interesting. Women delight in making culinary discoveries so here's your chance to dazzle them with an interesting little number. Often an attractive starter, with a few additions, can make a pretty main dish. Consider a cold dish with a concentration of pretty salads and hot breads, or something hot, subtly sauced and served with perfectly cooked rice. I usually dispense with a first course but, if you choose not to, go for something simple that you can arrange on a plate. Make food pretty, a little calorie-conscious if you like, but stylish.

Weekend lunch parties are definitely different, and Sunday lunch parties are becoming very popular. Whole families can be invited on this occasion and since they may be coming quite a distance, it's best not to be too tight with the time. As a rule, these lunch parties are best set up in the dining room when all ages can sit round the table – up to 12 is nice if your table will take the number. Here is a good chance to splash out on a big joint of meat and include some old-fashioned puddings. Bring on a cheeseboard to linger over. You'll find parents tend to stay round the table while children disappear to watch television, or play in the garden. Weekend lunch parties tend to start later and go on longer, probably ending up with a cup of tea before everyone goes home.

Offer wine when friends arrive and stick to it through lunch;

bottles of mineral water should be available too – drivers might like to drink spritzers. In summer a wine cup is light and refreshing and iced tea or coffee would be welcome too, especially if served in large ice cool glass jugs.

Herbs and Leaves

When it comes to making food look good, fresh herbs always have the edge – leafy, cool and wonderfully aromatic. Add them at the last minute and use in simple ways.

- Purple chive flowers are pretty for sprinkling over leafy green salads. Leave them whole or break into tiny pieces.
- Add shapely strawberry or blackcurrant leaves or sprigs of lemon balm to a platter of fresh fruits.
- Decorate soft white goat's cheeses with leaves of coriander or summer savory pressed on to the surface; then add a sprinkling of paprika or poppy seeds for contrast.

- Slip polished bay leaves (rub them with oil) under hard cheeses and vine leaves under soft ones, to decorate a cheese board.
- Cut a block of butter in half, run the prongs of a fork along the surface (to make a pattern) and add leaves of soft herbs such as mint or basil or a single coriander leaf. Or cut butter into pats and top each pat with a small piece of fresh herb.
- Let herbs float in your vinaigrette – chopped chives are pretty, and torn basil leaves look very elegant when the dressing is passed around in a bowl.
- Scatter leaves over vegetable or pasta salads – fresh basil or lamb's lettuce look dramatic.
- Use sprays of fresh herbs – coriander, mint, chives, fennel or dill – to garnish cold foods instead of always chopping them.

Salad Extras

A carefully prepared green salad is one of the basics – it serves almost every occasion. Keep it simple or dress it up – there are dozens of ways to make a green salad interesting and different. For the dressings, turn to page 141 and 185.

- Mix salad leaves including some unusual ones like brown-tipped oakleaf lettuce, frilly-edged frisée or torn radicchio for the red colour.
- Scatter dark snipped cress, leaves of watercress or lamb's lettuce over paler green iceberg or Chinese leaves. Or add colour in the form of snipped chive flowers, petals of nasturtium or golden marigolds.
- Add vegetables, blanched so they are still crunchy – mange-touts, asparagus tips or broccoli spears. Try samphire grass which looks spriggy but when dipped in boiling water comes up the most amazing vivid green and looks especially pretty if you add halved cherry tomatoes.
- Include fruits – they are fresh-tasting and blend with any vinaigrette. Try slices of kiwi fruit or banana or halved and seeded green grapes.
- Include the crunch of nuts – especially cashews, pine nuts, chopped walnuts or pecans – or tiny crisp croûtons or grilled, crumbled bacon rashers. A sprinkling of sunflower seeds is nice too.
- Add contrast with the white of broken pieces of feta, white stilton or cheshire cheese or tiny boiled quail's eggs, shelled and halved.
- Don't forget cucumber slices, sliced mushrooms or radishes, grated carrots, or chunks of ripe avocado for flavour.
- Lastly, consider adding contrasting flavours (sometimes bitter) like leaves of rocket or dandelion, herbs such as coriander, basil or chopped chives and sweet red onion in rings, spring onions (white and green) or sliced young leeks.

On Ice

Delicious tea, chilled or iced and laced with lemon and a swirl of sugar, is wonderfully refreshing and easy to make. All you have to do is follow the rules for hot tea, adding an extra spoonful of tea (or a tea bag) to the pot, and brew for about 8 minutes – no longer or the tannin comes out. Put plenty of ice cubes in a jug and sprinkle over a spoonful of fine sugar. Stir, then pour the tea through a strainer directly on to the ice cubes. This will cool the tea right down. Stir and top up with chilled water to taste, then serve in glasses with ice and a slice of lemon.

It's as simple as that, but of course there are all kinds of refinements. What tea you use depends on your own taste, but most experts agree that a non-astringent tea blend like Ceylon makes the best iced tea. And naturally flavoured teas – some scented, others with pieces of fruit such as lemon, strawberry, mango or vanilla – are all very refreshing.

A pretty garnish makes all the difference. If lemon slices are too tangy for your taste, try a slice of orange or a cucumber stick instead. Add sprigs of fresh mint, crushed a little to release the flavouring oils, or borage. With the simple addition of lemon or orange slices, tea can be sipped from the glass, but once greenery is added it's best to offer straws. For longer drinks, mix the tea liquid with equal parts of unsweetened apple juice, again adding ice and a slice of lemon.

Iced coffee is my own favourite drink. I don't think I could get through hot summer days without it. After lunch and in the evening, particularly when the weather is humid, iced coffee is at its most refreshing. I should emphasize that freshly ground coffee is best because it has an astringent, pick-me-up effect that you just don't get with instant granules.

Using my method you should make the coffee ahead, let it cool and refrigerate it ready for serving. Two things are very important. The first is that you use the filter method – either a machine or simply a pot with the filter set over the top. This is because you get an absolutely clear brew with no coffee grounds. Secondly, you should choose a dark continental roast with beans ground filter fine. This is because the strong flavour comes through best when served cold.

I don't make my coffee extra strong; I make it in just the same way as for a hot cup. And while I like to serve the chilled coffee over ice in pretty glasses, I don't dilute it over cubes in a jug to cool it down. When the weather starts looking good, brew your coffee the evening before. Sweeten the coffee while hot if that's how you like it – the sugar dissolves quickly in a hot liquid. Leave it in the coffee jug, then when it has cooled to room temperature put it in the refrigerator overnight to chill.

To serve, pour into ice-filled glasses. I personally like to top up my black coffee with a dash of chilled milk from the refrigerator. Making coffee this way means you can offer your guests a choice – black on ice (very continental) or white with milk. A dash of rum or brandy is a delicious addition. Or you can add a spoonful of softly whipped cream to each glass of chilled black coffee (it will float) and serve with straws – this looks very pretty.

FRESH SALMON MOUSSE

SERVES 6

1 piece salmon, about 550 g
  (1¼ lb)

75 ml (3 fl oz) cold water

15 g (½ oz) powdered gelatine

150 ml (¼ pint) mayonnaise

150 ml (¼ pint) natural yogurt

juice 1½ lemons

2 tablespoons chopped fresh
  chives

salt and freshly milled pepper

½ level teaspoon paprika

300 ml (½ pint) double cream

extra paprika, to garnish

P Can be prepared ahead: keep
refrigerated for up to 24 hours.

This is one of the best recipes I've come across, with flakes of fish to provide texture. A ring-shaped mould is my preference for serving, and I find a good dusting of red paprika and green chives make it look very appetizing.

Rinse the salmon piece and place in a saucepan. Add cold water to cover and then remove the salmon piece. Bring the water to the boil, replace the salmon in the saucepan and, when water reboils, boil for 1 minute only and draw off the heat. Cover with the pan lid and leave in a cool place overnight.

Next day the salmon will be perfectly cooked and quite cold. Lift from the pan, remove the skin and bones and flake the flesh.

Measure the cold water into a saucepan and sprinkle in the gelatine. Let stand for 5 minutes, then stir over low heat until the gelatine has dissolved – do not boil. Measure the mayonnaise and yogurt into a large mixing bowl and stir to blend. Add the dissolved gelatine and mix through. Let stand for about 30 minutes or until the mixture begins to show signs of setting.

Fold in the flaked salmon, lemon juice, half the chopped chives, a good seasoning of salt and pepper and the paprika. Whip the cream to soft peaks and fold into the mixture. Check the seasoning and pour into a 1.7 litre (3 pint) ring (or decorative) mould and spread level. Cover and refrigerate until set. **P**

Unmould (see page 120) on to a serving plate. Sprinkle the top with the remaining chives and add a dusting of paprika before serving.

MUSHROOM PÂTÉ

SERVES 6

900 g (2 lb) open cup or brown
  cap mushrooms

1 medium onion

2-3 cloves garlic

25 g (1 oz) butter

1 tablespoon soy sauce

To get a good, strong taste, the chopped mushrooms must be gently cooked, well softened and reduced – then tangy ingredients are added. The pâté comes up dark-coloured, but don't let that put you off – the flavour is delicious.

Trim the mushrooms and remove stalks. With a sharp kitchen knife, chop the mushrooms finely. Peel and finely chop the onion, and peel and chop the garlic. Melt the butter in a frying

1 tablespoon red wine vinegar

1 level teaspoon dried thyme

salt and freshly milled pepper

225 g (8 oz) curd cheese

P Can be prepared ahead: cover and refrigerate up to 24 hours.

pan, add the onion and soften – about 5 minutes. Add the garlic and mushrooms and continue to cook gently uncovered until the mushrooms are quite soft and any liquid has evaporated – about 20 minutes. The mushrooms will be quite dark in colour.

Stir in the soy sauce, vinegar, thyme and a seasoning of salt and pepper. Draw off the heat and cool.

Turn the curd cheese into a mixing bowl, add the mushroom mixture and blend – the cheese will take the colour of the mushrooms. Leave the mixture as a coarse pâté, or purée on a food processor or blender for a smoother mixture.

Spoon into a serving dish, cover and refrigerate for at least 1-2 hours. **P** Serve with warm French bread – no butter.

SWISS CHEESE TART

SERVES 6

1 recipe quantity tender crumb
  shortcrust (see right)

175 g (6 oz) Gruyère cheese

3 eggs (size 2)

1 egg yolk (size 2)

300 ml (½ pint) double cream

150 ml (¼ pint) milk

salt and freshly milled pepper

grated nutmeg

P Can be prepared ahead: reheat in a heated 160°C (325°F or gas no. 3) oven for 15 minutes.

For a tender, cooked-through pastry crust, use a metal flan tin with a push-up base and set the tart on a preheated baking sheet (see recipe instructions). The filling is creamy, and the cheese must be Gruyère for its delicious melting quality. Serve slices of the tart on a plate with large, crisp sprigs of watercress alongside.

Roll out the prepared pastry on a lightly floured work surface and use to line a 22.5cm (9 inch) flan tin with a removable base. Trim the edges. Prick the base with a fork, line with a circle of greaseproof paper and cover with a layer of 'baking beans'. Chill for 20 minutes.

Heat the oven to 190°C (375°F or gas no. 5) and put a baking sheet in the oven to heat. Place the chilled pastry shell in its tin directly on the hot baking sheet and bake for 20 minutes.

Meanwhile, grate the Gruyère cheese and set aside. In a mixing bowl, combine the eggs, egg yolk, double cream and milk and whisk to break up the eggs. Strain into a jug and season with salt, freshly milled pepper and a grating of nutmeg.

When baking time is complete, remove the pastry shell from the oven and lift out the baking beans and paper. Remove the pastry shell from the tin and replace on the baking sheet. Sprinkle in the cheese and pour in the custard.

Replace the tart in the oven and bake for a further 20 minutes or until the custard has set. Serve warm. **P**

TENDER CRUMB SHORTCRUST

MAKES A 225 g (8 oz) QUANTITY

225 g (8 oz) plain flour

pinch salt

150 g (5 oz) butter

1 egg (size 2)

2 tablespoons cold water

2 teaspoons white wine vinegar

A little vinegar keeps the pastry crust tender and you don't taste it at all. For really good results here, do the rubbing in and chill the mix – then the ingredients are really cold for mixing the dough.

Sift the flour and salt into a good sized mixing bowl. Add the butter cut in pieces and rub in with the fingertips. Combine the egg, water and vinegar – in a measure it should reach 75 ml (3 fl oz). Add all at once to the dry ingredients and stir with a table knife to form a rough dough in the bowl.

With floured fingers, draw the dough into a ball and turn on to a lightly floured work surface. Knead two or three times just to smooth the surface. Place in a polythene bag and refrigerate for at least 30 minutes (or overnight) before rolling out.

An oven heated to 190°C (375°F or gas no. 5) is the correct temperature for baking unless the recipe states otherwise.

In a food processor: put the flour, salt and chilled butter (cut in pieces) in the food processor bowl and process to fine crumbs. Turn the mixture into a bowl. Add the combined egg, water and vinegar and mix by hand to a dough.

For 175 (6 oz) pastry: use 175 g (6 oz) plain flour, pinch salt, 90 g (3½ oz) butter, 1 egg (size 3), 1 tablespoon cold water and 1 teaspoon white wine vinegar.

COURGETTE MOULDS WITH BASIL VINAIGRETTE

SERVES 6

450 g (1 lb) courgettes

1 medium onion

3 tablespoons grapeseed or other mild oil

2 tablespoons chopped fresh basil leaves

225 g (8 oz) curd cheese

2 eggs (size 2)

50 g (2 oz) fresh white breadcrumbs

salt and freshly milled pepper

A flavoursome combination, this actually tastes better warm than cold. Lining the moulds with the thinnest strips of courgette and adding basil leaves to the dressing makes these look very professional.

Wash and trim the courgettes but do not peel. Take one courgette and slice it lengthways into fine strips – a swivel-bladed vegetable peeler gives the best results. Soften the strips by placing them in a colander and pouring through boiling water from the kettle. Press the strips dry in absorbent kitchen paper. Lightly oil 6 individual moulds, about 150 ml (¼ pint) capacity, and line each one with two softened courgette strips. Set aside while preparing the filling.

25 g (1 oz) grated Parmesan cheese

For the vinaigrette dressing

salt and freshly milled pepper

1 level teaspoon wholegrain mustard

2 tablespoons wine vinegar

6 tablespoons olive oil

6-8 fresh basil leaves

P Can be prepared ahead: cover and refrigerate for no longer than 8 hours. Let come to room temperature before baking.

Cut the remaining courgettes up coarsely. Peel and finely chop the onion. Heat the oil in a frying pan, add the onion and soften over low heat – 5-8 minutes. Add the courgettes, cover and cook gently until they are barely tender – about 10 minutes. Let the mixture cool, then add the basil.

Heat the oven to 180°C (350°F or gas no. 4).

Turn the curd cheese into the bowl of a food processor. Add the eggs and process for a moment to blend. Then add the courgette mixture with the juices from the pan, the breadcrumbs, a seasoning of salt and pepper and the grated cheese. Cover and blend to a coarse purée. Spoon the mixture into the prepared moulds. **P**

Set the filled moulds in a deep roasting tin and add boiling water to come about 2.5 cm (1 inch) up the sides of the moulds. Cover with kitchen foil. Set in the heated oven and bake for 20 minutes.

Let cool for 5-10 minutes, then loosen the sides and unmould. Serve warm with a vinaigrette made by mixing a seasoning of salt and pepper, the mustard and vinegar in a small bowl. Add the oil in a stream and mix to an emulsion. Stir in torn basil leaves for flavour.

PASTA AND SMOKED CHICKEN SALAD WITH YOGURT DRESSING

SERVES 6

225 g (8 oz) pasta bows

2 tablespoons olive oil

1 bunch (6-8) spring onions

1 medium cucumber

350 g (12 oz) smoked chicken or ham

150 ml (¼ pint) natural yogurt

1 tablespoon tarragon wine vinegar

salt and freshly milled pepper

2 tablespoons chopped fresh chives

watercress leaves or lamb's lettuce, to garnish

The intricate curls and twists of pasta shapes are perfect for holding salad dressings – I always think the 'bows' are particularly attractive. Take care to slightly undercook pasta for salads; you will find the shapes absorb the dressing and continue to soften as the salad stands.

Bring a large pan of salted water to the boil. Add the pasta, stir until reboiling and cook for 6-8 minutes or until just tender, then drain. Turn the pasta into a large mixing bowl, add the oil and mix through. Let cool for about 10 minutes.

Trim the spring onions, then chop all the white part and some of the green stems. Peel the cucumber, halve lengthways and scoop out the centre seeds using a teaspoon. Cut the cucumber lengthways and then across into small dice. Cut the smoked chicken or ham into pieces. Add the spring onions, cucumber and chicken or ham to the pasta. **P**

Combine the yogurt, wine vinegar, a seasoning of salt and

P Can be prepared ahead: cover and refrigerate for no longer than 8 hours.

pepper and the chopped chives. Add to the pasta and turn the ingredients until well mixed. Turn the salad into a serving bowl and scatter watercress or lamb's lettuce leaves over before serving.

MIXED LEAF SALAD WITH BACON AND WHITE STILTON

SERVES 6

5 slices white bread

1 iceberg lettuce

225 g (8 oz) mixed salad leaves – oak leaf, frisée, lamb's lettuce and rocket with fresh chervil is a good choice

350 g (12 oz) rashers streaky bacon

2 tablespoons grapeseed or other mild oil

175-225 g (6-8 oz) white Stilton or Cheshire cheese

2 tablespoons tarragon wine vinegar

1 level teaspoon wholegrain mustard

salt and freshly milled pepper

6 tablespoons extra virgin olive oil

P Can be prepared ahead: keep in an airtight container.

Use a supermarket bag of mixed salad leaves here – it's the best way to get the variety. Interesting additions make appetizing contrasts with crisp bacon, crumbled cheese and crunchy croûtons. A delicious hot weather main dish salad – full of different textures.

Heat the oven to 160°C (325°F or gas no. 3).

Trim the crusts from the bread, then cut the slices in small dice. Spread on a baking tray and dry off in the heated oven for 30-40 minutes or until golden and quite crisp. Let cool. **P**

Remove the centre core from the iceberg lettuce and, with a kitchen knife, cut it into crisp chunks. Pick over and rinse the salad leaves, then shake dry and refrigerate tightly tied in a polythene bag so they crisp up.

Trim the bacon rashers, then snip with scissors into small pieces. Blanch the bacon bits in boiling water for 1 minute, then drain well. Fry the bacon gently in a pan with the grapeseed oil to draw the fat and crisp the bacon pieces. Drain on absorbent kitchen paper.

Crumble the cheese into chunky pieces.

In a bowl, whisk the tarragon vinegar, mustard and a seasoning of salt and pepper. Add the olive oil and whisk to an emulsion.

Turn the salad leaves into a serving bowl. Add the dressing and toss to shine the leaves. Sprinkle over the bacon bits, crumbled cheese and crunchy croûtons and serve.

LEMON CHICKEN WITH SWEET RED PEPPERS

SERVES 6

6 skinned chicken breast fillets

finely grated zest and juice 1 lemon

200 ml (7 fl oz) chicken stock

2 red sweet peppers

25 g (1 oz) butter, at room temperature

25 g (1 oz) plain flour

salt and freshly milled pepper

150 ml (¼ pint) double cream

decorated pastry triangles, to garnish (see page 102)

Chicken breasts are the part that everybody likes to eat, but without the carcass you will have to make the stock with a cube. I've added a strong flavour of lemon and used red pepper, which is the sweetest of the pepper colours, to contrast with the other flavours.

Heat the oven to 160°C (325°F or gas no. 3). Arrange the chicken fillets in a single layer in a shallow baking dish. Add the lemon zest to the stock and pour over the chicken. Cover the baking dish with kitchen foil. Set in the heated oven and bake for 20-30 minutes or until the chicken is tender.

Meanwhile, quarter the sweet peppers lengthways and remove the seeds. Arrange on a baking tray and grill until the skins are blistered and charred. Cover and leave for about 10 minutes by which time they should be cool enough to handle. Peel off the skins and chop the peppers coarsely. Keep warm.

Transfer the chicken pieces to a warmed serving platter and keep hot. Strain the cooking liquid into a saucepan and bring to the boil. Simmer rapidly for about 10 minutes to reduce and concentrate the flavour. On a plate, blend the butter and flour together to make a soft paste. Draw the pan off the heat, add the butter paste in small pieces and stir to blend. Return the pan to the heat and bring to the boil, stirring all the time to make a smooth sauce. Season with salt and pepper, and add the lemon juice and the cream. Reheat, add the peppers and pour over the chicken.

Add hot pastry triangles just before serving.

SPICED COCONUT LAMB

SERVES 6

900 g (2 lb) lean boneless lamb

1 large onion

3-4 cloves garlic

50 g (2 oz) butter

2 level teaspoons grated fresh root ginger

You should have a reasonable collection of spices in the cupboard to make this subtly spiced and pleasant recipe. The coconut cream is more unusual but is essential as it thickens the sauce and adds a smooth rich flavour. This same recipe can be made with pork fillet.

Trim the lamb and cut into small pieces. Peel and finely slice the onion. Peel and crush the garlic to a purée. Heat the butter

1 level teaspoon turmeric

2 level teaspoons ground cumin

1 level teaspoon mild chilli
  powder

8 whole green cardamom pods

4 whole cloves

300 ml (½ pint) water

300 ml (½ pint) single cream

50 g (2 oz) creamed coconut

50 g (2 oz) sultanas

fresh coriander leaves, to
  garnish

in a 25 cm (10 inch) frying pan (one with a lid), add the onion and fry gently until soft and golden. Stir in the mashed garlic, grated ginger, turmeric, cumin, chilli powder, crushed cardamom pods and the cloves. Fry for a further few moments to draw out the flavouring oils from the spices.

Add the meat and turn in the hot butter and spices. Stir in the water and cream and bring to a simmer, then cover with the pan lid and cook gently, stirring occasionally, for 1 hour or until the meat is tender.

Remove the pan lid and add the creamed coconut broken in pieces and the sultanas. Stir over low heat until the sauce thickens. Turn into a hot serving dish and garnish with coriander leaves. Serve with hot pilau rice.

PILAU RICE

SERVES 6

350 g (12 oz) basmati rice

1 medium onion

25 g (1 oz) butter

600 ml (1 pint) hot water

1½ level teaspoons salt

1 level teaspoon turmeric

1 level teaspoon ground
  coriander

1 bay leaf

3 cloves

50 g (2 oz) flaked almonds

A fine quality rice like basmati is very reliable and always cooks to perfectly separated grains. Using this method you'll find the mixture has plenty of flavour too because the spiced liquid is absorbed as the rice cooks. Fork the mixture up gently before serving.

Wash the rice grains thoroughly and drain well. Peel and finely chop the onion. Melt the butter in a medium saucepan, add the chopped onion and fry for a few moments to soften. Add the rice and stir into the butter and onion.

Stir in the water. Add the salt, turmeric, ground coriander, bay leaf and cloves. Bring to a simmer, stirring, then cover with the pan lid and cook over low heat for 15 minutes or until the rice is just tender and liquid absorbed. Draw off the heat and leave undisturbed for a further 5 minutes.

Meanwhile, toast the almonds (see page 210).

Fork the flaked almonds into the rice before serving.

MARINATED YELLOW PEPPERS WITH BULGAR WHEAT SALAD

SERVES 6

6 yellow sweet peppers

175 g (6 oz) bulgar wheat

400 ml (¾ pint) cold vegetable stock

2 medium onions

5 tablespoons olive oil

1 level teaspoon castor sugar

grated zest and juice 1 lemon

salt and freshly milled pepper

50 g (2 oz) seedless raisins

50 g (2 oz) pine nuts

350 g (12 oz) sliced pastrami, for serving

For the lemon dressing

100 ml (4 fl oz) olive oil

juice 2 lemons

salt and freshly milled pepper

Sweet peppers make attractive containers for interesting stuffings. These are filled and served cold with sliced pastrami; if your guests are vegetarian make it smoked salmon or slices of mozzarella cheese.

Take a slice from the top of each yellow pepper, leaving the stalk intact, and reserve. Shave the base of each pepper so it stands level and remove the seeds from inside each one. Pack the peppers close together in a deep-sided baking dish or casserole and set aside while preparing the stuffing.

Measure the bulgar wheat into a bowl and cover with the cold vegetable stock. Let soak for 1 hour – the bulgar wheat will swell and double in size. Drain the wheat in a colander, pressing out excess stock. Reserve the stock. Turn the bulgar wheat into a mixing bowl.

Peel and finely slice the onions. Heat 2 tablespoons of the oil in a frying pan, add the onions and sprinkle with the sugar. Cook gently, stirring occasionally, for about 20 minutes or until the onions are quite soft and beginning to take a golden colour. Draw off the heat. Add the grated zest and juice of the lemon, the remaining oil and a good seasoning of salt and pepper. Pour this hot dressing over the bulgar wheat and mix through. Add the seedless raisins and pine nuts and mix. Taste for seasoning.

Heat the oven to 180°C (350°F or gas no. 4).

Spoon the stuffing into each pepper case, filling them to the brim and pressing it in gently. Cover with the pepper lids. Add 4 tablespoons of the reserved stock to the baking dish. Cover the baking dish with foil or casserole lid. Set in the heated oven and bake for 45 minutes or until the peppers are tender. Remove from the oven and leave the peppers, covered, until quite cold – preferably overnight. **P**

Lift the peppers from the baking dish and arrange on a serving platter. In a mixing bowl, combine the olive oil, lemon juice and a seasoning of salt and pepper for the dressing. Add 3-4 tablespoons of the cold stock from the baking dish. Drizzle the dressing over the peppers and let marinate at room temperature for about 1 hour.

Add slices of pastrami to the platter before serving.

HERB-CRUMBED CHICKEN WITH MUSTARD DIPPING SAUCE

SERVES 6

6 skinned chicken breast fillets

1 egg (size 2)

*1 tablespoon grapeseed or
  other mild oil*

seasoned flour

*100 g (4 oz) fresh white
  breadcrumbs*

*1 tablespoon chopped fresh
  parsley*

*1 level teaspoon dried mixed
  herbs*

grated zest 1 lemon

salt and freshly milled pepper

50 g (2 oz) butter

2 lemons, for serving

For the dipping sauce

150 ml (¼ pint) soured cream

*2 level tablespoons wholegrain
  mustard*

½ level teaspoon salt

P Can be prepared ahead: keep
refrigerated for up to 6 hours.

*The crumbs used here need to be fresh and not dried so they
will absorb the butter and bake to a crunchy, crisp finish. In a
food processor, fresh bread slices can be reduced to crumbs in a
matter of seconds and they freeze well – it's worthwhile having
some on hand for a recipe like this.*

Heat the oven to 200°C (400°F or gas no. 6).

Trim the chicken pieces neatly. Crack the egg on to a
shallow plate, add the oil and mix with a fork. Spoon the
seasoned flour on to a second plate. Combine the breadcrumbs,
parsley, dried mixed herbs, grated lemon zest and a seasoning
of salt and pepper in a bowl. Melt the butter, add to the crumb
mixture and stir with a fork until the crumbs are butter-coated.

Turn the chicken fillets first in seasoned flour, then dip in
the beaten egg and finally coat with the buttered crumbs. Press
the crumb coating on firmly. Cover and refrigerate for at least
1 hour **P**

Arrange the chicken pieces on a buttered tray, spacing them
apart. Set in the heated oven and bake for 30 minutes or until
the chicken is tender and the coating crisp and golden.

Meanwhile, combine the soured cream, mustard and salt for
the sauce, cover and chill.

Arrange the chicken on a heated platter. Cut the lemons into
wedges and use as a garnish. Serve the mustard dipping sauce
separately.

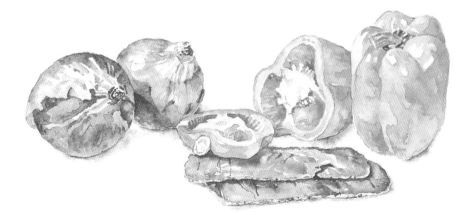

CHICKEN BREASTS STUFFED WITH APPLE AND SAGE

SERVES 8

8 chicken breast fillets with skins on

40 g (1½ oz) butter

3 red-skinned dessert apples

1 tablespoon cranberry jelly

For the stuffing

1 small onion

15 g (½ oz) butter

50 g (2 oz) fresh white breadcrumbs

225 g (8 oz) curd cheese

4-6 fresh sage leaves, or ½ level teaspoon rubbed dried sage

salt and freshly milled pepper

2 red-skinned dessert apples

Take care to pick out chicken breast fillets with their skins on so you can tuck this delicious curd cheese and grated apple mixture underneath. Avoid frozen chicken fillets at all costs: they stew in the oven instead of baking and the results are nothing like so good.

Heat the oven to 180°C (350°F or gas no. 4).

Partially loosen the skin on each chicken breast with your fingertips to form a pocket. Set aside while preparing the stuffing.

Peel and finely chop the onion. Melt the butter in a saucepan, add the onion and cook gently to soften. Draw off the heat and stir in the breadcrumbs with a fork. Turn the curd cheese into a mixing bowl. Add the breadcrumb mixture, the finely chopped sage leaves (or rubbed sage) and a good seasoning of salt and freshly milled pepper. Quarter and core the apples, leaving on the skins, then grate coarsely and add. Mix the ingredients thoroughly.

Take a dessertspoon of the stuffing and spoon into the pocket under the skin on each chicken fillet. Fold the thinner ends of the breasts underneath to form neat rounded shapes. Arrange close together in a well-buttered baking dish. **P**

Brush the chicken breasts with 15 g (½ oz) of the butter, melted. Set in the heated oven and bake for 30-35 minutes or until golden brown.

Meanwhile, core the apples leaving them whole, then slice across. Melt the rest of the butter in a frying pan. Add the apple slices and fry for 2-3 minutes, turning them over once or twice. Draw off the heat, add the cranberry jelly and stir until the jelly is melted and the apple slices are glazed.

Transfer the chicken breasts to a heated serving platter. Add the juices from the baking dish to the apple slices and stir to blend. Spoon the apple slices and pan juices around the chicken and serve.

P Can be prepared ahead: cover and refrigerate for up to 8 hours.

BAKED PARCELS OF SALMON WITH HERB BUTTER

SERVES 6

6 salmon steaks or cutlets, cut at least 2.5 cm (1 inch) thick

juice 1 lemon

4 tablespoons olive oil

4 tablespoons chopped coriander or chives

freshly milled pepper

1 leek

2 small carrots

100-125 g (4-5 oz) butter

milled sea salt

1 tablespoon lemon juice

P Can be prepared ahead: chill no longer than 12 hours.

Individual salmon portions can be wrapped and baked in the oven for serving hot; I like using greaseproof paper, in preference to foil, because the paper bakes translucent and you can almost see the contents. You can replace the vegetable shreds with blanched asparagus tips or mange touts, if you like.

Place the salmon cutlets in a shallow dish large enough for them to lie in one layer. In a bowl mix the lemon juice, oil, half the chopped herbs and a seasoning of freshly milled pepper.

Pour over the salmon cutlets, turn them in the mixture and let marinade for 1 hour. Meanwhile, trim the leek to 25 mm (1 inch) of the white stem, split lengthways and rinse well. Pare and cut the carrot in fine slices lengthways. Cut both vegetables into fine shreds. Place in a saucepan, cover with boiling water and simmer 3 minutes to blanch. Drain and return to the pan with 25 g (1 oz) of the butter and soften over gentle heat.

Cut 6 squares of greaseproof paper, each large enough to enclose one salmon portion. Brush each sheet with a little olive oil. Place a salmon piece in the centre of one sheet, season with salt and top with a forkful of the vegetable mixture. Draw opposite sides of the paper square over the fish and fold closed, then fold ends underneath to make a neat parcel. Repeat with each salmon portion. Arrange parcels in one layer in a baking dish or on a baking tray. **P**

Heat the oven to 180°C (350°F or gas no. 4). Set the baking dish or tray of salmon parcels in the oven, and bake for 15-20 minutes. Warm the remaining butter with the lemon juice, then add the rest of the chopped herbs. Open up the parcels and transfer salmon to hot serving plates. Pour over the melted lemon butter.

Overleaf: Baked parcels of salmon with herb butter

BEEF CASSEROLE WITH PARSLEY DUMPLINGS

SERVES 6

900 g (2 lb) lean braising steak

seasoned flour

½ level teaspoon dried mixed herbs

2 medium onions

25 g (1 oz) butter

1 tablespoon olive oil

1 level teaspoon castor sugar

6 carrots

1 bay leaf

few sprigs fresh thyme

piece pared orange zest

400 ml (¾ pint) beef or vegetable stock

225 ml (8 fl oz) red wine

1 level tablespoon concentrated tomato purée

salt and fresh milled pepper

1 teaspoon wine vinegar

For the dumplings

175 g (6 oz) self-raising flour

salt and freshly milled pepper

½ level teaspoon dried mixed herbs

2 tablespoons chopped fresh parsley

2 tablespoons grapeseed or other mild oil

1 egg (size 2)

1-2 tablespoons water

I find there really is no need to seal the beef for this kind of traditional casserole. Instead I fry the onions to a golden brown – they provide a good basic flavour and it's all much less trouble. Dumplings are always popular and will be feather-light if you weigh the dry ingredients in advance, but mix and add them straight to the cooking pot.

Trim the meat and cut into neat pieces, then roll in mixed seasoned flour and dried herbs. Place the floured meat in a casserole dish. Peel and thinly slice the onions. Heat the butter and oil in a frying pan, add the onions, sprinkle with the sugar and fry gently until the onions are softened and golden – about 20 minutes. Add the onions to the meat, leaving any pan dripping behind.

Heat the oven to 160°C (325°F or gas no. 3).

Peel and slice the carrots on the bias and add to the casserole along with the extra flavourings by way of bay leaf, thyme and pared orange zest. Add the stock, wine, concentrated tomato purée, a seasoning of salt and pepper and the vinegar. Cover, set in the heated oven and cook for 2 hours or until the meat is tender. **P**

Raise the oven heat to 180°C (350°F or gas no. 4). Sift the flour and a seasoning of salt and pepper into a bowl. Add the dried and fresh herbs. Combine the oil, egg and water. Add all at once to the dry ingredients and mix with a fork to a soft dough. Turn on to a floured surface and divide the dough into 8 portions. Roll each portion into a dumpling and place on top of the meat and vegetables (do not submerge). Recover the casserole and cook for a further 15-20 minutes.

P Can be prepared ahead: cool, cover and refrigerate for up to 24 hours. Reheat before adding dumplings.

MARINATED BEEF WITH A SPICED CRUST

SERVES 12

1 piece rolled silverside of beef, about 2.2 kg (5 lb)

For the dry marinade

50 g (2 oz) salt

1 level tablespoon ground black pepper

1 level tablespoon dry mustard powder

1 level tablespoon celery seasoning

½ level tablespoon dried thyme

½ level tablespoon ground cloves

2 cloves garlic

For the wet marinade

150 ml (¼ pint) grapeseed or other mild oil

150 ml (¼ pint) red wine vinegar

2 level tablespoons concentrated tomato purée

Several days are required to marinate this joint – first in a dry spice blend and then in an oil and vinegar mix – but the trouble is well worth the delicious flavour. Roast the meat to rare in preference to well done and it will taste very tender.

Your piece of silverside should be ready rolled and tied for roasting. Dry the outside well with absorbent kitchen paper. Combine the salt, pepper, mustard powder, celery seasoning, dried thyme and ground cloves in a bowl. Peel and finely chop the garlic and add to the mixture. Rub the outside of the joint well with this dry spice blend – you won't need it all but it keeps well and can be used another time. Wrap the beef joint in greaseproof paper and refrigerate overnight, or better ,still for 48 hours.

Combine the oil, vinegar and tomato purée for the wet marinade. Unwrap the beef joint and place it in a large freezer bag. Add the wet marinade and tie the bag closed. Leave the meat to marinate in the refrigerator for up to 24 hours, turning the bag once or twice to keep the meat moist. **P**

Heat the oven to 220°C (425°F or gas no. 7).

Lift the meat from the bag, reserving the marinade mixture in a bowl for basting, and set the beef joint in a roasting tin – no dripping or fat is required. Place in the heated oven and roast for 20 minutes. Reduce the oven heat to 180°C (350°F or gas no. 4) and continue roasting, allowing 20 minutes per 450 g (1 lb) for rare and 25 minutes per 450 g (1 lb) for medium done. Spoon over a little of the reserved marinade once or twice during the roasting time. When cooked the outside should be crusty and brown with the inside still pink.

Let the joint stand for 10 minutes so the meat juices can settle before carving. Serve with onion marmalade (see page 58) as a relish.

ONION MARMALADE

SERVES 6-8

900 g (2 lb) large onions

2 cloves garlic

4 tablespoons grapeseed or other mild oil

150 ml (¼ pint) red wine

1 level tablespoon wholegrain mustard

2 tablespoons red wine vinegar

1 level tablespoon light muscovado sugar

salt and freshly milled pepper

This is a relish, not a keeping preserve. Store it in the refrigerator and use within a week or so. It's a dark, sweet and spicy mixture that can be served with any cold meats or poultry and it's nice with pâté too.

Peel the onions and slice thinly, then separate the onion rings. Peel and finely chop the garlic. Heat the oil in a large frying pan, add the onion rings and soften over low heat for about 10 minutes. Add the garlic, red wine, wholegrain mustard, red wine vinegar, sugar and a seasoning of salt and freshly milled pepper.

Bring the contents to the boil. Stir well, then reduce the heat to a gentle simmer. Cover with the pan lid and cook for 30 minutes or until the onions are well softened.

Remove the pan lid and increase the heat. Cook, stirring occasionally, until the onion mixture is thick and well browned. Allow to cool before serving. **P**

CRANBERRY CROWN ROAST OF PORK

SERVES 12

1 crown roast of pork, prepared using 2 loins of pork with at least 6 bones on each

150 ml (¼ pint) red wine

300 ml (½ pint) vegetable stock or water

1 level tablespoon cornflour

2 tablespoons cold water

salt and freshly milled pepper

For the cranberry stuffing

450 g (1 lb) fresh or frozen cranberries

100 g (4 oz) castor sugar

150 ml (¼ pint) water

100 g (4 oz) fresh white breadcrumbs

50 g (2 oz) seedless raisins

grated zest 1 orange

1 level teaspoon salt

Tangy bright red cranberries are the perfect foil for the rich flavour of pork. This is an impressive roast with a delicious cranberry and raisin stuffing that, incidentally, is also good for roast turkey or chicken.

Heat the oven to 180°C (350°F or gas no. 4).

Remove any trimmings from inside the pork crown (butchers sometimes tuck trimmings inside to plump out the shape). Set the joint in a roasting tin and wrap the bone ends in foil to prevent excess browning. Set in the heated oven and roast for 2-2½ hours.

Meanwhile, pick over and rinse the cranberries. Measure the sugar and water into a saucepan. Stir over low heat to dissolve the sugar. Add the cranberries, bring to a simmer and cook gently for about 10 minutes or until the skins pop and the berries are soft. Measure the breadcrumbs, seedless raisins, orange zest, salt, a seasoning of pepper and the cinnamon into a bowl. Add half the cranberry mixture and the butter, melted. Stir with a fork to blend the ingredients.

About 1 hour before the pork roast is done, spoon the stuffing into the centre of the crown, pushing it down gently

freshly milled pepper

¼ level teaspoon ground cinnamon

50 g (2 oz) butter

and doming the top. Complete the cooking time – when the juices run clear (not pink), the pork is done. Lift the roast on to a warmed serving platter and remove the foil from the bone ends; keep hot. Pour off excess fat from the roasting tin and set the tin over direct heat. Add the wine and boil up to reduce while stirring up the pan drippings. Add the stock and 2-3 tablespoons of the reserved cranberries to bring up the colour. Blend the cornflour with the cold water to make a paste, stir into the pan juices and bring to a simmer. Taste, and season.

Spoon the remaining cranberries into the centre of the crown roast. Strain the gravy into a hot serving jug. Carve the roast by slicing between the bones.

HONEY ROAST LAMB WITH HONEY MINT SAUCE

SERVES 12

1 leg of lamb, about 2.9 kg (6 lb)

2 level tablespoons plain flour

1 level teaspoon salt

freshly milled pepper

½ level teaspoon ground cinnamon

1 large onion

1 large carrot

1 heaped tablespoon clear honey

400 ml (¾ pint) dry cider

1 level tablespoon cornflour

2 tablespoons cold water

For the honey mint sauce

225 ml (8 fl oz) white wine vinegar

2 tablespoons clear honey

4-6 tablespoons finely chopped fresh mint

When home-produced lamb is available, choose a succulent leg of Welsh or Scottish lamb. Add this glaze and a honey sweet mint sauce for a special treat.

Heat the oven to 180°C (350°F or gas no. 4). Trim the joint. Combine the flour, salt, a seasoning of freshly milled pepper and the ground cinnamon and rub it well into the lamb on all sides. Peel the onion and carrot and cut in thick slices. Lay these in the bottom of a roasting tin and place the meat on top.

Set the lamb in the heated oven and roast, allowing 25 minutes per 450 g (1 lb). Turn the joint over about halfway through so that the meat cooks evenly.

Meanwhile, make the honey mint sauce. Bring the vinegar and honey to a simmer and draw off the heat. Stir in the freshly chopped mint. Let cool. **P**

About 30 minutes before the end of the cooking time, lift the joint from the roasting tin. Pour off any fat, leaving pan drippings and vegetables behind. Replace the meat, best side up. Spread the honey over the surface and add the cider to the tin. Replace in the oven and complete the roasting time, basting once or twice with the juices in the tin.

Lift the meat on to a hot serving platter and let stand for 10 minutes for the juices to settle. Meanwhile, blend the cornflour with the cold water and stir into the juices in the roasting tin. Bring to a simmer over direct heat and stir for a few moments, then strain the gravy into a hot jug. Serve the roast lamb with the hot gravy and honey mint sauce.

AMBROSIA FRUIT BOWL

SERVES 6-8

6 oranges
1 medium pineapple
50 g (2 oz) castor sugar
1 level tablespoon cornflour
2 tablespoons cold water
1 tablespoon lemon juice
2-3 tablespoons rum

P Can be prepared ahead: keep refrigerated no longer than overnight.

This refreshing combination of fruits glows yellow and orange. Pineapple are always a delicious buy, and it's nice to have a recipe that uses up a whole fruit. The addition of rum emphasizes the flavours beautifully.

Take a slice from the top and base of each of five oranges and, using a sharp knife, cut round and round (like an apple) to remove the outer peel and white pith. Hold the fruit over a mixing bowl (to catch the juices) and cut into each one between the dividing membranes, lifting out the fruit segments. Put the orange segments into a serving bowl. Strain the orange juice into a measuring jug and reserve.

Using a vegetable peeler, remove the outer zest from the remaining orange and cut into very fine shreds. Add the juice of the orange to the measuring jug. Cut away the peel from the pineapple and slice first into thin wedges and then across into pieces. Add the pineapple to the orange segments.

Make the reserved orange juice up to 300 ml (½ pint) with water and pour into a saucepan. Stir in the sugar and shredded orange zest and set over the heat. Blend the cornflour with the cold water and stir into the contents of the saucepan. Bring to the boil, stirring all the time so the mixture thickens evenly. Draw off the heat and add the lemon juice and rum. Cool for 5 minutes, then pour over the fruits. Cool completely, then cover and refrigerate for several hours before serving. **P**

CREAMED RICE WITH CANDIED FRUITS

SERVES 6

75 g (3 oz) pudding rice
600 ml (1 pint) milk
3 tablespoons cold water
15 g (½ oz) powdered gelatine
75 g (3 oz) castor sugar
3 egg yolks (size 2)
2 level tablespoons chopped candied peel – citron, orange and lemon
2 level tablespoons cut up glacé cherries

Here, plump grains of pudding rice thicken and absorb milk to make a creamy, old-fashioned pudding, but then glacé fruits and nuts are added and the mixture is served cold, to become an elegant dessert.

Put the rice and milk in a medium saucepan and bring to a simmer, then cook gently, stirring frequently, until the rice grains are tender and the mixture is thick and creamy – about 30 minutes.

Meanwhile, measure the water into a small cup and sprinkle in the gelatine. Let soak for 5 minutes.

When the rice mixture is cooked, draw the pan off the heat. Add the soaked gelatine and stir until it has dissolved – the

2 level tablespoons chopped blanched almonds

1 teaspoon vanilla essence

300 ml (½ pint) double cream

For the caramel sauce

4 heaped tablespoons granulated sugar

300 ml (½ pint) water

juice 1 lemon

P Can be prepared ahead: keep the rice moulds refrigerated for no longer than overnight. Keep the sauce in a cool place.

heat of the rice mixture will be sufficient to do this. Add the sugar, then beat in the egg yolks one at a time. Turn the contents of the pan into a mixing bowl and set aside to cool, stirring once or twice.

Reserve a few chunky pieces of fruit for decoration, and stir the remainder into the creamed rice along with the nuts and vanilla essence. Whip the cream to soft peaks and fold into the rice and fruit mixture.

Place one or two pieces of the reserved fruit in the base of six individual moulds or one larger 1.1 litre (2 pint) mould, and spoon in the rice mixture. Tap the moulds gently so the mixture levels out. Refrigerate for several hours. **P**

To make the caramel sauce, measure the sugar into a dry saucepan, set the pan over moderate heat and stir until the sugar has melted and turned to a golden caramel. Draw off the heat and add a little of the water – take care as the mixture will bubble up furiously with the addition of a cold liquid. Return the pan to the heat and stir in the remaining water to make a thin caramel syrup. Add the lemon juice and allow to cool. **P**

Unmould on to serving plates, and serve with the caramel sauce or thin pouring cream.

CHILLED LEMON SOUFFLÉ

SERVES 6

4 eggs (size 2)

2 egg yolks (size 2)

75 ml (3 fl oz) cold water

15 g (½ oz) powdered gelatine

finely grated zest and juice 3 lemons

100 g (4 oz) castor sugar

300 ml (½ pint) double cream

toasted flaked almonds (see page 210), to decorate

This is a particularly good recipe, with a tart, lemony flavour and light texture. Chilled as a soufflé it looks grand, but you could also pour the mixture into a bowl and serve it as a mousse – with a fresh fruit sauce like strawberry or raspberry, for instance.

Fix a band of folded greaseproof paper around the outside of a 1.1 litre (2 pint) soufflé dish. Tie the paper in position with string and set the soufflé dish on a large plate so that it can be easily handled.

Separate the eggs, cracking the yolks into a large mixing bowl and the whites into a second smaller bowl. Add the extra 2 egg yolks to the other yolks. Measure the cold water into a saucepan and sprinkle in the gelatine. Let soak for 5 minutes, then stir over low heat until the gelatine has dissolved – do not boil. Draw off the heat.

Add the finely grated lemon zest, lemon juice and 75 g (3 oz) of the sugar to the egg yolks. Set the mixing bowl over a saucepan one-quarter filled with hot water (the water should not touch the base of the bowl) and whisk until the mixture is

P Can be prepared ahead: keep refrigerated for up to 8 hours.

thick and light. Remove the bowl from the heat. Hold the pan of dissolved gelatine over the mixing bowl, pour it in in a steady stream and whisk into the lemon mixture. Let the mixture cool, whisking occasionally, for about 20 minutes.

Whisk the egg whites to stiff peaks, sprinkle in the remaining sugar and whisk until glossy. Whip the cream to soft peaks. Fold first the cream and then the egg whites into the lemon mixture. Turn into the prepared soufflé dish. Cover and refrigerate for at least 3 hours. **P**

Let stand at room temperature for 30 minutes, then gently peel away the paper collar. Decorate with toasted flaked almonds in concentric rings on top only. This is delicious with pouring cream.

APPLE STREUSEL PIE

SERVES 6

175 g (6 oz) tender crumb shortcrust (see page 44)

700 g (1½ lb) sharp-flavoured dessert apples

50 g (2 oz) castor sugar

1 level tablespoon cornflour

25 g (1 oz) seedless raisins

icing sugar, to decorate

For the streusel topping

100 g (4 oz) plain flour

75 g (3 oz) butter, at room temperature

50 g (2 oz) light muscavado sugar

3 level tablespoons toasted, chopped hazelnuts (see page 210)

Here's an apple pie with a difference – there's a pastry crust with an apple and raisin filling, but on top is a crunchy crumble mixture that includes chopped hazelnuts.

On a lightly floured surface, roll out the pastry and use to line a 22.5 cm (9 inch) pie plate, leaving a 2.5 cm (1 inch) rim of pastry hanging over the edge. Make the pie rim higher by folding the overhanging pastry underneath, then pinch and twist with the fingers to form a stand-up rim around the plate. Put the pastry shell to chill while you make the filling. **P**

Heat the oven to 200°C (400°F or gas no. 6).

Peel, core and slice the apples. In a bowl, mix together the sugar and cornflour. Soften the raisins in hot water for a few minutes, then drain. Arrange the apple slices in the pastry shell, sprinkling the layers with the sugar mixture and the raisins. Mound the slices in the pie centre.

Measure the flour for the topping into a mixing bowl. Add the butter and rub in with the fingertips. Add the sugar and continue to rub in until the mixture forms coarse crumbs. Add 2 tablespoons of the chopped hazelnuts. Cover the apples with the topping and press down lightly. Sprinkle with the remaining nuts.

Set the pie in the heated oven and bake for 20 minutes. Lower the oven heat to 190°C (375°F or gas no. 5) and bake for a further 20-25 minutes or until the apples are tender – test with a knife.

Cool the pie to room temperature, then dust with icing sugar and serve.

QUEEN OF PUDDINGS

SERVES 6

100 g (4 oz) fresh white
    breadcrumbs

175 g (6 oz) castor sugar

finely grated zest 1 large lemon

600 ml (1 pint) milk

50 g (2 oz) butter

4 eggs (size 2)

3 level tablespoons raspberry
    jam

P Can be prepared ahead. Cool,
then refrigerate for up to 4 hours.
Bring back to room temperature
before adding meringue.

When meringue is used as a dessert topping, less sugar is used to make a lighter mixture that's soft in the middle, and it is best eaten hot. I like to have the custard base baked beforehand with the topping added just before serving – while the meringue browns, the rest of the pudding warms through perfectly.

Put the breadcrumbs in a mixing bowl and add 50 g (2 oz) of the sugar and the lemon zest. Bring the milk and butter to the boil, pour over the crumb mixture and leave to soak for 15 minutes.

Heat the oven to 180°C (350°F or gas no. 4). Well butter a 1 litre (1¾ pint) baking dish – shallow rather than deep to allow plenty of room for the meringue topping.

Separate the eggs, mixing the yolks into the soaked breadcrumbs and putting the whites together in a mixing bowl. Pour the custard mixture into the prepared dish. Set in the heated oven and bake for 20-30 minutes or until the custard has set – test by giving the dish a gentle shake. Carefully spread the raspberry jam over the surface of the warm custard – if the jam is at all stiff, heat it a little first. **P**

Whisk the egg whites until stiff. Sprinkle in half the remaining sugar and whisk to a glossy meringue. Using a metal spoon, fold in the remaining sugar. Swirl the meringue over the top of the pudding and return to the oven to brown and crisp it – about 15 minutes. Serve warm.

TRIFLE WITH SYLLABUB

SERVES 6-8

100 ml (4 fl oz) dry white wine

pared zest and juice 1 lemon

225 g (8 oz) fresh or thawed
    frozen raspberries

150 g (5 oz) castor sugar

1 baked trifle sponge layer (see
    page 64)

6 egg yolks (size 2)

1 level tablespoon cornflour

600 ml (1 pint) milk

Instead of a whipped cream topping, spoon a wine and lemon syllabub over your trifle and the result is scrumptious. Start this recipe well in advance – you must let the sponge cake really soak and the topping should be well chilled before serving.

Put the wine and lemon zest in a bowl and let soak for several hours or overnight.

Crush the raspberries with 25 g (1 oz) of the sugar to make a purée. Split the trifle sponge cake into two layers and sandwich with the crushed berries. Sprinkle over the juice. Cut into pieces and put in the bottom of a glass serving bowl.

In a mixing bowl, beat the egg yolks, half the remaining

300 ml (½ pint) double cream

flaked almonds, toasted (see page 210)

sugar and the cornflour until smooth and light. Heat the milk in a saucepan until hot. Gradually stir the hot milk into the egg yolk mixture, blend well and strain the mixture back into the rinsed milk saucepan. Set over low heat and bring just to the boil, stirring constantly as the custard thickens to a coating consistency. Draw off the heat at once and place the base of the pan in a bowl of cold water to lower the temperature. Stir occasionally as the custard cools, then pour over the trifle sponge cake. Cover and refrigerate overnight. **P**

Remove the lemon zest from the wine and add the lemon juice, the rest of the sugar and the double cream to the wine. Whisk the syllabub until thick and light, then spoon over the trifle and swirl attractively. Refrigerate for at least 2-3 hours. Sprinkle with the toasted flaked almonds just before serving.

TRIFLE SPONGE LAYER

MAKES ONE 20 cm (8 inch) LAYER

65 g (2½ oz) plain flour

1 level tablespoon cornflour

2 eggs (size 2)

75 g (3 oz) castor sugar

1 tablespoon hand-hot water

This kind of open-textured sponge cake readily soaks up fruit juices or flavouring sprinkled over the surface. In addition to trifles, it is also good split and filled with whipped cream and fresh fruit for tea.

Heat the oven to 190°C (375°F or gas no. 5). Grease and flour a 20 cm (8 inch) sponge layer tin. Sift the flour and cornflour together twice and set in a warm place.

Crack the eggs into a mixing bowl, add the sugar and place over a saucepan one-quarter filled with hot (not boiling) water. Whisk until the mixture leaves a good trail as it drops from the whisk. Remove the bowl from the heat. Whisk for a moment or two longer – the mixture should be thick and foamy. (If using electric beaters, there is no need to place the bowl over hot water for whisking.) Sift the flour mixture evenly over the surface and fold in lightly using the cutting edge of a metal tablespoon. When the flour is half mixed, add the tepid water (to lighten the mixture) and fold until the ingredients are blended.

Turn the mixture into the prepared cake tin and spread level. Set in the heated oven and bake for 20-25 minutes. Let cool in the tin for 2 minutes, then loosen the sides and turn on to a wire cooling tray. Let cool completely. **P**

P Can be prepared ahead: keep in an airtight container.

AFTERNOON TEAS

Wheaten scones

Cheddar scones

Scotch pancakes

Potted cheese with walnuts

Cinnamon raisin bread

Wholemeal banana pecan bread

.

Strawberry shortcake

American chocolate cake

Baked lemon cheesecake

Citrus tarts – lemon or lime

Fruit and cream roulade

Mincemeat crumble cake

Raisin orange pound cake

Luscious fruit cake

.

Cinnamon glazed gingercake

Almond and chocolate chip cake

Apple frangipane tart

Almond shortcrust

Walnut and banana cake

Dutch apple cake

Chocolate rum cake

.

Highlanders

Chocolate creams

Hazelnut thins

Wheatmeal digestives

Rolled oat and raisin cookies

AFTERNOON TEAS

We British are famous for our afternoon teas. It was the Duchess of Bedford who invented the idea in the early 19th century – a welcome break between 4 and 4.30 in the afternoon when a cup of fragrant tea and something dainty to eat offers the perfect moment to stop everything and relax. Afternoon tea parties are very sociable, slightly decadent and great fun. They offer an excellent way of introducing yourself to the neighbours, getting a group meeting together or just catching up with friends.

This is a time for your prettiest china, your best silver and tray or tablecloths. In choosing foods, go for items that are delicate and light and include savouries – simple potted spreads that can be served with fingers of hot toast or warm cheese scones. Traditional items like hot toasted muffins or crumpets, in a basket lined with a cloth should be cut in halves or quarters so they are easy to pick up and eat in the fingers.

Some teatime specialities like scones are best served freshly made – have the mixture made up to the 'rubbed-in' stage, then mix and bake as close to serving time as possible. Teabreads, pound cakes and richer fruit cake are good keepers and all will slice better if made a day or so in advance, which helps to relieve last minute baking sessions. Include some of these and make sure they have cooled completely before they are wrapped.

A filled and iced layer cake is a special treat – there is absolutely nothing like the homemade version – make it the centrepiece on the table, then cut in slices and serve with forks. Layer cakes, small iced cakes and pastries all give that delicious feeling of indulgence which is really the essence of this occasion.

A spread including a choice of scones or sandwiches, a teabread, two kinds of cake and a biscuit is a nice balance to set on the table. Prepared items, especially sandwiches, should be kept covered until serving time; with an overwrap of clear film, you could set food on trays or plates up to 4 hours in advance.

Family teas are nice sitting round the table, especially when children are present. On the other hand tea served from the trolley gives you more manoeuvrability, and when the weather is

Previous pages: clockwise, Wholemeal banana pecan bread, Dutch apple cake, wheaten scones, wheatmeal digestives and rolled oat and raisin cookies

warm, tea can be wheeled into the garden. There must always be plenty of room to sit comfortably and small tables should be set up at guests' elbows for putting plates and cups on.

For a crowd you can plan your tea buffet-style and set all the eats on a sideboard. Two golden rules for buffet teas are that everything should be small, no more than two-bite-size, and everything should be ready spread and topped – scones with savoury topping or whipped cream with a decorative strawberry, cakes in miniature or small slices. It's easier for guests if knives are not required for cutting or spreading although a fork for taking a sweet cake or fruit tartlet is acceptable. Have tea pots and cups and accessories at one end of the buffet table. Let guests collect eats, a cup of tea and then manoeuvre to find a place to sit.

Offer two kinds of tea such as Indian and China, with milk, sugar and lemon or orange slices. Be selective and adventurous with the teas you choose – Darjeeling, Assam or Lapsang Souchong. Brew tea just before serving so it tastes its most refreshing. Have a jug of boiling water for topping up the pot and an old-fashioned slop bowl for discarding tea leaves.

TIME FOR TEA

Tea is a totally natural drink with a wide variety of flavours. It really is worth trying out different ones – tea suits any time of the day or evening. At a specialist shop you may be able to buy pure teas which are unblended. These are top of the scale, usually large leaf; they will need a longer infusion time and they make a lighter coloured brew. Pure teas have a directness of flavour that's quite unique: they're more expensive but you will need less in the pot. Most prepacked teas are blended.

Teas are blended for consistency and often for particular occasions – such as a breakfast blend – and there are many excellent house blends. Scented and exotic teas are regular teas with flavouring added – mango, vanilla, lemon, orange or cinnamon. They are very refreshing. Earl Grey is the most famous scented tea. Choose different teas for different occasions and you might even try blending your own – *Assam* with *Earl Grey* is delicious.

Assam: full-bodied and pungent (needs milk). Serve for afternoon tea on a cold day or as an excellent breakfast tea.

Ceylon: delicate in flavour. It is good hot with lemon or better still with a slice of orange and is great for iced tea.

Darjeeling: known as the champagne of teas with a delicate muscatel flavour. It is a delicious tea for lunch or afternoon.

Keemun: aromatic flavour. This is a traditional breakfast tea that's coming back in fashion.

Yunnan: pale amber colour and delicately-flavoured (no milk). This is good for lunch or after dinner.

Oolong: fragrant peach-like flavour (no milk). This is good for after dinner.

Lapsang Souchong: strong smokey taste. It is very thirst-quenching on a hot afternoon.

Jasmine: soothing, fragrant brew mixed with jasmine flowers (no milk). Its good digestive properties make it an excellent after dinner tea and it is also delicious for iced tea.

Earl Grey: a blend with a distinctive scented taste. It is refreshing with sweet cakes at teatime; mix it with other teas if you find the flavour overpowering.

Tea Sandwiches

These should be dainty, two-bite size and absolutely fresh. Make sandwiches attractive by using contrasting bread slices, cutting them in neat ways and then adding a fresh looking garnish.

● For closed sandwiches use a brown or wheatgerm loaf which has a lighter texture and is easier to cut than a wholemeal loaf. Plain white, milk or bran breads are also suitable as are currant or malt bread which make delectable sweet sandwiches.

● Bread should be thinly sliced. If you buy a loaf from the local baker ask him to put it through the fine slicer.

● Use soft-from-the-fridge spreads – usually in tubs – or cream butter first to soften it. Then spread bread slices right to the edge so the butter acts as a waterproof coating and prevents fillings from making bread slices soggy.

● Don't overfill sandwiches (see ideas below) – no more than the thickness of one bread slice is about right. Remember that several paper-thin slices of meat or cheese is better than one thick slab.

● Delay cutting off the crusts until nearer serving time and sandwiches will keep fresher. Stack, wrap in foil and refrigerate, you can make sandwiches 3-4 hours ahead.

● For serving, trim sandwiches and cut into squares, fingers or triangles with a sharp kitchen knife dipped in hot water or an electric carving knife. Arrange on a serving platter, overlapping so you can see the fillings. Keep covered tightly with clear film and refrigerate until serving time.

● Add an edible garnish to the sandwich platter – sprigs of watercress, halved cherry tomatoes, cucumber sticks or trimmed spring onions for instance.

Include these ideas . . .

● Use one brown and one white slice for each sandwich; then cut in squares or triangles and reverse alternate sandwiches on the platter for a brown and white effect.

● Use three bread slices – white with a brown slice in the centre or vice versa. Make the first layer lettuce only and second the chosen filling. Cut in fingers and arrange on their sides for a ribbon effect.

● Use two slices (brown is best) – cut in quarters to make chubby square sandwiches. Stack, then lay on sides in neat rows.

● Split fancy finger rolls or tiny cob dinner rolls and they can be topped with any sandwich filling. Don't put back the tops or they get too big – keep them in halves.

The spreads – try to get a balance and offer a choice – one fish or meat and one egg or salad filling . . .

● taramosalata with cucumber slices

● egg salad with cress or watercress

● cream cheese seasoned with chopped fresh chives or spring onions

● paper-thin slices smoked ham with wholegrain mustard

● houmous with black olives and crisp lettuce

● smooth liver pâté with chopped gherkins

● cream cheese with chopped dates or banana (sweeten the cream cheese with a little thin shred marmalade) on currant or malt bread.

WHEATEN SCONES

MAKES 24

225 g (8 oz) wholemeal flour

225 g (8 oz) plain flour

¼ level teaspoon salt

2 level teaspoons bicarbonate of soda

4 level teaspoons cream of tartar

75 g (3 oz) butter

25 g (1 oz) castor sugar

1 egg (size 2) made up to 300 ml (½ pint) with milk

extra plain flour, for dusting

P Can be prepared ahead: cover and keep cool for up to 3-4 hours.

Use a flour dredger to dust these scones liberally with flour before they go into the oven and they will bake with soft tender crusts – it's the traditional Scottish way.

Sift both the flours, the salt, bicarbonate of soda, and cream of tartar into a mixing bowl. Tip in the bran from the sieve. Add the butter cut in pieces and rub in with fingertips. Stir in the sugar. **P**

Heat the oven to 200°C (400°F or gas no. 6).

Mix the egg and milk with a fork to break up the egg. Add to the dry ingredients all at once. Using a table knife, mix to a soft dough – do not overmix. Turn on to a floured surface and, using floured fingers, knead about three turns, just to smooth the underside.

Turn the dough smooth side up and pat or roll out to a thickness of not less than 10 mm (½ inch). Stamp out rounds of the dough using a 5 cm (2 inch) floured cutter – cut scones close together to get as many as possible from the original rolling. Collect the trimmings and press together to make the last few.

Arrange the scones on floured baking trays, then dust the scones with flour. Place immediately in the heated oven and bake for 12 minutes or until well risen and firm to the touch. Transfer to a wire cooling tray to cool for 15-20 minutes.

Split and serve warm with preserves and a bowl of whipped double cream.

CHEDDAR SCONES

MAKES 24

450 g (1 lb) self-raising flour

¼ level teaspoon salt

4 level teaspoons baking powder

75 g (3 oz) butter

100 g (4 oz) Cheddar cheese

1 egg (size 2), made up to 300 ml (½ pint) with milk

A floured kitchen knife is the best tool for cutting a cheese scone dough – it's more economical and you get all the scones from the first rolling which means every one will rise evenly.

Heat the oven to 200°C (400°F or gas no. 6).

Sift the flour, salt and baking powder into a large mixing bowl. Add the butter, cut in pieces, and rub in with fingertips. Grate the cheese and stir in.

Mix the egg and milk with a fork to break up the egg. Add the wholegrain mustard and mix. Add to the dry ingredients all

1 level teaspoon wholegrain
  mustard

at once and, using a table knife, mix to a soft but not sticky dough in the bowl. Turn on to a floured work surface and knead about three turns, just to smooth the surface.

Pat or roll out the dough to a thickness of not less than 10 mm (½ inch). Using a floured knife, cut the dough first into squares and then into triangles. Arrange on floured baking trays and dust the scones with flour.

Place in the heated oven and bake for 12 minutes or until well risen. Transfer to a cooling tray.

When barely cool, split and butter for serving. Or leave until cold, then spread with seasoned soft cheese and top with thinly-cut slices of egg, tomato or cucumber and a decorative herb garnish.

SCOTCH PANCAKES

MAKES 24

225 g (8 oz) self-raising flour

½ level teaspoon salt

2 level teaspoons baking
  powder

25 g (1 oz) castor sugar

1 egg (size 2)

1 rounded teaspoon golden
  syrup

225 ml (8 fl oz) milk

oil for greasing

Including a little golden syrup among the ingredients is the secret of an evenly browned surface – the hallmark of good Scotch pancakes. A heavy frying pan or the traditional griddle is the other essential item.

Sift the flour, salt, baking powder and sugar into a medium mixing bowl. Make a well in the middle and add the lightly mixed egg, golden syrup and milk. Using a wooden spoon, stir from the centre of the bowl, gradually drawing the flour in from around the sides. Beat to a smooth mixture.

Heat a heavy frying pan over moderate heat; the pan should warm up slowly until quite hot. Grease the surface using a pad of crumpled absorbent kitchen paper dipped in a saucer of oil. Drop dessertspoons of the mixture (from the point of the spoon) on to the hot pan. When bubbles start to break on the surface of the pancakes and the underside is golden, flip them over with a palette knife and cook the second side. As they come from the pan, slip the pancakes between the folds of a clean teacloth to keep them warm and soft. Prepare all the mixture in the same way, remembering to grease the pan with oil each time.

Serve the Scotch pancakes freshly made and warm, with butter and preserves.

POTTED CHEESE WITH WALNUTS

SERVES 6

225 g (8 oz) red (coloured) Cheshire cheese

100 g (4 oz) unsalted butter, or equal parts butter and curd cheese

freshly milled pepper

pinch ground mace

2 tablespoons sweet sherry or port

25 g (1 oz) shelled walnuts

P Can be prepared ahead: cover and refrigerate for up to 1 week.

This smooth, old-fashioned cheese spread has walnuts added for interest. If you have a moment to toast the walnuts, the flavour will be more intense. You can vary the taste using different cheeses, and do bear in mind that potted cheese also makes very good toasted cheese.

Grate the cheese as finely as possible. Put the butter, or butter and curd cheese, in a mixing bowl. Add the grated cheese, a seasoning of freshly milled pepper and the mace. Mix until smooth and well blended. Beat in the sherry or port. Chop the walnuts and mix in.

If using a food processor, start by grating the cheese into the processor bowl. Add the butter, freshly milled pepper, mace and sherry or port. Cover and process until smooth. Stir in the walnuts by hand.

Turn the mixture into a serving crock. **P** Serve with hot toast – no butter. For variations, use Double Gloucester, Wensleydale or Cheddar cheese, and add extras such as chopped fresh chives or snipped raisins.

CINNAMON RAISIN BREAD

MAKES 2 SMALL LOAVES

450 g (1 lb) strong white flour

1 × 7 g sachet easy blend dried yeast

1 level teaspoon castor sugar

225 ml (8 fl oz) mixed equal parts milk and water, hand hot

½ level teaspoon salt

1 level teaspoon ground cinnamon

50 g (2 oz) butter

25 g (1 oz) light muscovado sugar

1 egg (size 2)

50 g (2 oz) shelled walnuts

175 g (6 oz) seedless raisins

It is impossible to write about teas without at least one reference to a yeast risen bread, and a fruit bread like this is well worth the effort if there's going to be a crowd around to appreciate it. The unusual method encourages a good volume – raisin bread should be very light and open textured; slices are good for sandwiches and toasting.

Sift 100 g (4 oz) of the flour into a small bowl. Add the dried yeast, castor sugar and the mixed milk and water. Whisk to a smooth mixture and let stand for 20 minutes or until frothy.

Meanwhile, sift the remaining flour, the salt and cinnamon into a large mixing bowl. Add the butter cut in pieces and rub in with fingertips. Stir in the brown sugar. Add the yeast liquid and the lightly mixed egg and mix to a rough dough in the bowl. Turn on to a clean work surface and knead very thoroughly for about 10 minutes. Shape into a ball and replace in the mixing bowl. Cover with a cloth and leave at room temperature to rise until the dough has doubled – about 1 hour.

Chop the walnuts.

Turn risen dough out and press all over with the knuckles to flatten. Distribute the walnuts and raisins over the surface. Squeeze and knead the dough to mix the fruit and nuts through. Divide the dough in half. Flatten each piece to an oblong, turn the short sides into the centre and roll up tightly from an open end. Place the loaves, seam down, in greased 450 g (1 lb) loaf tins. Cover and leave at room temperature until the dough has risen to about 10 mm (½ inch) above the rim of the tins.

Heat the oven to 200°C (400°F or gas no. 6).

Place the risen loaves in the heated oven and bake for 20-25 minutes. Unmould and rub the tops with a buttered paper for a soft, shiny crust. Let cool completely. **P**

WHOLEMEAL BANANA PECAN BREAD

MAKES 1 LOAF

225 g (8 oz) self-raising wholemeal flour

100 g (4 oz) butter

100 g (4 oz) light muscovado sugar

50 g (2 oz) sultanas

50 g (2 oz) shelled pecans or walnuts

450 g (1 lb) bananas (weight with skins on)

2 eggs (size 2)

This is a teabread and very quick to make because it's raised with baking powder. Teabreads are always better the second day when they slice without crumbling. Banana keeps this recipe moist and it stores well, too.

Heat the oven to 180°C (350°F or gas no. 3).

Grease a 22.5 × 12.5 × 7.5 cm (9 × 5 × 3 inch) loaf tin and line with a strip of greaseproof paper cut the width of the base and long enough to overlap the opposite ends.

Sift the flour into a mixing bowl, then tip in any bran remaining in the sieve. Add the butter cut in pieces and rub in with fingertips. Add the sugar and sultanas. Reserve 4 pecans (or walnuts) for decoration and chop the remainder. Add the chopped nuts to the mixing bowl and mix.

Peel the bananas and mash with a fork. Add the mashed bananas to the dry ingredients along with the eggs. Using a wooden spoon, mix everything to blend, then beat well for 1 minute to make a soft consistency – no extra liquid will be required.

Turn the mixture into the prepared tin and spread level. Arrange the reserved pecans (or walnuts) on top. Set in the heated oven and bake for 1-1¼ hours. Let cool in the tin 5 minutes, then loosen the sides and lift out using the baking paper ends to help. Leave until completely cold then store for 24 hours before cutting. **P** Serve sliced and buttered.

STRAWBERRY SHORTCAKE

SERVES 6-8

450 g (1 lb) fresh strawberries

1 level tablespoon castor sugar

150 ml (¼ pint) double cream

icing sugar, for the top

For the shortcake

225 g (8 oz) plain flour

2 level teaspoons baking
  powder

pinch salt

75 g (3 oz) butter

1 egg (size 2)

3 tablespoons milk

40 g (1½ oz) castor sugar

15 g (½ oz) melted butter, for
  brushing

Serve shortcake freshly baked and warm – if circumstances allow, get the ingredients assembled, then mix and bake as close to serving time as possible. Notice the layers are brushed with melted butter which makes them easy to separate as they come from the oven. You can fill this with other fruits, but in my opinion, nothing beats strawberry shortcake.

Select eight of the best strawberries for decoration and set aside. Slice the remaining berries into a bowl, sprinkle with the castor sugar and leave for at least 1 hour to draw out the juices.

Heat the oven to 200°C (400°F or gas no. 6). Thoroughly butter a 20 cm (8 inch) round sponge cake tin and line with a circle of greaseproof paper.

Sift the flour, baking powder and salt into a large mixing bowl. Add the butter, cut in pieces, and rub in with fingertips. Lightly mix the egg, milk and castor sugar. Add all at once to the dry ingredients and, using a fork, mix everything to a rough dough in the mixing bowl. Turn on to a lightly floured surface and knead two or three turns – just to smooth the surface.

Divide the dough in half and pat each portion out to a round to fit the tin. Using floured fingertips, press one round of dough over the base of the prepared tin. Brush the surface liberally with the melted butter. Place the second round of dough on top and press gently to fit.

Set in the heated oven and bake for 15 minutes. Turn on to a wire cooling tray and gently separate the layers with a knife. Cut the shortcake top into 6-8 neat divisions.

Whip the cream to soft peaks. Place the warm shortcake base on a serving plate and spoon over the sliced strawberries and juices from the bowl. Add the whipped cream, then the top layer of shortcake, placing divisions in correct order. Dust with icing sugar and decorate with the reserved berries.

AMERICAN CHOCOLATE CAKE

MAKES A 22.5 cm (9 inch) CAKE

250 g (9 oz) self-raising flour

25 g (1 oz) cocoa powder

1 level teaspoon bicarbonate of soda

½ level teaspoon salt

1½ level teaspoons baking powder

75 g (3 oz) plain chocolate

100 ml (4 fl oz) boiling water

175 g (6 oz) butter

100 g (4 oz) castor sugar

175 g (6 oz) light muscovado sugar

3 eggs (size 2)

1 teaspoon vanilla essence

225 ml (8 fl oz) natural yogurt

6-8 tablespoons apricot jam

For the soured cream frosting

75 g (3 oz) plain chocolate

15 g (½ oz) butter

2 tablespoons soured cream

225 g (8 oz) icing sugar

pinch salt

few drops vanilla essence

Deep and well flavoured, this recipe uses yogurt to mix and it really brings out the rich chocolate taste. This is no ordinary sponge, it's a party piece, and you will need a large spring clip tin to bake it in.

Heat the oven to 160°C (325°F or gas no. 3).

Butter a 22.5 cm (9 inch) spring clip tin and line the base with a circle of greaseproof paper.

Sift the flour, cocoa powder, bicarbonate of soda, salt and baking powder on to a plate. Break the chocolate into a small bowl, add the boiling water and stir until the chocolate has melted and the mixture is smooth.

In a large mixing bowl, cream the butter with both sugars until soft and light. Lightly mix the eggs and vanilla essence and gradually beat into the creamed mixture. Stir in the melted chocolate and then the yogurt. Place a sieve over the mixing bowl, spoon in the flour mixture and sift over the creamed ingredients. Fold in the flour lightly and evenly using the cutting edge of a metal tablespoon.

Turn the mixture into the prepared tin and spread level. Set in the heated oven and bake for 50-60 minutes or until a skewer comes out clean. Cool in the tin for 10 minutes, then run a spatula around the sides to loosen and transfer to a wire cooling rack. Leave until cold.

Break the chocolate for the frosting into a medium bowl. Add the butter and set over a saucepan of hot (not boiling) water until melted. Remove the bowl from the heat and stir in the soured cream. Sift in the icing sugar, add the salt and vanilla essence and beat to a smooth frosting.

Slice the chocolate cake twice to make three layers. Sandwich them with the apricot jam. Swirl the frosting over the top and around the sides of the cake.

Let the finished cake stand several hours before slicing and serving – I find it cuts best the next day. **P**

BAKED LEMON CHEESECAKE

SERVES 8-10

6 trifle sponge cakes

450 g (1 lb) curd cheese

50 g (2 oz) butter, at room temperature

100 g (4 oz) castor sugar

2 level tablespoons plain flour

3 eggs (size 2)

finely grated zest 2 lemons

50 ml (¼ pint) soured cream

3 passion fruits, to decorate

P Can be prepared ahead: refrigerate overnight.

Using trifle sponge cakes to line the baking tin provides a soft cake base. It's quicker than making pastry and much nicer than biscuit crumbs. Cheesecake needs at least 24 hours to mature, so bake it at least the day before serving.

Heat the oven to 160°C (325°F or gas no. 3).

Butter a 22.5 cm (9 inch) spring clip tin and line the base with thin slices of trifle sponge cake, trimming the slices to fit the shape of the tin. Press down firmly.

Turn the curd cheese into a large mixing bowl, add the butter and beat until well mixed. Reserve 1 tablespoon of the sugar; combine the remaining sugar with the flour, add to the creamed mixture and beat well. Separate the eggs, cracking the whites into a separate bowl and beating the yolks into the creamed mixture one at a time. Stir in the grated lemon zest and soured cream. Whisk the egg whites until stiff, sprinkle in the reserved sugar and whisk until glossy. Fold the whites into the cheese mixture.

Pour into the prepared tin and spread level. Set in the heated oven and bake for 45 minutes or until the mixture is set. Cool in the baking tin. Cover and refrigerate for at least 4 hours before serving. **P**

Slice open the passion fruits and scoop the pulp and seeds over the top of the cheesecake just before serving.

CITRUS TARTS – LEMON OR LIME

MAKES 12

1 recipe quantity almond shortcrust (see page 83)

3 kiwi fruits or 6 fresh strawberries

candied citrus zest (see below)

For the filling

75 g (3 oz) castor sugar

25 g (1 oz) butter

finely grated zest and juice 1 lemon or 2 limes

2 eggs (size 2)

150 ml (5 fl oz) double cream

Individual pastry shells have always been popular for special occasions. These are filled with a tangy citrus cream and topped with fresh fruits.

Heat the oven to 190°C (375°F or gas no. 5).

Roll the pastry out thinly and use a 7.5 cm (3 inch) cutter to stamp out 12 rounds, using up all the trimmings. Press the pastry rounds over the outside of 12 fluted tartlet (or brioche) moulds. Prick the base of each with a fork and arrange open ends down on a baking tray.

Set in the heated oven and bake for 10-12 minutes – the pastry will take the pretty fluted shapes. Remove from the tins and let cool completely.

Put the sugar, butter, finely grated lemon or lime zest and

P Can be prepared ahead: keep refrigerated for up to 4 hours.

juice in a mixing bowl. Set over a saucepan of simmering water (the water must not touch the base of the bowl) and stir until the butter is melted and the sugar dissolved. Break the eggs with a fork and strain into the mixing bowl. Cook, stirring frequently, until the mixture thickens – about 10 minutes. Remove from the heat and allow to cool.

Whip the cream to soft peaks and fold into the cold lemon mixture. Spoon into the tartlet shells. Refrigerate for at least 1 hour. **P** Top with a slice of kiwi or halves of strawberries and candied zest before serving.

● **Candied citrus zest** Pare the thinnest strips of zest from a lemon or lime using a swivel-bladed vegetable peeler, then shred very finely with a kitchen knife. Alternatively, use a lemon zester. Place the zest in a saucepan and cover with cold water. Bring to a simmer and blanch for 2-3 minutes, then drain. Measure 2 level tablespoons castor sugar and 1 tablespoon water into the saucepan and stir over low heat to dissolve the sugar. Then bring to a simmer, add the blanched zest and cook gently for 2-3 minutes or until the zest is glazed. Fork out the candied zest and strew over the tops of tarts or other sweet dishes.

FRUIT AND CREAM ROULADE

CUTS INTO 8 SLICES

40 g (1½ oz) plain flour
1 level tablespoon cornflour
pinch salt
1 egg yolk (size 2)
2 level tablespoons ground almonds
75 g (3 oz) + 1 level tablespoon castor sugar
2 eggs (size 2)
icing sugar for the top
For the filling
300 ml (½ pint) double cream
225 g (8 oz) fresh or frozen raspberries

This very light sponge rolls beautifully without any cracks – you'll find the method unusual. If you flavour the cream with liqueur this could be a dessert.

Heat the oven to 220°C (425°F or gas no. 7).

Grease an oblong 33.5 × 23.5 cm (13½ × 9½ inch) biscuit tin (with edges) and line with a strip of greaseproof paper long enough to cover the base and overlap the opposite ends.

Sift the flour, cornflour and salt twice and set aside. In a mixing bowl combine the egg yolk, ground almonds and 1 tablespoon of the sugar and blend until creamy. Add the whole eggs and the rest of the sugar. Set the bowl over a saucepan one-quarter filled with hot (not boiling) water and whisk until the mixture is thick and light. Remove from the heat and whisk for a few moments more. Add the sifted dry ingredients and fold in lightly using the cutting edge of a metal tablespoon.

Turn the mixture into the prepared tin and spread level – pay attention to the corners. Set in the heated oven and bake

P Can be prepared ahead: keep refrigerated no longer than overnight.

for 8 minutes. Cool for 1 minute, then loosen sides and turn on to a cloth. Cover with a second cloth and leave until quite cold.

Strip off the baking paper and turn the sponge over so the top crust is uppermost. Whip the cream to soft peaks and spread evenly over the surface. Cover with the raspberries (fruits that are frozen will thaw in the cake). Roll up from a long side. Cover and refrigerate for at least 4 hours (best when frozen fruits are used) to allow the cream to set firm. **P**

Dust with icing sugar before serving. This looks pretty cut on the bias, like a French loaf.

MINCEMEAT CRUMBLE CAKE

MAKES A 22.5 cm (9 inch) CAKE

2 dessert apples
225-350 g (8-12 oz) mincemeat
175 g (6 oz) self-raising flour
pinch salt
100 g (4 oz) butter, at room temperature
100 g (4 oz) castor sugar
2 eggs (size 2)
½ teaspoon vanilla essence
1-2 tablespoons milk
For the crumble topping
100 g (4 oz) self-raising flour
75 g (3 oz) butter
75 g (3 oz) castor sugar
25 g (1 oz) flaked almonds

A crunchy crumble topping on a rich cake base makes a nice contrast of textures – the bonus is the mincemeat and apple in the middle. Everyone will want this recipe!

Heat the oven to 180°C (350°F or gas no. 4).

Grease a 22.5 cm (9 inch) spring clip tin. Sift the flour for the crumble topping into a bowl. Add the butter and cut in with two table knives using a scissor-like movement until the mixture looks like coarse crumbs. Add the sugar and flaked almonds and set aside.

Peel, quarter and core the apples, then dice finely and mix into the mincemeat. Sift the flour and salt for the cake on to a plate. In a mixing bowl, cream the butter with the sugar until soft and light. Lightly mix the eggs and vanilla essence and add to the creamed mixture a little at a time, beating well after each addition – add a little of the flour along with the last few additions of egg. Gently fold half the remaining flour into the mixture, then add the rest of the flour and the milk and mix until blended.

Spoon the cake mixture into the prepared tin and spread level. Fork the apple and mincemeat mixture evenly over the cake mixture, then sprinkle the crumble topping evenly over the filling and cake. Place in the heated oven and bake for 45-50 minutes. Allow to cool in the tin before opening the sides. **P**

RAISIN ORANGE POUND CAKE

MAKES 1 LOAF CAKE

200 g (7 oz) plain flour

25 g (1 oz) cornflour

2 level teaspoons baking
  powder

75 g (3 oz) icing sugar

pinch salt

100 g (4 oz) seedless raisins

100 g (4 oz) butter, at room
  temperature

100 g (4 oz) castor sugar

grated zest and juice 1 orange

2 eggs (size 2)

icing sugar, for dusting

One or two simple cake recipes are always useful to have — not everyone wants rich fillings and frostings. This traditional pound cake has a soft crumb and a subtle orange flavour, and it slices beautifully.

Heat the oven to 160°C (325°F or gas no. 3).

Grease a 22.5 × 12.5 × 7.5 cm (9 × 5 × 3 inch) loaf tin and line with a strip of greaseproof paper cut the width of the base and long enough to overlap the opposite ends.

Sift the flour, cornflour, baking powder, icing sugar and salt on to a plate. Coarsely chop the raisins with a knife. Cream the butter with the castor sugar and grated orange zest in a large mixing bowl until soft and light. Squeeze the orange juice and make up to 75 ml (3 fl oz) with water. Lightly mix the eggs and gradually beat into the creamed mixture a little at a time – add a spoonful of the flour mixture along with the last addition of egg. Fold in half the remaining flour using the cutting edge of a metal tablespoon. Add the rest of the flour with the chopped raisins and orange juice and mix to a soft consistency.

Spoon the mixture into the prepared tin and spread level. Set in the heated oven and bake for 50-60 minutes or until firm to the touch and golden. Let cool in the baking tin for 10 minutes, then loosen the sides and lift the cake out using the paper ends. Cool on a wire tray. When quite cold, dust with icing sugar. Store 24 hours before slicing. **P**

LUSCIOUS FRUIT CAKE

**MAKES A 22.5 cm (9 inch)
  SQUARE CAKE**

350 g (12 oz) tenderized dried
  apricots

350 g (12 oz) sultanas

100 g (4 oz) glacé pineapple

225 g (8 oz) whole candied
  lemon and orange peel

50 g (2 oz) stem ginger

50 g (2 oz) shelled Brazil nuts

350 g (12 oz) plain flour

A rich fruit cake but not the usual one – here you'll find dried apricots, glacé pineapple, stem ginger and Brazil nuts, for instance. This is baked as a square cake because it's the easiest shape to cut and slice neatly.

Chop the apricots and place in a mixing bowl with the sultanas. Rinse the sugar coating from the pineapple, candied peel and stem ginger and press dry in absorbent kitchen paper. Chop the pineapple, peels and ginger and add to the mixing bowl. Chop the nuts and add. Sift the flour and salt on to a square of greaseproof paper. Add 2 tablespoons of the flour to the prepared fruits and mix.

1 level teaspoon salt

275 g (10 oz) butter, at room
  temperature

275 g (10 oz) castor sugar

5 eggs (size 2)

2 tablespoons stem ginger
  syrup

Heat the oven to 140°C (275°F or gas no. 1). Grease and line a 22.5 cm (9 inch) square cake tin.

In a bowl, cream the butter with the sugar until soft and light. Lightly mix the eggs and beat into the creamed mixture a little at a time. Add half the sifted flour and fold in with the cutting edge of a metal spoon. Add the remaining flour, the fruit mixture and ginger syrup and mix to a medium soft consistency.

Spoon the mixture into the prepared cake tin. Spread level and hollow out the centre slightly. Place in the heated oven and bake for 4 hours – the cake should be evenly risen and golden. Let cool in the tin for 24 hours before turning out. **P** Cut in slices for serving.

CINNAMON GLAZED GINGER CAKE

CUTS INTO 24 PIECES

225 g (8 oz) self-raising flour

1 level tablespoon ground
  ginger

1 level teaspoon ground
  cinnamon

½ level teaspoon bicarbonate
  of soda

100 g (4 oz) butter

100 g (4 oz) light muscovado
  sugar

2 eggs (size 2)

3 tablespoons clear honey

5 tablespoons milk

100 g (4 oz) sultanas

50 g (2 oz) chopped glacé
  ginger

For the glaze

225 g (8 oz) icing sugar

¼ level teaspoon ground
  cinnamon

juice ½ orange

This is my ginger cake recipe for special occasions – dark and spicy with a cinnamon-flavoured glaze. Bake, wrap and store for a day or so, then ice, if you want a really moist texture.

Heat the oven to 160°C (325°F or gas no. 3). Grease a 27.5 × 17.5 × 2.5 cm (11 × 7 × 1 inch) oblong baking tin, or small roasting tin, and line with a strip of greaseproof paper cut the width of the base and long enough to overlap opposite ends.

Sift the flour, ginger, cinnamon and bicarbonate of soda into a mixing bowl. Add the butter cut in pieces and rub in with fingertips. Add the sugar and mix. In a small bowl combine the eggs, honey and milk and mix with a fork. Add to the dry ingredients and, using a wooden spoon, beat well to make a smooth, shiny mixture. Stir in the sultanas and chopped ginger.

Pour into the baking tin and spread level. Set in the heated oven and bake for 1 hour. Let cool in the baking tin for 30 minutes, then turn out on to a wire cooling tray and leave until cold.

Sift the icing sugar and cinnamon for the glaze into a mixing bowl. Add sufficient orange juice to mix to a stiff consistency. Set the bowl over a saucepan of hot (not boiling) water and soften the glaze to a coating mixture. Pour over the gingercake and spread evenly. Let stand until the glaze has hardened.

Store the cake for at least 24 hours, then cut in squares for serving. **P**

ALMOND AND CHOCOLATE CHIP CAKE

MAKES 1 LOAF CAKE

150 g (5 oz) plain flour

2 level teaspoons baking
  powder

175 g (6 oz) soft tub margarine

175 g (6 oz) castor sugar

100 g (4 oz) ground almonds

3 eggs (size 2)

½ teaspoon almond essence

2 tablespoons milk

50 g (2 oz) plain chocolate,
  chopped in small pieces

15 g (½ oz) flaked almonds

icing sugar, for dusting

It couldn't be easier – this recipe uses an 'all in one' mix with soft tub margarine for easy blending. The ground almonds keep the cake moist and provide flavour while the chunky bits of plain chocolate are a lovely surprise.

Heat the oven to 160°C (325°F or gas no. 3).

Grease a 22.5 × 12.5 × 7.5 cm (9 × 5 × 3 inch) loaf tin and line with a strip of greaseproof paper cut the width of the base and long enough to overlap opposite ends.

Sift the flour and baking powder into a large mixing bowl. Add the margarine, sugar, ground almonds, eggs, almond essence and milk. Using a wooden spoon, stir first to blend the ingredients, then beat well for 1 minute to get a smooth cake mixture. Stir in the chocolate pieces. Spoon the mixture into the prepared loaf tin and spread level. Tap the surface of the mixture with knuckles dipped in water to moisten it, then sprinkle with the flaked almonds.

Set in the heated oven and bake for 1 hour or until the cake is well risen and golden. Let cool in the tin for 5 minutes, then turn on to a wire cooling tray. Let cool completely, then store for 24 hours. **P** Dust with icing sugar and serve cut in slices.

APPLE FRANGIPANE TART

CUT INTO 8-10 SLICES

1 recipe quantity almond
  shortcrust (see right)

75 g (3 oz) butter, at room
  temperature

75 g (3 oz) castor sugar

2 eggs (size 2)

100 g (4 oz) ground almonds

4 tart dessert apples

2 tablespoons sieved apricot
  jam

1 tablespoon lemon juice

Here sliced apples are baked on top of an almond cream in a pastry crust. Nuts and fruits are always a good combination and you can vary the fruits – fresh plums or apricots could replace the apples if they are halved, stoned and arranged attractively.

Roll out the prepared pastry and use to line a 22.5 cm (9 inch) round flan tin (preferably with a loose base). Chill while preparing the filling.

Heat the oven to 190°C (375°F or gas no. 5) and put a baking sheet on the oven shelf.

In a medium mixing bowl, cream the butter with the sugar until soft and light. Add the eggs and ground almonds and mix to a smooth, soft paste. Spoon the mixture into the pastry shell and spread level.

Core the apples, leaving them whole, then peel and cut in

half lengthways. Slice the apples thinly, keeping the slices in order. Then press the apples gently to fan out the slices. Lift the apple slices off the chopping board with a palette knife and lay on the almond filling attractively from edge to centre. Press lightly into the filling.

Set in the heated oven (directly on the baking sheet) and bake for 15 minutes. Then lower the oven heat to 180°C (350°F or gas no. 4) and bake for a further 20-25 minutes or until the filling is set and golden – test in the centre.

Meanwhile, in a saucepan combine the apricot jam with the lemon juice and set over low heat. Stir to melt and blend, then bring to the boil and boil for 1 minute. While the tart is still hot from the oven, paint the top with the hot apricot glaze – this will help to protect the fruit and retain the colour. Let cool completely. **P**

ALMOND SHORTCRUST

MAKES SUFFICIENT PASTRY to line a 25 cm (10 inch) tart tin or 12-16 individual tartlet cases

200 g (7 oz) plain flour

25 g (1 oz) ground almonds

100 g (4 oz) butter

50 g (2 oz) sifted icing sugar

finely grated zest ½ lemon

1 egg yolk (size 2)

2 tablespoons cold milk

A melt in the mouth, tender pastry, this is best used for sweet tarts and tartlets. Sprinkle flour on the work surface from a dredger to minimize the amount used – too much extra flour spoils the light texture of the pastry.

Sift the flour into a good-sized mixing bowl and add the ground almonds. Add the butter cut in pieces and rub in with fingertips. Add the sifted icing sugar and the grated lemon zest and mix.

In a small bowl combine the egg yolk and milk and mix with a fork. Add all at once to the dry ingredients and, using a table knife, mix to a rough dough in the bowl. With floured fingers draw the pastry into a ball and turn on to a lightly floured work surface. Knead two or three times just to smooth the surface. Place in a polythene bag and refrigerate for at least 30 minutes (or overnight) before rolling out.

An oven heated to 190°C (375°F or gas no. 5) is the correct baking temperature unless the recipe states otherwise.

In a food processor: put the flour, ground almonds, sifted icing sugar and grated lemon rind in the processor bowl and buzz to mix. Add the chilled butter, cut in pieces, and process to fine crumbs. Turn the mixture into a bowl. Add the combined egg and milk and mix by hand to a dough.

WALNUT AND BANANA CAKE

CUTS INTO 12 SLICES

225 g (8 oz) self-raising flour

1 level teaspoon baking powder

100 g (4 oz) butter

50 g (2 oz) shelled walnuts

175 g (6 oz) light muscovado
  sugar

50 g (2 oz) seedless raisins

450 g (1 lb) ripe bananas
  (weight with skins on)

2 eggs (size 2)

finely chopped walnuts, to
  decorate

Using a ring mould for baking – plain or fluted – gives you an alternative shape for a teatime cake. With a glaze drizzled over the top, it looks unusual and pretty.

Heat the oven to 180°C (350°F or gas no. 4). Butter a 1.7 litre (3 pint) ring mould.

Sift the flour and baking powder into a medium mixing bowl. Add the butter cut in pieces and rub in with fingertips. Chop the walnuts and add with the sugar and raisins and mix through.

Peel the bananas and mash with a fork. Add the mashed bananas and eggs to the dry ingredients. Using a wooden spoon, stir to blend the mixture and then beat well to get a soft cake mixture – no liquid will be required. Turn the mixture into the prepared cake tin and spread level.

Set in the heated oven and bake for 35-40 minutes or until well risen. Let cool in the tin for 5 minutes, then turn on to a wire cooling tray and leave until completely cold.

Sift the icing sugar for the glaze into a bowl. Add the lemon juice and mix to a smooth coating consistency. Pour over the cake and allow to run down the sides. Sprinkle finely chopped walnuts over the moist glaze and leave to dry. **P** Cut in slices for serving.

DUTCH APPLE CAKE

CUTS INTO 6 PIECES

175 g (6 oz) self-raising flour

1 level teaspoon baking powder

pinch salt

75 g (3 oz) castor sugar

1 egg (size 2)

6 tablespoons milk

2 tablespoons grapeseed or
  other mild oil

For the apple topping

450 g (1 lb) sharp-flavoured
  dessert apples

25 g (1 oz) melted butter

By using oil in this recipe, there is no more work than just mixing together the ingredients, yet the end result is a light, fluffy cake. The top is decorated with rows of sliced apple and a spicy mixture of sugar and cinnamon – you can do the same recipe with halved plums.

Heat the oven to 200°C (400°F or gas no. 6). Grease a 27.5 × 17.5 cm (11 × 7 inch) oblong baking or roasting tin and line with a strip of paper cut the width of the base and long enough to overlap the opposite ends.

Sift the flour, baking powder and salt into a mixing bowl. Add the sugar. Combine the egg, milk and oil in a second bowl, then pour into the flour mixture. Using a wooden spoon, stir to blend the ingredients, then beat well for 1 minute to get

50 g (2 oz) light muscovado
  sugar

½ level teaspoon ground
  cinnamon

a soft cake mixture. Pour the mixture into the prepared baking tin and spread level.

Peel, core and thickly slice the apples. Brush the top of the cake mixture all over with the melted butter, then arrange apple slices over the surface in neat rows. Sprinkle with the mixed sugar and cinnamon.

Set in the heated oven and bake for 35 minutes. Let cool in the baking tin for 2 minutes, then loosen the sides and lift out using the baking paper ends to help. Let cool completely. **P** Cut into portions for serving.

FLAKY PASTRY

MAKES A 225 g (8 oz) QUANTITY

225 g (8 oz) strong white flour

pinch salt

175 g (6 oz) butter

150 ml (¼ pint) cold water

2 teaspoons lemon juice

Easier to make than puff pastry, this works just as well when it's a crisp, flaky texture that you want. The pastry is best made 24 hours ahead and well chilled so the fat firms up, enabling you to cut better shapes. Use for pie crusts and wrapping.

Sift the flour and salt into a good sized mixing bowl. Add 25 g (1 oz) of the butter and rub in with the fingertips. Have the remaining butter well chilled and grate on a coarse grater directly into the flour – dip the butter block into the flour as you grate to keep the pieces separate. Stir the flour and fat with the fingertips to separate the pieces – do not rub in.

Measure the water and add the lemon juice. Add all at once to the dry ingredients and, using a table knife, mix to a rough dough in the bowl. With floured fingers, draw the mixture together and turn on to a floured board. Do not knead – simply press the dough into a rectangle.

Roll out the dough to an oblong three times longer than it is wide. Fold by turning the bottom third up over the centre and the top third down over both. Press the edges to seal, and give the dough a half turn – so the open ends are top and bottom. Repeat the process, then wrap and chill for at least 30 minutes.

Give two more rolls and folds, and the pastry is ready to use. Cover and chill for at least 30 minutes. **P**

An oven heated to 200°C (400°F or gas no. 6) is the right baking temperature unless the recipe states otherwise.

P Can be prepared ahead: make up to 1 day in advance.

HIGHLANDERS

MAKES 18

100 g (4 oz) plain flour

50 g (2 oz) rice flour (see recipe)

100 g (4 oz) unsalted butter, at room temperature

50 g (2 oz) castor sugar

demerara sugar, for coating

With the same buttery, crisp texture as ordinary shortbread, this roll of dough is coated in demerara sugar, then sliced so that each baked shortbread biscuit has a crunchy, sugary rim.

Sift the flour and rice flour on to a plate. (Rice flour gives shortbread the traditional sandy texture. If it's not available, make up the amount with extra flour.) Cream the butter with the sugar in a bowl until soft and light. Add half the flour and beat until smooth. Sift the remaining flour on to a clean work surface. Turn the creamed mixture on top and with fingertips, draw the remaining flour into the mixture.

If using a food processor, start by putting the flour, rice flour and sugar into the processor bowl. Cover and mix for 30 seconds. Add the chilled butter cut in dice. Cover and process to a rough dough. Turn on to a clean work surface and draw the dough together with fingertips.

Shape the shortbread into a 'rope' about 4-5 cm (1½-2 inches) thick. Sprinkle the demerara sugar on to a square of greaseproof paper. Roll the shortbread in the sugar to coat on all sides. Cover and refrigerate for at least 1 hour until firm. **P**

Heat the oven to 190°C (375°F or gas no. 5).

Using a sharp knife, cut the shortbread rope across into 5 mm (¼ inch) slices. Arrange on ungreased baking sheets (spacing them apart) and prick each one with a fork. Set in the heated oven and bake for 10 minutes to set. Then lower the oven heat to 160°C (325°F or gas no. 3) and bake for a further 10 minutes to dry off. Let cool on the baking sheet for 1 minute, then transfer to a wire cooling tray. When completely cold, store in an airtight tin.

P Can be prepared ahead: keep dough refrigerated overnight.

CHOCOLATE CREAMS

MAKES 36 FILLED COOKIES

100 g (4 oz) plain chocolate

50 g (2 oz) granulated sugar

225 g (8 oz) butter

150 g (5 oz) light muscovado sugar

350 g (12 oz) plain flour

These old-fashioned teatime cookies are sandwiched in pairs with a smooth chocolate cream. You'll find a food processor helps with the making of these.

Break the chocolate in pieces and put in a food processor bowl along with the granulated sugar. Process to a fine powder. Turn on to a plate and reserve.

Cut the butter into the processor bowl, add the soft brown

For the filling

50 g (2 oz) butter

50 g (2 oz) icing sugar

50 g (2 oz) chocolate sugar
  mixture (see recipe)

P Can be prepared ahead: store
in an airtight tin.

sugar and process until soft. Add the flour and 100 g (4 oz) of the chocolate sugar mixture and process to a dough. Turn on to a floured work surface, knead for a moment, then wrap. Chill until the dough is firm.

Heat the oven to 190°C (375°F or gas no. 5). Grease at least two baking sheets.

Take walnut-sized pieces of dough and roll into balls. Arrange on the baking sheets (you will have to bake these in batches). Flatten each ball with a wet fork. Set in the heated oven and bake for 10-12 minutes or until firm. Cool for 2 minutes on the baking sheet and then transfer to a wire cooling tray. Let cool completely. **P**

Combine the butter for the filling with the sifted icing sugar and remaining chocolate sugar mixture until creamy. Spread the filling over half the baked cookies and sandwich with the remainder.

HAZELNUT THINS

MAKES ABOUT 48

50 g (2 oz) shelled hazelnuts

50 g (2 oz) granulated sugar

225 g (8 oz) butter

100 g (4 oz) castor sugar

300 g (11 oz) plain flour

P Can be prepared ahead: keep
dough refrigerated for 2-3 weeks.

Once prepared, the dough for these crisp biscuits can be refrigerated for 2-3 weeks, or even frozen, and it only takes a moment to slice off a batch and bake them. Hazelnut thins are slim and elegant – you could serve them with a dessert or after dinner coffee.

Toast and chop the hazelnuts (see page 210). Turn the hazelnuts and granulated sugar into the bowl of a food processor and process until fine. Turn on to a plate and reserve. Slice the butter into the processor bowl, add the sugar and process until soft and light. Add the flour and reserved hazelnut mixture and blend to a smooth dough.

Turn the dough on to a lightly floured board and divide in half. Shape each piece of dough into a roll about 22.5 cm (9 inches) long. Wrap in greaseproof paper and flatten slightly – by running your hand along the top of the roll. Refrigerate for several hours or until the dough is quite firm. **P**

Heat the oven to 190°C (375°F or gas no. 5).

Using a sharp knife, slice biscuits thinly from the dough. Place on greased baking sheets. Set in the heated oven and bake for 10-12 minutes or until just beginning to brown. Cool on the sheets for 2 minutes, then transfer to a wire cooling tray. When completely cold, these can be stored in an airtight tin.

WHEATMEAL DIGESTIVES

MAKES 24

175 g (6 oz) wholemeal flour

pinch salt

2 level teaspoons baking
  powder

50 g (2 oz) medium oatmeal

50 g (2 oz) butter

40 g (1½ oz) white cooking fat

40 g (1½ oz) castor sugar

3 tablespoons milk

A traditional recipe for digestive biscuits, this uses wholemeal flour and oatmeal for a coarse texture. These homemade biscuits are not as sweet as those you buy. They are good on their own but especially nice spread with butter and topped with a sliver of Cheddar cheese.

Heat the oven to 200°C (400°F or gas no. 6).

Measure the wholemeal flour, salt, baking powder and oatmeal into a large bowl and mix together. Beat down the butter and white cooking fat on a plate to soften and blend. Add in small pieces to the dry ingredients and rub in with fingertips. Stir in the sugar. Add the milk and mix to a rough dough in the mixing bowl. Turn on to a floured work surface and knead lightly once or twice just to smooth the surface. Let the dough rest for 10 minutes under the upturned bowl.

Roll out the dough to a thickness of about 5 mm (¼ inch). With a plain round 6 cm (2½ inch) cutter, stamp out the biscuits. Gather up and reroll the trimmings until the dough is used up. Arrange the biscuits on greased baking sheets and prick all over with a fork. Set in the heated oven and bake until lightly coloured – about 12 minutes. Let cool on the sheets for 2 minutes, then transfer to a wire cooling tray. **P**

ROLLED OAT AND RAISIN COOKIES

MAKES 30

100 g (4 oz) self raising
  wholemeal flour

pinch salt

100 g (4 oz) rolled oats

50 g (2 oz) seedless raisins

25 g (1 oz) chopped walnuts

100 g (4 oz) butter

100 g (4 oz) soft brown sugar

2 tablespoons clear honey

1 tablespoon water

Take care to get the correct yield when cookie making; I find it helps to spoon out the mixture first, then shape.

Heat oven to 180°C (350°F or gas no. 4). Sift wholemeal flour and salt into a mixing bowl. Tip in any bran remaining in the sieve. Add the rolled oats, seedless raisins and walnuts.

Measure the butter, soft brown sugar, honey and water into a saucepan. Set over low heat and stir until ingredients are melted and runny, but not hot. Pour into the sifted ingredients and mix well. Let stand 10 minutes. Take teaspoons of the mixture and roll into balls. Arrange cookies on greased baking trays, spacing them apart   about 12 per tray.

Set in the heated oven and bake 10 minutes or until lightly coloured. Let cool on the baking tray 1 minute, then transfer to a cooling rack. When quite cold store in a closed tin.

SUPPER
PARTIES

Leek and mussel soup

Bean and vegetable broth

Spinach salad with hot bacon dressing

Roasted pepper salad with salami

Green lentil and bacon salad with avocado

Cheese soufflé crêpes

·

Stir-fried chicken with cashew nuts

Vegetarian stir-fry

Fettucine with avocado

Fresh noodles with smoked salmon and cream

Grilled sea trout with wholegrain mustard butter

Grilled salmon steaks with soured cream and chives

Hot seafood platter

Prawn pilaff

Spinach and ricotta crêpes

Seafood crêpes

Hungarian cabbage crêpes

Couscous with spicy sweet pepper sauce

Boston baked beans with smoked pork sausage

Boston brown bread

·

Baked fresh figs

Hot apple pastries

Dark chocolate soufflés

Banana brûlées

SUPPER PARTIES

Supper parties are on the up and up. Because there is less pressure and more freedom of choice, the hostess feels less on trial, as she doesn't have to achieve the supposed culinary heights required for a dinner party.

A supper party gives you a chance to be more adventurous with your recipes. It is a time for hearty chowders and filling broths with crusty bread in winter or, when the new vegetables appear on the market, a time to chance your arm with a delicious warm salad that requires a last minute dressing. For suppers you can try out a few recipes that tend to get excluded from dinner parties simply because they can't be prepared ahead; you can experiment with pasta dishes, a Chinese stir-fry, grilled salmon, or filled crêpes, and serve with a wonderful mixed salad tossed in your own special dressing. It's the perfect occasion too to try out a dish you've tasted on holiday, served with an appropriate wine – you could invite in fellow travellers to see if you've got it right. A friend told me she enjoyed giving supper parties because it never mattered so much if things went a bit wrong.

With dishes like these, the trick is to get the preparation ready ahead – all the slicing and chopping and the measuring. Set your ingredients out like a chef's *mis en place*; it saves time. Washed salad leaves and herbs, whole or freshly chopped, will stand up beautifully in the refrigerator as will prepared vegetables. If you use wine in the recipe, you can drink the rest with the meal. With everything to hand, even down to the garnish, you are less likely to get flustered or forget something if you get distracted. Let guests come into the kitchen; this is just the kind of occasion when they could lend a hand – it can only add warmth to the occasion.

Offer something light and pretty for dessert, such as a hot fruit dish or delicious pastry. Prepare a pretty cheeseboard that's something of a talking point – a single piece of some beautiful locally produced cheese, a delicious goat's or ewe's milk cheese. There's an increasing number of wonderful cheeses produced up and down the country – you'll find them in specialist cheese shops and delicatessens – and a recent discovery of yours would interest guests.

Informal suppers are a time for chatting, tasting and discussion, and for sitting round the table. If it's the kitchen table, that's best of all.

CUTTING IT FINE

Let guests linger over a stylish cheese board – with just a little throught it can be arranged beautifully.

● Avoid too much choice – it's better to have two or three decent sized pieces of cheese than a confusion of smaller bits. A hard cheese, something semi-soft and a blue cheese are a good selection, or go for a theme and serve British cheese only – there's a wide variety to choose from.

● Give cheese space on the cheese board. It's a good idea to set blue cheese on a separate plate with its own knife. For a buffet, set cheeses on rush mats and dispense with the board; they will look very pretty.

● Fruit makes an attractive addition to the cheese board – a bunch of grapes, a cluster of fresh strawberries, fresh dates or cherries add colour and appeal.

● A mixture of your own, like herbed cheese (page 145), makes an intriguing addition. Fork it into a ramekin dish and top with a herb garnish.

● White, soft, unripened cheese can be subtly garnished with a herb leaf and a dusting of paprika, chopped walnuts or flower petals to give it a lift.

● Make up mini kebabs of fruits and serve with cheese for a delicious surprise. Try black grapes, whole strawberries, kiwi chunks and pineapple pieces speared on satay sticks in alternate colours, to be handed round separately.

● Simple crusty bread is best with cheese – a mixed grain loaf, poppy seed plait or baguette. For a special occasion, thinly sliced walnut or close-textured raisin bread and wheatmeal digestives (page 88) are delicious.

JUST FRUITS

Some of the most refreshing and attractive desserts are just combinations of fresh fruits. These are easily prepared and have everything going for them – colour, flavour and simplicity.

● Combine fresh raspberries with tangy redcurrants, in the proportions of 450 g (1 lb) raspberries to 100 g (4 oz) redcurrants. If the redcurrants are too tart for your taste, toss the fruits with 1 level tablespoon castor sugar before serving.

● Heap seeded black or green grapes in individual serving glasses and top each with a generous spoonful of chilled Greek-style yogurt. Sprinkle with light muscovado sugar and let stand for 5 minutes so the sugar begins to dissolve.

● Cut a fresh pineapple in half lengthways, then scoop out the flesh (keeping shells intact) and dice into bite-sized pieces. Mix with sliced strawberries and pile back into the shells for serving.

● Arrange whole strawberries with their hulls on a platter along with fresh pineapple chunks or green grapes (anchored on cocktail sticks). Add a bowl of fromage frais for dipping into.

● Slice strawberries into a serving bowl, sprinkle with the juice of 2 oranges and leave for at least 1 hour to macerate. Or combine sliced kiwi fruits and strawberries and treat the same – the colours are stunning.

● Offer fresh raspberries with a soft cream cheese. Fashionable mascarpone is delicious – it's a fresh soft cheese from Italy with a creamy texture that's not unlike clotted cream. An alternative could be whipped double cream combined with natural yogurt in equal parts.

● Slice one or two sweet, ripe melons (Ogen or Charentais) in quarters. Deseed, then cut away the peel and slice the quarters like an apple. Arrange slices around the edge of a platter and fill the centre with a choice of soft fruits such as fresh raspberries, blueberries or blackberries.

LEEK AND MUSSEL SOUP

SERVES 6

1.5 kg (3 lb) fresh mussels

1-2 stalks celery

1 bay leaf

1 sprig fresh thyme

100 ml (4 fl oz) dry white wine

450 g (1 lb) leeks

2 medium onions

1 large potato

25 g (1 oz) butter

900 ml (1½ pints) vegetable stock

salt and freshly milled pepper

2 tablespoons chopped fresh coriander or parsley

150 ml (¼ pint) single cream

P Can be prepared ahead: cool, cover and chill for up to 6 hours.

Add shellfish to a simple vegetable soup and you have a great combination. Here the green of leeks with their mild onion flavour matches up perfectly with fresh mussels. I've prepared the same soup substituting sliced scallops and the result was delicious. This is an easy way of producing a simple fish soup without having to prepare a fish stock.

Wash and scrub the mussels in several changes of cold water; discard any open ones. Scrub and string the celery, cut up and put in a large saucepan with the herbs and wine. Add the mussels straight from the rinsing water. Cover with the pan lid and set over high heat to steam the mussels open – it takes only a few minutes. Shake the pan occasionally. Discard mussels that have not opened and remove the remaining mussels from their shells. Strain the liquid from the pan and pour it over the mussels to keep them moist.

Split and rinse the leeks, then shred all the white part and some of the green. Peel and chop the onions, and peel and dice the potato. Melt the butter in a saucepan, add the chopped onions and leeks and soften over gentle heat for about 10 minutes. Add the potato, stock and seasoning, and bring to a simmer. Cover and cook gently until the vegetables are tender – about 20 minutes.

Ladle the soup mixture into a food processor or blender and purée until smooth. **P**

Return the soup to the pan, reheat and check seasonings. Add the mussels and reserved liquid, the chopped coriander or parsley and the cream and heat through for serving.

BEAN AND VEGETABLE BROTH

SERVES 6

175 g (6 oz) dried haricot beans

2 onions

2 cloves garlic

2 red sweet peppers

4 carrots

225 g (8 oz) green beans

3 tablespoons olive oil

Broths are colourful and pretty, and the vegetables are left in pieces, so take the time and trouble to cut them in small neat pieces as you are preparing everything. Serve this like a minestrone, with grated Parmesan cheese for sprinkling.

Soak the beans overnight in cold water to cover, then drain. Peel and finely chop the onions. Peel the garlic and chop finely. Halve, deseed and dice the red pepper. Peel the carrots and dice quite small. Trim and shred the green beans.

1.7 litres (3 pints) vegetable
 stock

few leaves of spinach or chard

25 g (1 oz) small 'soup' pasta

salt and freshly milled pepper

2 tablespoons chopped fresh
 parsley

grated Parmesan cheese, for
 serving

P Can be prepared ahead: cool,
cover and refrigerate for up to 6
hours. Reheat before adding
spinach or chard.

Heat the oil in a large saucepan. Add the onions and soften gently without allowing them to take any colour. Add the garlic and stir for a moment, then add the sweet peppers, carrots, drained haricot beans and the stock. Bring to a simmer, cover with the pan lid and cook gently for 50 minutes or until the beans are almost tender. **P**

Wash the spinach or chard and pull out the centre rib, then roll the leaves in a bundle and shred across in ribbons. Add the green beans to the soup pot and simmer for 5 minutes. Then add the shredded spinach or chard and pasta and simmer until the pasta is tender – about 5 minutes.

Check the seasoning with salt and pepper and sprinkle with chopped parsley. Serve with a bowl of grated Parmesan for sprinkling over.

SPINACH SALAD WITH HOT BACON DRESSING

SERVES 4

225-350 g (8-12 oz) fresh
 spinach

2 ripe avocados

6 rashers streaky bacon

3 tablespoons grapeseed or
 other mild oil

2 tablespoons red wine vinegar

½ level teaspoon toasted
 sesame seeds (see page 210)

freshly milled pepper

Tender fresh spinach is required here – the small leaves of Italian spinach are excellent. You can add a few fresh dandelion leaves or lamb's lettuce if you like. The hot bacon dressing wilts the leaves slightly so this should be prepared and served at once.

Pick over and wash the spinach in several changes of cold water, then shake dry. Pull away the stalks and tear large leaves into smaller pieces. Halve and stone the avocados, then peel and slice them thinly. Place the spinach leaves and avocado slices in a large serving bowl.

Trim the rinds from the bacon rashers and dice the bacon. Put in a dry frying pan and set over low heat to draw out the bacon fat. Allow the bacon pieces to get really crisp, then with a perforated spoon transfer the bacon from the pan to a plate, leaving the hot drippings behind. Add the oil to the pan, then the vinegar and sesame seeds. Stir over low heat until the dressing is hot. Season with freshly milled pepper and draw the pan off the heat.

Scatter the crisp bacon over the salad, then drizzle over the hot dressing. Serve at once – a hot dressing makes delicate greens wilt more quickly.

Overleaf: Cheese soufflé crêpes

ROASTED PEPPER SALAD WITH SALAMI

SERVES 6

4-5 sweet peppers – a mixture
of red and yellow only

1 medium onion

6-8 tablespoons olive oil

2 level teaspoons castor sugar

1 tablespoon crumbled fresh
thyme leaves

salt and freshly milled pepper

juice 1 lemon

225-350 g (8-12 oz) thinly
sliced Italian salami

Grilling peppers brings up the flavour and makes it easy to peel off the skins. Once the skins are gone, the colours look much stronger – use red and yellow peppers only for this salad as they are very dramatic and the sweetest-tasting.

Heat the grill to hot and set the grill pan about 7.5 cm (3 inches) from the heat source. Quarter the sweet peppers lengthways and remove the seeds. Arrange the pieces on a baking tray (you will have to prepare these in batches) and set under the heat until the skins are blistered and charred. Cover with a cloth and leave for about 10 minutes by which time they should be cool enough to handle. Peel off the charred skins. Place the pepper pieces close together in a shallow serving dish – rows of alternate colours are nice.

Peel and slice the onion. Heat 2 tablespoons of the oil in a frying pan, add the onion and sprinkle with the sugar. Cook gently until the onion is softened and just beginning to colour. Sprinkle in the thyme and stir through. Add a seasoning of salt and plenty of pepper, the remaining oil and the lemon juice. Bring to a simmer and pour over the peppers. Leave to marinate for up to 6 hours. **P** Do not refrigerate.

Serve with the slices of salami offered separately – let guests pick at the salad and eat the salami.

GREEN LENTIL AND BACON SALAD WITH AVOCADO

SERVES 4

175 g (6 oz) green lentils

salt and freshly milled pepper

100 g (4 oz) streaky bacon, in
one piece

4 tablespoons olive oil

1 medium onion

2 cloves garlic

2 level teaspoons castor sugar

2 tablespoons red wine vinegar

2 tablespoons soy sauce

2 ripe avocados

The dressing for this salad is interesting because you actually make it in the frying pan using the bacon drippings with spices and condiments for extra taste. The dressing needs to be spicy because lentils (like all pulses) absorb lots of taste. Serve as a starter salad with hot breads.

Rinse and drain the green lentils (no need to soak), then place in a saucepan with cold salted water to cover. Bring to the boil. Reduce the heat, cover and simmer gently for 10-15 minutes or until just tender. Drain and turn into a mixing bowl.

Trim the bacon and cut in dice (cut-up streaky rashers will do but diced bacon looks best). Heat 1 tablespoon of the oil and the diced bacon in a frying pan and cook gently to draw out the bacon fat. Peel and slice the onion, and peel and chop the

P Can be prepared ahead: marinate overnight.

garlic. Add the onion to the pan, sprinkle with the sugar and fry until the onion is soft and golden – about 5 minutes. Stir in chopped garlic, the remaining oil, the red wine vinegar and soy sauce. Add a good seasoning of salt and pepper. Bring to a simmer and tip over the lentils. Stir well. Cover and let marinate for at least 1 hour in a cool place. **P**

Halve the avocados and remove the stones. Peel off the skins and cut the flesh in thick slices. Arrange the avocado slices on one side of a serving platter and add the lentil and bacon salad to the other. Serve with hot breads.

CHEESE SOUFFLÉ CRÊPES

SERVES 6

12 prepared crêpes (see page 104)

40 g (1½ oz) butter

3 level tablespoons plain flour

225 ml (8 fl oz) milk

salt and freshly milled pepper

grated nutmeg

50 g (2 oz) Gruyère cheese

1 level teaspoon wholegrain mustard

2 eggs (size 2)

2 egg whites (size 2)

50 g (2 oz) melted butter with 1 teaspoon toasted sesame seeds (see page 210) for serving

P Can be prepared ahead: cover and refrigerate for up to 3 hours.

These are very dramatic – a cheese soufflé mixture inside folded crêpes actually pushes them up. Have everything ready, then bake and transfer them straight on to hot serving plates.

Have the crêpes ready prepared and stacked – there is no need to reheat them at this stage. Set aside while preparing the cheese filling.

Melt the butter in a saucepan over low heat. Stir in the flour and cook for 1 minute, then gradually stir in the milk, beating well to make a smooth sauce. Season with salt, pepper and a little nutmeg and draw off the heat. Grate the cheese and stir into the sauce until melted – the heat of the sauce will be sufficient to do this. Add the mustard and taste for flavour: it should be quite pronounced.

Separate the eggs, beating the yolks into the sauce and putting all the egg whites together in a bowl. Whisk the whites to stiff peaks. Add one spoonful to the cheese mixture and blend through, then turn the cheese mixture into the remaining whisked whites and fold through gently to make a light soufflé filling. **P**

Heat the oven to 200°C (400°F or gas no. 6). Lightly butter two baking trays.

Place a tablespoon of the soufflé filling on one side of each crêpe. Fold the uncovered half over to cover the soufflé mixture and place on the baking trays – six crêpes on each baking tray.

Set in the heated oven and bake for 8 minutes or until well risen. Transfer at once to warm serving plates and drizzle over the melted butter with toasted sesame seeds. Serve with a crisp green salad and hot bread.

STIR-FRIED CHICKEN WITH CASHEW NUTS

SERVES 3-4

2 skinned chicken breast fillets

1 red sweet pepper

1 bunch (6-8) spring onions

2 stalks celery

100 g (4 oz) mange-touts

2 tablespoons grapeseed or
  other mild oil

50 g (2 oz) shelled cashew nuts

For the sauce

1 level tablespoon cornflour

2 level teaspoons grated fresh
  root ginger

2 tablespoons light soy sauce

1 teaspoon clear honey

juice ½ lemon

100 ml (4 fl oz) water

salt and freshly milled pepper

A crunchy mixture of vegetables, chicken and nuts in a soy and ginger sauce. This is the kind of recipe that's fun when the occasion is informal – you can prepare and assemble the ingredients ahead but cooking must be done at the last minute. Serve with hot saffron rice topped with a sprinkling of chopped spring onions.

Cut the chicken into fine shreds with a sharp knife. Halve and deseed the sweet pepper, then cut into shreds similar in size to the pieces of chicken. Trim the spring onions and finely chop all the white part and some of the green stems. Scrub and string the celery, then shred. Top and tail the mange-touts. Measure the cornflour, fresh root ginger, soy sauce, honey, lemon juice and water for the sauce into a small bowl. Mix until smooth and season with salt and pepper. Set the ingredients aside until ready for cooking. **P**

Set a wok or 25 cm (10 inch) frying pan over the heat and, when hot, add the oil. Swirl it around the pan. Add the chicken and stir-fry for 3-4 minutes or until the pieces are white. Add the red pepper, spring onions, celery, mange-touts and cashews and stir-fry for several minutes more – anything for 3-6 minutes depending on the heat and the pan. Stir up the sauce ingredients and pour into the pan. Stir until the sauce is thickened and the ingredients are glazed. Turn into a hot dish for serving.

VEGETARIAN STIR-FRY

SERVES 4

450 g (1 lb) prepared vegetables
  – mange-touts, courgettes,
  green beans and sweet
  peppers (see recipe)

100 g (4 oz) small pasta shapes

3 tablespoons grapeseed or
  other mild oil

4 eggs (size 2)

1 tablespoon red wine vinegar

salt and freshly milled pepper

Crisp-cooked vegetables tossed with pasta are here topped with garlic croûtons and lightly poached eggs. As the egg breaks the yolk blends deliciously with the other ingredients.

Prepare the vegetables for stir-frying – to a similar size for even cooking. Trim mange-touts and leave whole. Trim and slice courgettes into matchstick strips. Shred beans finely. Halve, deseed and shred peppers – red ones are a pretty contrast. **P** Set a large bowl to warm in the oven at lowest heat.

Add the pasta to a saucepan of boiling salted water and stir until reboiling. Cook for 5 minutes or until just tender, then drain. Turn into the warmed bowl and add 1 tablespoon of the

1 level tablespoon coarsegrain mustard

garlic croûtons (see below)

grated Parmesan cheese

oil to keep the pasta separate.

Put the eggs in a pan of cold water, bring to the boil and simmer for 6-8 minutes. Drain and cover with cold water to arrest further cooking.

Set a wok or 25 cm (10 inch) frying pan over the heat and when hot add the remaining oil. Swirl it around the pan. Add the prepared vegetables and stir-fry for 5-6 minutes depending on the heat and the pan. Using a perforated spoon, add the vegetables to the pasta bowl. Add the vinegar, seasoning and mustard to the cooking pan and bring to a simmer. Pour over the vegetables and pasta and toss to mix.

Spoon into four individual warmed bowls and top each serving with a shelled egg, garlic croûtons and a sprinkling of Parmesan cheese.

● **Herb or garlic croûtons:** Croûtons are made with white bread slices cut in medium-sized dice, then fried in hot butter until crisp and golden. Try sprinkling them with chopped herbs. Or, for a garlic flavour, heat butter with a crushed clove of garlic for 1 minute without browning, then add the bread cubes. Drain croûtons on absorbent kitchen paper and serve straight away.

FETTUCINE WITH AVOCADO

SERVES 4

3 ripe avocados

juice 1-2 lemons

150 ml (¼ pint) double cream

225-350 g (8-12 oz) fettucine or tagliatelle

salt and freshly milled pepper

1 egg yolk (size 2)

grated Parmesan cheese, for serving

Avocado might seem an unusual partner for pasta but this is delicious. Make sure the avocados are ripe, when they have a soft buttery texture that melts into the sauce.

Cut the avocados in half and remove the stones. Using a spoon, remove the avocado flesh and chop up coarsley. Put the avocado in a bowl with the juice of 1 lemon to keep the green colour. Put the cream in a large serving bowl and set in the oven at lowest heat to warm through.

Add the pasta to a saucepan of boiling salted water and stir until reboiling. Cook for 6 minutes or until the pasta is just tender, then drain.

Add the egg yolk to the warmed cream and stir through. Tip in the hot cooked pasta and toss – the heat of the pasta will be sufficient to thicken the egg and cream sauce. Add a good seasoning of salt and freshly milled pepper. Add the prepared avocado along with sufficient lemon juice to sharpen up the flavour. Toss to mix and serve at once, with grated Parmesan for sprinkling.

FRESH NOODLES WITH SMOKED SALMON AND CREAM

SERVES 4

225 g (8 oz) smoked salmon

225 g (8 oz) fresh green tagliatelle

15 g (½ oz) butter

150 ml (¼ pint) double cream

1 tablespoon chopped fresh dill, or 1 level teaspoon dried dillweed

freshly milled black pepper

squeeze lemon juice

A mouth-watering combination, this looks pretty when you shred the smoked salmon in strips to match the noodles. The flavour is defininitely best when fresh pasta is used. I tend to treat this as an indulgent supper dish, but it also makes a very good dinner party first course when it would go twice as far.

Roll each smoked salmon slice up tightly, then shred across and shake the strips to separate them. Bring a large saucepan of salted water to a rolling boil, add the pasta and stir until the water reboils, then cook for 2 minutes (dried pasta takes 6 minutes). When the pasta is cooked, drain at once in a colander.

Put the butter, cream and dill into the hot saucepan and let the butter melt. Add a seasoning of freshly milled pepper and return the pasta to the pan. Toss to combine with the cream and dill sauce. Add the smoked salmon strips and a squeeze of lemon juice to sharpen up the flavour. Toss again and serve at once, with extra freshly milled pepper over the top.

GRILLED SEA TROUT WITH WHOLEGRAIN MUSTARD BUTTER

SERVES 6

1 × 1.5 kg (3 lb) sea trout, or farmed pink rainbow trout

100 g (4 oz) butter

3 level tablespoons wholegrain mustard

salt and freshly milled pepper

Sea trout are seasonal and available only in summer, but at other times of the year cook farmed rainbow trout this way. Make sure your grill pan can cope with a whole fish and don't start until almost serving time – the fish is surprisingly quickly cooked.

Have the fishmonger gut the fish leaving on the head – remove the head only if it's a question of fitting the fish on to the grill pan. With a sharp knife, slash through the thickest part of the fish three times on each side – this aids the cooking and makes serving easier. Melt the butter in a saucepan and stir in the mustard to make a thick well-flavoured mixture.

Heat the grill to moderately hot and set the grill pan about 7.5 cm (3 inches) from the heat source. Place the fish on the grill rack and season with salt and freshly milled pepper.

Spread lavishly with about half the mustard butter, pushing it into the knife cuts. Place the fish under the grill and cook for 10 minutes – the skin will char and crisp up. Carefully turn the fish over. Season and spread the remaining mustard butter on the second side. Replace under the grill and cook for about 8 minutes – the second side requires less time.

Transfer the fish to a warm platter. Cut along the back and lift the flesh off the bone – the deep cuts will encourage portions to come away in neat pieces.

GRILLED SALMON STEAKS WITH SOURED CREAM AND CHIVES

SERVES 4

4 salmon steaks, cut about 2.5 cm (1 inch) thick

25 g (1 oz) butter

seasoned flour

150 ml (¼ pint) soured cream

juice ½ lemon

salt and freshly milled pepper

1 tablespoon chopped fresh chives

Have salmon steaks for grilling cut at least 2.5 cm (1 inch) thick (thin steaks dry out quickly) then keep the cooking heat to moderate and these will be perfect. Cook and serve in the same dish if you can.

Heat the grill to moderate and set the grill rack about 7.5 cm (3 inches) below the heat source. Put the butter in a rectangular flameproof serving dish (or cast iron gratin dish) and set under the heat to let the butter melt. When the butter is hot, lay in the salmon steaks and immediately turn them over so both sides are butter coated. Cook under the grill for 3-4 minutes.

Turn the salmon steaks again, baste with the melted butter and then dust with seasoned flour. Replace under the grill and cook for a further 5-6 minutes or until the steaks are golden and the flesh flakes when you press it gently near the bone.

Transfer the salmon to a hot serving platter. Set the gratin dish over direct heat and stir the soured cream into the buttery juices. Add the lemon juice, a seasoning of salt and pepper and the chives. Stir until bubbling and hot, then pour over the salmon steaks and serve.

HOT SEAFOOD PLATTER

SERVES 6

450 g (1 lb) smoked haddock
  fillet

450 g (1 lb) fresh halibut fillet

300 ml (½ pint) dry white wine

150 ml (¼ pint) water

225 g (8 oz) smoked mussels or
  cooked fresh mussels
  removed from their shells

40 g (1½ oz) butter

40 g (1½ oz) plain flour

salt and freshly milled pepper

1 egg yolk (size 2)

150 ml (¼ pint) double cream

50-75 g (2-3 oz) Gruyère cheese

decorated pastry triangles, to
  garnish (see below)

This platter combines smoked and fresh fish with pieces cut portion-size so serving is easier. Each person gets a little smoked and fresh fish with a few smoked mussels and crisp pastry triangles as a bonus.

Heat the oven to 160°C (325°F or gas no. 3).

Trim the fish, removing any skin and bones, and cut each fish into six serving pieces. Arrange the fish pieces (except mussels) in a large frying pan, add the wine and water and bring to a simmer. Cover with the pan lid and poach gently for 6-8 minutes or until the fish is cooked. With a perforated spoon, transfer the fish to a hot serving platter, grouping the white and smoked fish together. Sprinkle over the mussels. Cover with kitchen foil and keep warm in the heated oven.

Strain the fish poaching liquid and make up to 400 ml (¾ pint) with water if necessary. Melt the butter in a saucepan, stir in the flour and cook over low heat for 1 minute. Gradually stir in the hot fish liquid, beating well all the time to make a smooth sauce. Bring to a simmer, stirring, season with salt and freshly milled pepper and cook gently for 3-5 minutes. Combine the egg yolk and cream in a bowl. Draw the pan off the heat, stir in the yolk and cream mixture and check the seasoning.

Heat the grill to hot. Spoon the sauce over the fish pieces. Grate the Gruyère cheese and sprinkle over the top. Place under the heated grill until bubbling and golden brown. Add hot pastry triangles just before serving – a few on the platter look decorative; otherwise, pass them separately to let guests help themselves.

● **Decorated pastry triangles:** Thaw 1 × approx 350 g packet of frozen pastry and roll out on a floured surface to 5 mm (¼ inch) thickness. With a sharp kitchen knife, cut out approximately twelve 5 cm (2 inch) triangles. Brush the pastry tops with egg glaze (1 egg yolk beaten with 1 tablespoon water), then sprinkle with sesame seeds. Arrange the pastry triangles on an ungreased baking tray and set in an oven heated to 200°C (400°F or gas no. 6). Bake for 10-15 minutes or until well risen, crisp and golden.

PRAWN PILAFF

SERVES 4

450 g (1 lb) cooked unshelled
  prawns

½ lemon

few parsley stalks

200 g (7 oz) peeled, cooked
  prawns

1 medium onion

1 red sweet pepper

75 g (3 oz) butter

225 g (8 oz) long-grain rice

salt and freshly milled pepper

2 tablespoons chopped fresh
  parsley

I've used a mixture of unshelled prawns and peeled prawns here – the crushed prawn shells are used to flavour the stock and, because the rice absorbs the cooking liquid, the pilaff has a delicious seafood taste.

Rinse and shell the prawns. Crush the shells and place in a saucepan with about 900 ml (1½ pints) cold water. Add a slice from the lemon and a few parsley stalks. Bring to a simmer and cook for 20 minutes to make a flavoured stock. Strain and reserve 600 ml (1 pint) for the recipe. **P** Combine all the prawns and set aside.

Peel and finally chop the onion. Deseed and chop the red sweet pepper. Melt 25 g (1 oz) of the butter in a medium saucepan, add the onion and sweet pepper and soften over the heat for about 5 minutes. Add the rice and stir until the grains are coated with butter. Pour in the reserved stock and bring to the boil. Season with salt and pepper. Lower the heat to a simmer, cover with the pan lid and cook gently for 20-30 minutes or until the rice grains are tender and the stock absorbed.

Melt the remaining butter in a frying pan, add the reserved prawns and heat through. Season with freshly milled pepper. Add the hot prawns and butter from the pan, the juice of the lemon and the chopped parsley to the cooked pilaff and fork through the rice. Serve with a green salad.

CRÊPES

MAKES 12

100 g (4 oz) plain flour
pinch salt
1 egg (size 2)
1 egg yolk (size 2)
300 g (½ pint) milk
1 tablespoon melted butter or grapeseed oil
oil for frying

Crêpes are suberb for making in advance. Here is something you could have on hand in the freezer, especially if you make a double batch. Or simply make the day before and store in the refrigerator ready for filling and serving.

Sift the flour and salt into a mixing bowl and make a well in the centre. Crack the egg and yolk into the centre and add half the milk. Using a wooden spoon, stir from the middle, keeping the liquid ingredients in the centre while gradually drawing in the flour from around the sides of the bowl. Beat to a smooth batter. Stir in the remaining milk and melted butter or oil. Alternatively, put the milk, eggs, melted butter or oil and flour (in that order) in the bowl of a food processor. Cover and blend. Switch off the machine, scrape down the sides of the bowl and blend again.

Strain the prepared batter into a jug – it should have the consistency of thin cream.

Heat a 15 cm (6 inch) omelette pan or crêpe pan very thoroughly, then rub round the inside with a pad of absorbent kitchen paper that has been dipped in a saucer of oil – keep the oil close at hand. Pour about 2 tablespoons of the crêpe batter (from the jug) into the centre of the hot pan and immediately lift and tilt the pan so that the batter spreads over the bottom thinly. When brown on the underside, loosen the crêpe with a spatula and turn to cook the second side, then turn out of the pan. Repeat until all the batter is used up – rubbing the hot pan with the oil pad between each crêpe. **P**

Crêpes for immediate use should be stacked and kept warm – on a plate set over a saucepan of simmering water is the old-fashioned and best method.

Freezing crêpes: Enclose a stack of cold crêpes in a freezer bag – they can be refrigerated for up to 3 days or frozen for 3 months.

● You can vary the basic crêpe batter by using wholemeal flour instead of plain for **Wholemeal crêpes**. They are darker in colour but very nice in savoury recipes. Or, use lager for the mixing liquid to make **Beer Batter crêpes**. These come up slightly crisp and very light and are excellent with fish or seafood fillings. Take care to let the froth subside and to measure the lager (not the froth) when you are making these.

P Can be prepared ahead: unroll a length of absorbent kitchen paper and turn each prepared crêpe directly on to it – the paper will absorb the greasy patches and keep crêpes light and dry.

SPINACH AND RICOTTA CRÊPES

SERVES 6

12 prepared crêpes (see left)

450 g (1 lb) fresh spinach, or 1 × approx 225 g packet frozen chopped spinach, thawed

225 g (8 oz) ricotta or curd cheese

salt and freshly milled pepper

40 g (1½ oz) butter

100 g (4 oz) fresh white breadcrumbs

50 g (2 oz) grated parmesan cheese

For the sauce

1 small onion

2 cloves garlic

2 tablespoons grapeseed or other mild oil

1 × approx 400 g can chopped tomatoes

1 tablespoon red wine vinegar

1 level teaspoon castor sugar

2 tablespoons chopped fresh herbs

P Can be prepared ahead: cover and refrigerate for up to 8 hours. Let come to room temperature before baking, or allow extra baking time.

Filled crêpes make an excellent supper dish so long as you choose interesting fillings. These are folded and served in a tangy tomato sauce – a good vegetarian recipe that could be made in large quantities for a hot buffet dish.

Have the crêpes prepared and stacked – there is no need to heat them at this stage.

Start with the sauce: peel and finely chop the onion. Peel and finely chop the garlic. Heat the oil in a saucepan, add the onion and cook gently to soften. Add the garlic and cook for a moment more, then stir in the contents of the tin of tomatoes, the red wine vinegar and sugar. Bring to a simmer and cook gently for 10-15 minutes to make a well-flavoured tomato sauce. Stir in the herbs and draw off the heat.

Heat the oven to 190°C (375°F or gas no. 5).

Pull away the centre rib from the fresh spinach and wash in several changes of cold water. Place in a large saucepan, cover and cook for 2-3 minutes until leaves wilt. Drain in a colander, pressing well to remove excess moisture, then chop the spinach finely. If using frozen spinach, cook according to the package directions, then drain.

In a mixing bowl, combine the ricotta or curd cheese, a good seasoning of salt and freshly milled pepper and the chopped spinach. Divide the spinach filling between the crêpes and fold into triangles. Arrange the filled crêpes in a well-buttered baking dish. **P**

Spoon the tomato sauce over the crêpes. Melt the butter, add the breadcrumbs and Parmesan and stir with a fork. Sprinkle the buttered crumbs around the sides of the dish. Set the crêpes in the heated oven and bake for 20-30 minutes or until golden brown and bubbling hot.

SEAFOOD CRÊPES

SERVES 6

12 prepared beer batter crêpes
  (see page 104)

25 g (1 oz) butter

50 g (2 oz) Gruyère cheese

For the seafood filling

225 g (8 oz) fresh scallops

225 g (8 oz) skinned halibut
  fillet

225 ml (8 fl oz) dry white wine

100 g (4 oz) peeled, cooked
  prawns

150 ml (¼ pint) single cream

40 g (1½ oz) butter

40 g (1½ oz) plain flour

salt and freshly milled pepper

P Can be prepared ahead: cover
and refrigerate for up to 8 hours.
Let come to room temperature
before baking, or allow extra
baking time.

Here's another way to present crêpes. These are filled and folded, then buttered and baked in the oven, without a sauce coating. They go very well with a carefully prepared crisp salad.

Have the crêpes ready prepared and stacked – there is no need to reheat them at this stage. Set aside while preparing the seafood filling.

Carefully remove the pink 'coral' from the scallops and reserve. Place the scallops with the halibut in a shallow pan (a frying pan is ideal), add the wine and bring to a simmer. Remove from the heat, add the reserved 'corals', cover with the pan lid and leave for 5 minutes to poach the fish.

With a perforated spoon, transfer the seafood to a mixing bowl. Flake the halibut and slice the scallops. Add the prawns. Replace the pan of poaching liquid over the heat and boil rapidly to reduce the quantity by half. Strain into a measuring jug and add sufficient cream to make the quantity up to 300 ml (½ pint).

Melt the butter in a saucepan over low heat. Stir in the flour and cook gently for 1 minute. Gradually stir in the wine and cream mixture, beating well all the time to make a smooth sauce. Bring to a simmer and cook for 2-3 minutes. Season with salt and pepper. Pour the sauce into the seafood mixture and allow to cool.

Heat the oven to 180°C (350°F or gas no. 4).

Divide the cooked filling between the crêpes. Fold the sides of the crêpes into the centre, then roll up to enclose the filling. **P**

Arrange the filled crêpes on a buttered baking tray, spacing them apart. Brush with butter, melted. Set in the heated oven and bake for 15 minutes to heat through. Grate the cheese, sprinkle over the crêpes and return to the oven to bake for a further 5 minutes. Serve hot.

HUNGARIAN CABBAGE CRÊPES

SERVES 6

1 recipe quantity crêpe batter (see page 104)

½ small cabbage

oil for frying

6 thin slices cooked ham

40 g (1½ oz) butter

25 g (1 oz) plain flour

300 ml (½ pint) milk

salt and freshly milled pepper

grated nutmeg

1 level teaspoon Dijon mustard

50 g (2 oz) Gruyère cheese

25 g (1 oz) grated Parmesan cheese

P Can be prepared ahead: cool, cover and refrigerate for up to 8 hours. Let come to room temperature before baking, or allow extra baking time.

These are a surprise and very good. Blanched cabbage shreds are added to the batter before making the crêpes. This makes them rather bulky so they can only be folded in half – in this case with a slice of ham inside. Once finished with a cheese sauce and grilled they are deliciously moist and quite filling.

Prepare the crêpe batter and set aside. Quarter the cabbage, cut away the hard core and shred finely across the leaves. Add the cabbage shreds to a saucepan of boiling water and simmer for 3 minutes to blanch, then drain well, pressing out all the moisture. Add to the crêpe batter.

Heat a small omelette or crêpe pan over medium heat. Grease the pan lightly with oil (using a small pad of absorbent kitchen paper dipped in a saucer of oil). Ladle in about 3 tablespoons of the batter and tilt the pan so the cabbage and batter spread evenly over the surface. When browned on the underside, turn to cook on the second side, then turn out of the pan. Repeat until all the batter is used up, to make about 12 cabbage crêpes.

Cut the ham slices in half and divide between the crêpes, placing the ham on the lighter, second cooked side. Fold the crêpes in half and place in a buttered baking dish.

Heat the oven to 180°C (350°F or gas no. 4).

Melt the butter in a saucepan over low heat. Stir in the flour and cook for 1 minute, then gradually stir in the milk, beating well to make a smooth sauce. Bring to a simmer and cook for 2-3 minutes. Season well with salt and pepper and a little grated nutmeg. Draw off the heat and add the mustard. Grate the Gruyère cheese and add to the sauce. Stir until cheese has melted – the heat of the sauce will be sufficient to do this. Pour the hot sauce over the crêpes to coat them. **P**

Sprinkle crêpes with grated cheese. Set the dish in the heated oven and bake for 20-25 minutes or until bubbling hot and brown.

Couscous with Spicy Sweet Pepper Sauce

SERVES 4

225 g (8 oz) couscous

300 ml (½ pint) water

1 level teaspoon salt

2-3 pieces pared lemon zest

2 tablespoons warmed olive oil

For the vegetable sauce

4-5 sweet peppers – a mixture of red and yellow

2 medium onions

2-3 cloves garlic

3 tablespoons olive oil

1 tablespoon crumbled fresh thyme leaves

225 ml (8 fl oz) water

1 level tablespoon concentrated tomato purée

1 level teaspoon light muscovado sugar

½ teaspoon chilli sauce

salt and freshly milled pepper

Couscous has little flavour of its own but the addition of a spicy vegetable sauce does the trick. Pass warmed pitta bread with this.

Measure the couscous into a bowl and stir in the water, salt and pared lemon zest. Let soak for 20 minutes or until the liquid is absorbed. Then rub the grains between the fingers until there are no lumps. Place the couscous in a steamer lined with cheesecloth or muslin and steam for 30 minutes over simmering water.

Meanwhile, heat the grill to hot and set the grill pan about 7.5 cm (3 inches) below the heat source. Quarter the peppers lengthways and remove the seeds. Arrange the pepper pieces on a baking tray and grill until the skins are blistered and charred. Cover with a cloth and leave for 10 minutes by which time they should be cool enough to handle. Peel off the charred skins.

Peel and slice the onions, and peel and chop the garlic. Heat the olive oil in a frying pan, add the onions and cook gently to soften – about 5 minutes. Stir in the garlic and thyme and fry for a few moments more. Combine the water, concentrated tomato purée, sugar and chilli sauce in a bowl. Pour into the pan and bring to a simmer. Add the peppers and simmer for about 10 minutes to reduce and concentrate the flavour. Check the seasoning with salt and freshly milled pepper.

Turn the couscous on to a hot serving platter and drizzle over the warm oil. Pour over the hot spicy pepper sauce and serve.

BOSTON BAKED BEANS WITH SMOKED PORK SAUSAGE

SERVES 6

450 g (1 lb) dried white haricot beans

1 piece bacon, about 700 g (1½ lb)

1 onion

2 cloves

25 g (1 oz) light muscavado sugar

2 tablespoons black treacle

1 level tablespoon concentrated tomato purée

1 level tablespoon prepared mustard

1 level teaspoon salt

freshly milled pepper

1 × 225 g (8 oz) smoked pork sausage ring

squeeze lemon juice

Homemade baked beans are very special, and the addition of a smoked pork sausage ring makes them substantial eating. It's not worth cooking small quantities but the beans do reheat very well. If you're inclined, tackle the Boston brown bread too – it's the traditional accompaniment.

Put the dried beans in a large bowl, cover generously with cold water and soak overnight. Soak the bacon piece in water to cover in another bowl.

Drain the beans and put in a saucepan with fresh cold water to cover – about 1.1 litres (2 pints). Bring to a simmer, cover with the pan lid and cook gently for 1 hour. Meanwhile, put the bacon piece in a second saucepan with fresh cold water to cover, bring slowly to the boil and simmer for 30 minutes. Drain the bacon piece and cut away the rind.

Heat the oven to 140°C (275°F or gas no. 1).

Transfer the beans and liquid to a large casserole. Peel the onion, stick the cloves into it and add to the beans with the bacon piece, pushing both down under the beans. In a small bowl, combine the sugar, treacle, tomato purée, mustard, salt and a seasoning of pepper with a ladleful of the liquid from the beans. Mix to blend and stir into the beans. Cover the casserole, set in the heated oven and cook for 2-3 hours.

Remove the skin from the smoked pork sausage and slash the sausage crossways several times with a knife (it looks more attractive). About 20 minutes before the end of the cooking time, add to the pot of beans.

Before serving, check the taste, adding a squeeze of lemon juice to sharpen up the flavour if you like. Serve the hot beans with slices of bacon and smoked sausage. Bowls of coleslaw tossed in vinaigrette and wholemeal or Boston brown bread are the best accompaniments.

BOSTON BROWN BREAD

MAKES 2 LOAVES

175 g (6 oz) wholemeal flour

175 g (6 oz) rye flour

1½ level teaspoons bicarbonate of soda

1½ level teaspoons salt

150 g (5 oz) cornmeal

100 g (4 oz) seedless raisins

250 g (9 oz) dark treacle

350 ml (12 fl oz) low-fat natural yogurt

100 ml (4 fl oz) water

P Can be prepared ahead: return the bread to the cans and steam for 10-15 minutes to warm through.

A dark bread made with wholemeal rye flour, cornmeal, treacle and raisins, Boston brown bread is sticky and delicious, the traditional accompaniment for Boston baked beans.

Boston brown bread is steamed to cook and food cans are the traditional container – use two 822 g (1 lb 13 oz) empty vegetable or fruit cans. Grease and flour both cans, then tap sharply to knock out excess flour. Select a saucepan with a lid that is large enough to take both cans and cover the bottom of the saucepan with a folded sheet of newspaper to keep the cans off the bottom of the pan.

Sift the wholemeal and rye flours, bicarbonate of soda and salt into a bowl. Add any bran remaining in the sieve, the cornmeal and raisins. Measure the treacle into a large mixing bowl, add the yogurt and water and stir to blend. Add the sifted dry ingredients and mix to a soft dough.

Spoon the mixture into the prepared cans, filling them three-quarters full. Cover each with a square of greased foil (folded with a pleat to allow the bread to rise) and tie on with string. Set in the steamer, add boiling water to come halfway up the sides of the cans and steam for 2 hours. Test the bread with a skewer – it should come out clean.

Let the bread cool in the containers for 10 minutes, then loosen the sides with a spatula and slip out on to a wire cooling tray. **P** Serve warm, cut in slices.

BAKED FRESH FIGS

SERVES 6

12 fresh figs

3 level tablespoons light muscavado sugar

175 ml (6 fl oz) port

These are frivolous and pretty. Fresh figs are a treat, and when served warm with a port and brown sugar syrup they are almost aromatic.

Heat the oven to 180°C (350°F or gas no. 4).

Rinse the figs and with a sharp knife cut a cross in the flesh of each fig at the stalk end. Arrange the fruit in a single layer (cut side up) in a roomy casserole or baking dish. Sprinkle over the sugar and pour in the port.

Cover the figs with the casserole lid or enclose the baking dish with foil. Set in the heated oven and bake for 20-25 minutes or until warmed through – the figs will open up like flowers while the sugar and port form a syrup.

Serve the figs warm with the syrup from the dish spooned over. Pass chilled whipped cream or thick natural yogurt.

HOT APPLE PASTRIES

MAKES 6

1 recipe quantity flaky pastry
  (see page 85)

3 dessert apples

beaten egg, to glaze

icing sugar, for dusting

These are incredibly easy. Surprisingly, rolling out the pastry is the only tricky part, but if you work on a cool surface it's much easier to handle.

On a lightly floured work surface, roll out the pastry not less than 5 mm (¼ inch) in thickness. Try to guide the pastry to an oblong about 20 cm (8 inches) wide and 30 cm (12 inches) long. Chill the rolled pastry (on a baking sheet) to firm it up. Then using a 10 cm (4 inch) round cutter, stamp out six rounds of pastry. Transfer the pastry rounds to a baking tray that has been rinsed with cold water.

Heat the oven to 200°C (400°F or gas no. 6).

Peel the apples, leaving them whole, and cut out the cores. Cut each apple in half lengthways, then slice the halves thickly – holding the slices in the correct order. Transfer one sliced apple half to the centre of each pastry circle. Brush the pastry edges with beaten egg.

Set the tray of apple pastries in the heated oven and bake for 30 minutes – the pastry will rise around the apples to form a border and will be golden brown.

Dust each pastry generously with icing sugar and pass under a hot grill for a few moments to caramelize the tops. Serve hot with chilled cream.

DARK CHOCOLATE SOUFFLÉS

SERVES 6

100 g (4 oz) plain chocolate

150 ml (¼ pint) soured cream

1 teaspoon vanilla essence

4 eggs (size 2)

50 g (2 oz) castor sugar

icing sugar, for the tops

The best way to serve these is to push a spoon into the centre of each hot soufflé and pour in a pool of warm chocolate sauce or chilled cream.

Select 6 individual ramekin or small soufflé dishes and butter them well. Break the chocolate into a large mixing bowl and set over a saucepan of hot (not boiling) water until melted. Remove the bowl from the heat. Stir in the soured cream and vanilla essence. Separate the eggs, cracking the whites into a separate bowl and beating the yolks into the chocolate mixture.

*1 recipe quantity warm
chocolate sauce (see page
136), or 225 ml (8 fl oz) single
cream*

P Can be prepared ahead: will
keep for up to 30 minutes before
baking.

Heat the oven to 200°C (400°F or gas no. 6).

Whisk the egg whites to a stiff snow, add the sugar and whisk again until glossy. Using a metal spoon, fold the whisked whites into the chocolate mixture. Spoon into the prepared dishes and arrange them on a baking tray. **P**

Set in the oven and bake for 10 minutes – the soufflés should remain soft in the centre. Dust with icing sugar and serve, with chocolate sauce or cream.

Banana Brûlées

SERVES 6

300 ml (½ pint) single cream

1 egg (size 2)

2 egg yolks (size 2)

25 g (1 oz) castor sugar

few drops vanilla essence

225 ml (8 fl oz) double cream

2 tablespoons natural yogurt

3 medium-size ripe bananas

squeeze lemon juice

4 level tablespoons demerara
  sugar

P Can be prepared ahead: keep
refrigerated overnight.

A variation on a classic theme, these custards are individually baked in ramekin dishes. Ideally, start the day before, so the custard and cream are well chilled; then you get the delicious contrast with the crunchy browned sugar topping.

Heat the oven to 160°C (325°F or gas no. 3).

Lightly butter six individual ramekins or small soufflé dishes and place in a large baking dish or roasting tin.

Heat the single cream almost to the boil. While cream is heating, lightly beat the whole egg, egg yolks, sugar and vanilla in a bowl. Stir in the hot cream and blend well. Strain the custard into a jug and pour into the prepared dishes, filling them not more than half full.

Fill the large baking dish or roasting tin to a depth of about 10 mm (½ inch) with warm water. Set the custards in the heated oven and bake for 25-30 minutes or until they are set. Cool, then refrigerate until chilled.

Whip the double cream to soft peaks and fold in the natural yogurt. Peel and mash the bananas with a squeeze of lemon juice. Spoon the banana over each chilled custard, cover with the whipped cream and spread the cream level. Refrigerate for several hours. **P**

About 1 hour before serving, sprinkle the tops generously with demerara sugar to cover the surface evenly. Place under a hot grill to melt the sugar – about 1 minute. Refrigerate until the sugar topping becomes crisp.

DINNER PARTIES

Celery and stilton soup

Orange, olive and raisin salad

Tomato and avocado terrine

Cucumber and chive mousse

.

Courgette-stuffed chicken breasts with red pepper sauce

Cured pork loin with raisin sauce

Pan-fried steaks with red plums

Honey-glazed duck with grapefruit and ginger sauce

Salmon wrapped in filo with chive butter

Slow roast pheasant with fried chicory

Venison pot roast

.

Long-grain and wild rice with mushrooms

Hot gratin of potatoes

Red cabbage with apple

.

White chocolate mousse in dark chocolate cases

Nesselrode iced bombe

Nesselrode topping

Curd cheese and sultana crêpes

Hot pineapple with orange shreds

Chocolate steamed pudding with chocolate sauce

DINNER
PARTIES

Choose guests thoughtfully for dinner parties. Being fewer in number, this is more of a select group specially chosen to enjoy a particular occasion. I always include two long-standing friends because they give me confidence and help the conversation along. A hostess friend of mine swears by a maximum of six round the table: after that, she claims, the conversation divides. I think she is right.

It's important not to feel that dinner party food must be as elaborate as in an expensive restaurant – that everything must be cooked in lashings of cream or wine, be flavoured with garlic and exotic spices or served in the latest style. Let restaurants get on with restaurant food. For your dinner parties, tackle dishes you are comfortable with, that are simple – you'll be surprised how many people prefer it. Keep the menu practical, with not too many courses – dinner parties are much more fun when the hostess is not flustered.

I find it easier to start by planning the main course. Once a decision has been reached it's usually not too difficult to add on a first and last course. Consider a dish that won't spoil if dinner is delayed – a meat dish in a sauce or gravy or some exotic casserole. Or go for something that is wrapped and then baked – in filo pastry or flaky pastry, or folded in crêpes and then topped with a sauce. These dishes stand up well to a short wait. It's more convenient to have a cold first course already on the table, but something hot presented after guests sit down is a pleasant surprise and it needn't be anything complicated – a gratin of vegetables or a light soup, perhaps. Give the menu a seasonal touch at some stage – in your choice of vegetables is a good place. It shows you've given the menu some thought.

Good planning is the key to success. Work out what you can cook the day before and what you must leave until the last moment. A pretty garnish or topping can be prepared ready in a polythene bag and stored in the refrigerator, then all you have to do is add it. Getting everything ready at the same time is the hardest bit, but if you note the cooking or reheating times of every recipe and make yourself a time-table you'll know when to start each one in relation to the others and you should finish with

Previous pages: Venison pot roast and red cabbage with apple

everything cooked and ready together. Don't hurry guests through a party menu – little breaks are nice. Use the gaps between courses to add the finishing touches – that little bit of garnish, for instance.

A choice of desserts makes an impressive ending. Most hostesses do this, but it's a nice idea to have one hot and one cold dish. A hot dish could be very simple – a fruit combination that is already assembled and simply popped in the oven after the main course is served. It's a good idea to bring on the cheeseboard and dessert together and let guests have a choice – not everyone has a sweet tooth and nobody will feel guilty refusing dessert if there's a cheeseboard to pick at.

If conversation is flowing, serve coffee at the table. Otherwise, arrange cups on a large tray and serve in the sitting room. Include low caffeine or decaffeinated coffee and interesting tea – Lapsang Souchong or a fruit-flavoured tea like mango will be surprisingly popular. Pass some delicious thin biscuits – your own hazelnut thins (see page 87) or any of the excellent ones you can buy – or unusual sweetmeats – glacé apricots or prunes d'agen. These are much nicer than chocolates.

START WITH SMOKED FISH

Smoked fish provides an easy and delicious first course as long as it's fresh and moist. This means keeping smoked fish covered (it dries very easily) and serving it at room temperature for the best flavour – take smoked fish from the refrigerator at least 30 minutes before serving. Experiment with tangy dressings – you'll find smoked fish takes them very well. Try these ideas.

● Offer smoked salmon with a vinaigrette made using lemon juice instead of vinegar; add a little grated lemon rind and very finely diced cucumber. Crinkle smoked salmon slices on plates, add a spoonful of dressing and a lemon wedge.
● Try smoked halibut slices with a soured cream and mustard sauce (see page 148, omitting the spring onions) sharpened with lemon juice and a seasoning of black pepper. Spoon the dressing along-side the smoked fish and sprinkle the dressing with chopped fresh chives.
● Smoked trout, which went out of fashion when it used to be on the bone, is now right back in again with pink trout fillets (no bones) that are easy to serve. Offer these with a ravigote sauce (vinaigrette with lots of herbs) or with a dill sauce such as you would normally serve with gravadlax.
● Make up an 'assiette' of smoked fish – on individual plates or on a single platter for guests to help themselves. You could include crinkled or rolled slices of smoked salmon or smoked sea trout, strips of smoked halibut, flakes of peppered smoked mackerel, fillets of smoked eel, thin slices of smoked cod's roe and smoked mussels tossed in a vinaigrette dressing. Add a discreet garnish of frisée and lemon wedges and pass horseradish soured cream sauce (see page 148) – it will look impressive.

SOUP OF THE EVENING

Soups made with the freshest ingredients are as much in favour as they ever were. Cream soups can look plain without something extra, but there's no need for anything complicated – simple additions are the most appetizing and are the easiest to add at the last minute.

- One or two wide leaves of flat-leafed parsley, coriander or watercress or the inner leaves of celery look pretty floating on the surface. Or stir shredded and softened leek or spinach into an appropriately-flavoured soup.
- Mix finely chopped fresh tarragon, dill, chives or basil into single cream and then pour into soup bowls to achieve a speckled 'pool' – this looks dramatic.
- Add texture with chopped fresh parsley or chives stirred in. Chopped parsley packed in ice cube trays with water and frozen (keep on hand) will dissolve instantly when added to hot soup, to release a parsley garnish. Or add flakes of your own favourite herb butter just before serving.
- Coarsely milled black pepper adds speckles to a plain soup. Pour in a swirl of cream, then add a few turns of the pepper-mill on the 'white'. Red paprika is an alternative.
- Top with crunchy croûtons – particularly vegetable soups. Trim crusts from bread slices, then cut bread in fine dice and fry in oil, stirring until crisp and golden. Add mashed garlic to the oil for flavour or sprinkle hot croûtons with fresh or dried herbs like oregano.
- Pulled bread pieces look even more attractive – drag bread pieces from thick slices in un-even bits, then treat as for croûtons.

PRESENTING VEGETABLES

Serve vegetables simply, and you can rely on them to add colour and flavour.

- The latest trend is to serve a simple combination of veget-ables on one large platter. Con-trast the choice (not more than three) and don't mix them – grouping the colours has more visual impact.
- The natural look is all the rage, so don't over-trim veget-ables (especially new summer ones). Include some of the stalks and the tails and any tiny green inner leaves. If they are small, leave vegetables whole.
- A nut of butter will give hot vegetables a shine or use a little olive oil.
- Flavour melted butter for tossing vegetables with sea-soned salt or pepper, whole-grain mustard, or snipped spring onion, chives or parsley.
- Add a contrast with slivered toasted almonds (see page 210), crumbled crisp bacon bits, sautéed onion rings or toasted sesame seeds (see page 210).
- Reach for the peppermill to garnish light-coloured veget-ables or purées – the coarse grains add texture. A sprinkling of paprika is pretty too.
- Heat soured cream with salt and freshly milled pepper and chopped fresh chives or grated cheese and pour over hot cooked vegetables.
- Use serving cases made from shortcrust pastry baked on fluted moulds (see page 120); single portions of vegetables can be spooned inside.
- Many cooked vegetables are delicious served cold or at room temperature; a sprinkling of salt and pepper and your favourite oil and vinegar dres-sing is all that is needed to enhance the flavours.

ARRANGING COLD MEATS

Given a little thought and with colourful extras, platters of cold meats or poultry can be arranged very attractively for a party. It's always less expensive to cook cold meats yourself, and given good-sized trays or plates it doesn't take long to put together appetizing presentations.

● Roast meat or poultry a day ahead for serving cold and let them cool in their own time – don't hurry by refrigerating.

● Carve when quite cold (not before or you lose precious juices), and slice meats thinly when they will taste more tender.

● Arrange slices on a platter by folding, rolling or crinkling up the slices rather than laying them flat, so you get textures and shapes.

● Arrange in combination with delicatessen smoked meats or salamis which are ready to serve; these add contrasts. A platter could include prosciutto wrapped around melon slices for instance.

Elegant extras could include any of these:

● scooped-out tomatoes filled with tarragon or mustard mayonnaise or horseradish cream.

● celery or carrot sticks or trimmed spring onions.

● fluted cucumber slices around the rim of the dish.

● onions – peeled and thinly sliced – in overlapping rings.

● chunks of white feta cheese tossed in a herb vinaigrette.

● tiny bunches of sugared black grapes set in lettuce cups – to show up the colour.

● fresh pineapple chunks rolled in chopped fresh mint or tomato quarters rolled in chopped fresh chives.

● hard-boiled egg halves topped with mayonnaise and sprinkled with toasted sesame seeds (see page 210) or just a little freshly milled pepper.

● apricot halves filled with cranberry or mint jelly according to the meats chosen.

● pickled fruits served in blanched orange peel cups (see page 195).

FROZEN ASSETS

Simple presentations suit frozen desserts best. Top quality ice creams and sorbets ready made are as good as anything you can prepare yourself, and you don't have to be content with just serving them plain from the container. Try these different scooping and moulding ideas.

● An ice cream or sorbet can be scooped out well ahead of time and stored in the freezer on trays lined with non-stick baking parchment ready for serving. Pile the scoops in a chilled glass bowl.

● Forget the individual serving glasses and present scoops of ice cream or sorbet on dessert plates with a slice or two of fresh fruit; on a plate there's more room for a pretty garnish.

● Consider thin slivers cut across a star fruit, the fanned-out slices of a cut strawberry, kiwi fruit or mango, a scattering of fresh raspberries or a spray of sugared redcurrants arranged alongside scoops of ice cream or sorbet.

● Press a prepared ice cream or sorbet (or two contrasting colours) into a chilled loaf pan and freeze firm. Then unmould and slice with a sharp knife dipped in hot water and wiped between cutting each slice. Slicing sorbets instead of scooping them looks elegant on dessert plates.

● Alternatively, press sorbets into shapely metal moulds and freeze; a hot cloth applied to the outside of the mould will loosen the sorbet without spoiling its contours. Use a ring mould and you could fill the centre with diced fresh fruits.

● Serve ice creams and sorbets with something crisp and sweet – like tuiles, langues de chat or those delicious macaroons twisted in their own papers called amaretti. Or make your own geneva wafers (see page 160), or hazelnut thins (see page 87).

UNMOULDING A MOUSSE

Whether yours is a savoury or sweet recipe, when the mixture is set with gelatine the method of turning it out of the mould on to a serving plate remains the same . . .

Run the point of a knife round the edge of a plain mould to loosen it; use wet fingers to draw back the mixture from a fluted mould. Either way, don't forget the centre of a ring mould.

Hold the mould level and dip up to the rim in a bowl of hot water (as warm as the hand can comfortably bear) for about 10 seconds. Dry the outside with a cloth.

Place the serving plate over the top of the mould and invert both plate and mould together. Then, holding both firmly together, give a sharp shake. If the mousse does not leave the mould, repeat the process.

It's a good idea to wet the surface of the serving plate with cold water before starting, then you can slide the mousse into position if it doesn't happen to come out dead centre.

Remember that the best moulds are metal ones because they conduct the heat more efficiently; when dipped in warm water the contents will quickly loosen. China or earthenware moulds are much more difficult to handle – best avoided as they are more decorative than practical.

CELERY AND STILTON SOUP

SERVES 6

1 head celery

1 medium onion

1 large potato

25 g (1 oz) butter

1 level teaspoon salt

1.1 litres (2 pints) vegetable
 stock

1 bay leaf

freshly milled pepper

100 g (4 oz) stilton cheese

150 ml (¼ pint) single cream

1 egg yolk (size 2)

P Can be prepared ahead: cool,
cover and refrigerate for up to 24
hours. Reheat for serving but do
not boil.

*Delicately flavoured and pale coloured, this soup perks up
considerably when a garnish is added – a few reserved celery
leaves from the inner stalks or a mixture of parsley and toasted
walnuts ground fine in the food processor is pretty.*

Separate the celery stalks, scrub them and pull away the
strings. Chop the stalks finely. Also chop up the green leafy
bits from inside the heart and reserve a few for the soup
garnish. Peel and finely chop the onion, and peel and dice the
potato.

   Melt the butter in a large saucepan. Add the onion and cook
gently to soften. Add the celery with most of the leafy bits and
stir through. Sprinkle with the salt, cover the pan and leave to
cook over low heat for about 15 minutes to draw out the celery
juices.

   Add the potato, stock, bay leaf and a seasoning of pepper.
Bring to a simmer, cover again and cook gently for about 40
minutes or until the vegetables are quite tender.

   Draw off the heat and remove the bay leaf. Crumble the
Stilton in pieces, add to the hot soup and stir through – the
cheese will melt. Ladle the soup into a food processor or
blender and purée. Or pass the soup through a coarse food
mill. **P**

   Combine the cream and egg yolk in a bowl, add a ladleful of
the hot soup and blend, then stir into the soup in the pan.
Check the seasoning before serving, garnishing with the
reserved celery leaves.

ORANGE, OLIVE AND RAISIN SALAD

SERVES 6

6 oranges

100 ml (4 fl oz) olive oil

50 ml (2 fl oz) dry sherry

1 tablespoon chopped fresh
 mint or thyme

salt and freshly milled black
 pepper

75 g (3 oz) stoned black olives

25 g (1 oz) seedless raisins

*The ingredients here betray a Mediterranean origin. This
pretty and fresh-tasting starter salad looks best with orange
slices overlapping on individual serving plates. It is also good as
a buffet salad with cold meats or fish.*

Using a vegetable peeler, thinly pare the zest from one orange.
Squeeze the juice and set aside. With a sharp knife, cut the zest
into thin shreds. Put the orange shreds in a saucepan and cover
with cold water. Bring to a simmer and blanch for about 3
minutes to tenderize, then drain well.

   In a mixing bowl combine the olive oil, dry sherry, reserved

P Can be prepared ahead: keep refrigerated for up to 6 hours.

orange juice, the orange shreds, herbs and a seasoning of salt and pepper.

Cut a slice from the top and bottom of the remaining oranges, then cut around to remove the peel and pith from the fruits. Cut the oranges across into thin slices and discard any pips. Layer the orange slices in a bowl. Scatter the black olives and raisins over. Spoon over the prepared dressing. Cover and refrigerate for at least 2 hours. **P**

Transfer the orange slices, olives and raisins with spoonfuls of the dressing on to individual plates for serving.

TOMATO AND AVOCADO TERRINE

SERVES 6

3 tablespoons cold water

15 g (½ oz) powdered gelatine

1 medium onion

600 ml (1 pint) tomato juice

salt and freshly milled pepper

1 level teaspoon castor sugar

1 tablespoon tarragon wine
  vinegar

4-6 ripe avocados

2-3 tablespoons lemon juice

fresh basil leaves or chopped
  chives, to garnish

For the dressing

75 ml (3 fl oz) mayonnaise

75 ml (3 fl oz) soured cream

salt and freshly milled pepper

2 tablespoons chopped fresh
  chives

P Can be prepared ahead. Keep refrigerated for no longer than 24 hours.

This looks nothing until it is sliced, when you see a blend of green, gold and bright red. Lay slices on serving plates and add a spoonful of the dressing and fresh herbs – leaves of basil or chopped chives are pretty.

Measure the water into a teacup and sprinkle in the gelatine. Let soak for 5 minutes. Peel and thinly slice the onion. Pour the tomato juice into a saucepan, add the sliced onion and bring to a simmer, then draw off the heat and leave to infuse for 10-15 minutes. Add the soaked gelatine and stir to dissolve – the heat of the tomato juice will be sufficient to do this. Add a seasoning of salt and freshly milled pepper, the sugar and vinegar. Strain into a jug and leave to cool.

Spoon a layer of the tomato jelly into the bottom of a 22.5 × 12.5 × 7.5 cm (9 × 5 × 3 inch) oblong tin or mould and chill to set firm.

Halve the avocados and remove the stones. With the tip of a knife blade, cut the skin along the centre back of each half, then peel off the skin to reveal the bright green flesh underneath. Cut the avocado in dice (not too small) and mix with the lemon juice to keep the colour.

Set about 150 ml (¼ pint) of the remaining jelly aside. Mix the drained diced avocado with the rest of the tomato jelly and pour into the tin. Chill until set firm.

Pour over the reserved jelly to seal the surface. Cover and refrigerate for at least 4 hours or until set. Combine the ingredients for the dressing and refrigerate. **P**

Unmould (see page 120) and cut in thick slices. Lay one slice on each serving plate, add a spoonful of the dressing and garnish with fresh herbs.

CUCUMBER AND CHIVE MOUSSE

SERVES 6

1 medium cucumber

salt and freshly milled pepper

1 bunch (6-8) spring onions

75 ml (3 fl oz) cold water

15 g (½ oz) powdered gelatine

2 tablespoons tarragon wine
    vinegar

450 g (1 lb) fromage frais

3 tablespoons chopped fresh
    chives

1 level teaspoon castor sugar

300 ml (½ pint) double cream

paprika, to decorate

P Can be prepared ahead: keep
refrigerated no longer than
overnight.

This is very light-textured and fresh-tasting on account of the fromage frais used in place of the traditional cream cheese. I think a ring shape is impressive – let guests help themselves. Or you could set the mixture in individual moulds, in which case I would dice the reserved cucumber, turn in vinaigrette and spoon over the top of each one.

Finely slice a quarter of the unpeeled cucumber and reserve for the decoration. Peel the remaining cucumber, then cut in half lengthways and scoop out the inner seeds using a teaspoon. Dice the flesh and place in a colander with a sprinkling of salt. Let stand for 1 hour, then rinse in cold water and press the cucumber dry in absorbent kitchen paper.

Trim the spring onions, then chop all the white and some of the green stems.

Lightly oil a 900 ml (1½ pint) ring mould.

Measure the water into a saucepan, sprinkle in the gelatine and let soak for 5 minutes. Set the pan over low heat and stir gently to dissolve the gelatine – do not boil. Draw off the heat and add the tarragon vinegar.

Turn the fromage frais into a mixing bowl. Add the diced cucumber, chopped spring onions, chopped chives, a good seasoning of salt and pepper and the sugar. Stir to mix. Add the gelatine mixture all at once and blend through. Whip the cream to soft peaks and fold in. Taste for seasoning.

Turn the mixture into the prepared mould and spread level. Cover and refrigerate for at least 2 hours. **P** Unmould (see page 120) and garnish with the reserved cucumber slices and a good sprinkling of paprika.

COURGETTE-STUFFED CHICKEN BREASTS WITH RED PEPPER SAUCE

SERVES 8

8 chicken breast fillets, with
  skins on

15 g (½ oz) butter

For the stuffing

1 small onion

15 g (½ oz) butter

50 g (2 oz) fresh white
  breadcrumbs

225 g (8 oz) curd cheese

2 tablespoons chopped fresh
  parsley

salt and freshly milled pepper

225 g (8 oz) courgettes

For the sauce

2 red sweet peppers

2 cloves garlic

½ level teaspoon sugar

salt and freshly milled pepper

150 ml (¼ pint) double cream

P Can be prepared ahead: cover
and refrigerate chicken and sauce
separately for up to 6 hours. Heat
the sauce for serving.

*A variation on chicken with apple and sage stuffing (see page
52), this is equally good. The stuffing of curd cheese and
courgettes here comes up green-flecked and the red sweet
pepper sauce adds a colourful contrast. An excellent dinner
party dish with lots of nice flavours.*

Partially loosen the skin on each chicken breast fillet with
fingertips to form a pocket. Set aside while preparing the
stuffing.

Peel and finely chop the onion. Melt the butter in a
saucepan, add the onion and cook gently to soften. Draw off
the heat and stir in the breadcrumbs with a fork. Turn the curd
cheese into a mixing bowl. Add the breadcrumb mixture, the
chopped parsley and a good seasoning of salt and pepper.
Rinse and trim the courgettes, then grate them coarsely. Add
to the stuffing mixture and blend the ingredients thoroughly.

Heat the oven to 180°C (350°F or gas no. 4).

Take dessertspoons of the mixture and spoon into the
pockets under the chicken skin. Fold the thinner ends of the
breasts underneath to form neat rounded shapes and arrange
close together in a buttered baking dish. **P**

Brush the chicken breasts with the butter, melted. Set in the
heated oven and bake for 30-35 minutes or until a rich golden
brown.

Meanwhile, cut the red peppers for the sauce into quarters
lengthways and remove the seeds. Arrange the pepper pieces
on a baking tray and set under a hot grill until the skins are
blistered and charred. Cover with a cloth and leave for 10
minutes by which time the peppers should be cool enough to
handle. Peel away the skins and cut the pepper flesh coarsely.
Peel and chop the garlic. Put the pepper flesh into a blender
and chop coarsely. Add the garlic, sugar, a seasoning of salt
and pepper and the cream and blend to a purée. **P** Pour into a
saucepan and heat through gently.

Transfer the chicken to a heated serving platter. Pass the
warm red pepper sauce separately.

CURED PORK LOIN WITH RAISIN SAUCE

SERVES 6

700 g (1½ lb) piece smoked
  cured pork loin

For the raisin sauce

100 g (4 oz) seedless raisins

400 g (¾ pint) unsweetened
  apple juice

25 g (1 oz) light muscovado
  sugar

pinch salt

1½ level tablespoons cornflour

2 tablespoons water

3 tablespoons wine vinegar

15 g (½ oz) butter

A raisin sauce has always been popular with ham or gammon cuts. Here I've used a smoked cured pork loin which is boneless, very lean and treated to a mild cure so there is no need for soaking.

Heat the oven to 160°C (325°F or gas no. 3).

Remove the meat covering (cured pork loin is usually vacuum-packed, often with cooking instructions supplied – follow these if you like). Put the piece of meat in a roasting tin and roast allowing 45 minutes per 450 g (1 lb) plus 15 minutes – no basting or turning is required.

Meanwhile, put the raisins in a saucepan with the apple juice, bring to a simmer and cook for 10 minutes to plump up the raisins. Add the sugar and salt. Blend the cornflour with the water. Add a little of the hot apple juice, stir to blend and then return the whole lot to the saucepan. Stir until the sauce has thickened and is boiling. Draw off the heat and add the vinegar and butter.

Let the cooked pork loin rest for 5 minutes (so the meat juices settle), then carve in slices and serve with the hot raisin sauce spooned over.

PAN-FRIED STEAKS WITH RED PLUMS

SERVES 6

6 beef fillet steaks

2 level tablespoons light
  muscovado sugar

2 tablespoons dark soy sauce

juice 1 lemon

1 tablespoon grapeseed or
  other mild oil

1 level teaspoon grated fresh
  root ginger

salt and freshly milled pepper

1 clove garlic

225 g (8 oz) red or purple
  plums

25 g (1 oz) butter

There is nothing new about serving fruits with meat and yet it's a combination that is frequently overlooked. Fruits look exotic and they make dishes interesting. Plums are a good choice here because they have such a brilliant colour and blend perfectly with the tangy marinade.

Trim the fillet steaks and place in a shallow dish. Combine the brown sugar, soy sauce, lemon juice, oil, grated fresh root ginger and a seasoning of salt and pepper in a bowl. Peel and chop the garlic and add. Mix the marinade and pour over the steaks. Cover and refrigerate for up to 8 hours or overnight, turning the steaks once or twice.

Halve and stone the plums. Melt the butter in a 25 cm (10 inch) frying pan. Lift the steaks from the marinade, add to the hot butter and fry, turning them once or twice – 5 minutes for rare, 6-8 minutes for medium done. Lift the steaks from the

150 ml (¼ pint) red wine

3 tablespoons redcurrant jelly

1 level teaspoon Dijon mustard

pan to a serving platter and keep warm.

Pour the red wine into the hot pan drippings and stir well to pick up any flavouring bits. Add the strained meat marinade, the redcurrant jelly and the mustard. Stir to break up the jelly and bring to a simmer. Add the plums and turn them in the hot liquid for a moment to tenderize them.

Spoon the hot plums and sauce over the steaks and serve.

HONEY-GLAZED DUCK WITH GRAPEFRUIT AND GINGER SAUCE

SERVES 6

4-5 duck breast fillets

1 tablespoon clear honey

1 tablespoon dark soy sauce

For the sauce

3 pink grapefruits

50 g (2 oz) granulated sugar

300 ml (½ pint) unsweetened grapefruit juice

2 tablespoons clear honey

2 tablespoons soy sauce

juice 1 lemon

1 level teaspoon grated fresh root ginger

1 level tablespoon cornflour

2 tablespoons water

P Can be prepared ahead: cool, cover and refrigerate the sauce for up to 6 hours. Reheat to simmering before adding the cornflour.

Duck breast fillets are quite large and will provide more than one serving so it's always best to offer them already sliced – in this case with a citrus and ginger sauce. You can experiment with this recipe – orange or pineapple (juice and fruit pieces) can be substituted for the grapefruit – but include the ginger every time.

Heat the oven to 200°C (400°F or gas no. 6). Prick the skin on each duck fillet with a fork. Blend the honey and soy sauce to make a glaze and brush it over each duck fillet. Set the duck fillets skin side up on a rack in a roasting tin. Set in the heated oven and cook for 30 minutes or until the skins are crisp.

Meanwhile, slice away the outer peel and white pith from the grapefruits, then with a sharp knife cut into the fruits between the membrane to lift out the segments; reserve them. Measure the sugar into a dry saucepan. Set over moderate heat and stir until the sugar has melted and turned to a caramel. Draw off the heat and add the grapefruit juice – cover your hand as the mixture will boil up furiously with the addition of a cold liquid. Replace the pan over the heat. Add the honey, soy sauce, lemon juice and grated root ginger. Stir until the mixture simmers and any lumps of caramel have dissolved away. **P**

Blend the cornflour with the water, stir into the contents of the pan and cook until the sauce thickens and clears, stirring constantly. Add the grapefruit segments.

Slice the duck breasts diagonally and place on a heated serving platter. Spoon over a little of the sauce and fruit segments. Serve the remaining sauce separately.

SALMON WRAPPED IN FILO WITH CHIVE BUTTER

SERVES 6

1 tail end piece salmon, about 700 g (1½ lb)

salt and freshly milled pepper

100 g (4 oz) butter, at room temperature

2 tablespoons chopped fresh chives

1 teaspoon lemon juice

6 sheets filo pastry, thawed

1 egg (size 2)

1 teaspoon water

25 g (1 oz) grated Parmesan cheese

P Can be prepared ahead: cover and refrigerate for up to 24 hours.

Individually wrapped portions of salmon look good for dinner parties. Filo pastry bakes beautifully crisp even underneath and when these are cut open the chive butter flows out.

Ask the fishmonger to fillet the tail end into two halves and to remove the skin. Season the salmon with salt and pepper and cut across into neat portions – you should get three nice pieces from each fillet.

In a bowl, cream the butter until soft, then beat in the chopped chives and lemon juice. Alternatively, put the ingredients in a food processor and blend to a smooth green herb butter. Put half the butter in a saucepan and melt over low heat; reserve for brushing the filo. Distribute the remaining herb butter over the pieces of salmon in flakes.

Heat the oven to 190°C (375°F or gas no. 5).

Lay the filo sheets out flat (in a stack) and cover with a damp cloth to prevent them drying out. Take the first sheet and brush all over with the melted herb butter. Fold the sheet in half lengthways and brush with butter again. Set a portion of salmon (buttered side up) about 2.5 cm (1 inch) in from the top end and fold the sides of the filo sheet in over the salmon to meet right along the length of the pastry. Fold the top 2.5 cm (1 inch) in over the salmon and roll to the end of the pastry to completely enclose it. Place on a buttered baking tray with the sealed ends underneath. Repeat with each portion of salmon and the remaining filo sheets. **P**

Lightly mix the egg and water and use to brush each filo parcel. Sprinkle with the grated cheese. Set in the heated oven and bake for 30-35 minutes or until golden brown. Serve hot.

SLOW ROAST PHEASANT WITH FRIED CHICORY

SERVES 6

3 pheasants

100 g (4 oz) butter

onion and carrot for the roasting tin

plain flour, for dredging

6 heads chicory

2-3 tablespoons seasoned flour

300 ml (½ pint) chicken or giblet stock

1 tablespoon redcurrant jelly

1 teaspoon red wine vinegar

salt and freshly milled pepper

I used to roast my pheasant the traditional way until a friend put me on to this method. I find it more reliable especially since my birds tend to come from the supermarket. Chicory makes a marvellous accompaniment – it's the bitter flavour that's so good.

Have the pheasants prepared ready for roasting; otherwise, truss them just like a chicken with trussing needle and string. There's no need to bother with bacon rashers over the breasts using this slow roast method.

Heat the oven to 160°C (325°F or gas no. 3).

Put 50 g (2 oz) of the butter in the roasting tin and let it melt, then, with a pastry brush, dab a little of the melted butter over the birds. Add a thickly sliced onion and carrot to the roasting tin (to flavour the gravy) and set the birds breast down on the sliced vegetables. Set the tin in the heated oven and roast for 1 hour. There is no need to baste.

Turn the birds breast side up, baste with the pan drippings and then lightly sprinkle with flour (from a flour dredger). Return to the oven to roast for a further 20 minutes to complete the cooking time.

Meanwhile, remove any damaged outer leaves from the chicory and trim the stalk ends. Add the whole heads to a saucepan of boiling salted water and simmer until barely tender – about 10 minutes. Drain thoroughly and allow to cool. **P**

Put the seasoned flour on a plate and roll each head of chicory in the seasoned flour. Melt the remaining butter in a roomy frying pan and, when hot and bubbling, add the floured chicory. Fry fairly quickly, turning the heads once or twice, until the chicory is brown and crisp.

Transfer the cooked pheasants to a hot serving platter, add the chicory (if there is room – otherwise place the chicory on a separate plate) and keep warm, uncovered.

Remove the vegetables from the roasting tin and set the pan over direct heat. Add the chicken or giblet stock and stir well to pick up all the flavouring bits. Add the redcurrant jelly, red wine vinegar (and mashed up pheasant livers if you have them) and simmer for 2-3 minutes to reduce and concentrate the flavour. Season with salt and pepper and strain. Serve this gravy with the pheasants.

VENISON POT ROAST

SERVES 8

1 boned and rolled venison
  joint, such as shoulder, about
  1.5-2 kg (3-4 lb)

2 tablespoons grapeseed or
  other mild oil

1 medium onion

1-2 carrots

2 stalks celery

25 g (1 oz) butter

2 bay leaves

pared zest and juice 1 orange

400 ml (¾ pint) hot stock

1 level tablespoon redcurrant
  jelly

150 ml (¼ pint) red wine

1 level tablespoon cornflour

2 tablespoons cold water

salt and freshly milled pepper

Venison is a very lean meat that suits the moist cooking method of a traditional pot roast and you capture all the delicious meat juices. Old-fashioned root vegetables would be nice for serving with this.

Heat the oven to 160°C (325°F or gas no. 3).

Rub the surface of the venison all over thoroughly with the oil. Peel and slice the onion thickly. Pare the carrots and slice lengthways. Scrub and string the celery stalks and cut in large pieces. Melt the butter in a fireproof casserole. Add the venison joint and turn to brown all sides in the hot butter. Lift the meat from the casserole.

Arrange the sliced onion, carrots, celery and bay leaves in the casserole to make a bed of vegetables. Replace the venison on top. Add a few pieces of pared orange zest and sufficient stock to cover the vegetables. Bring to a simmer over direct heat, then cover with the casserole lid and set in the heated oven. Cook for 1½-2 hours (allowing 30 minutes per 450 g (1 lb)). Remove the casserole lid for the last 15 minutes cooking time.

Lift the venison on to a hot serving platter. Strain the cooking juices into a saucepan and add any remaining stock. Add the orange juice, redcurrant jelly and red wine. Bring to a simmer, stirring well. Combine the cornflour and water in a small bowl. Add a little of the hot pan juice and mix, then return to the saucepan. Bring to a simmer, stirring until gravy has thickened. Season with salt and freshly milled pepper and serve with the sliced venison.

Long-grain and Wild Rice with Mushrooms

SERVES 6

1 medium onion

100 g (4 oz) wild rice

600 ml (1 pint) vegetable or chicken stock

1 level teaspoon salt

175 g (6 oz) long-grain rice

225 g (8 oz) button mushrooms

50 g (2 oz) butter

2 tablespoons chopped fresh parsley

A combination of long-grain and wild rice looks good on the dinner table – it's interesting. Wild rice must be cooked in stock, preferably with onion added, to bring out the flavour. Here both grains are cooked together so the mixture is easy to handle – then you add extras.

Peel and finely chop the onion. Place the onion and wild rice in a large saucepan. Add the stock and salt and let soak for 30 minutes.

Set the pan over moderate heat and bring to the boil. Reduce the heat, cover with the pan lid and simmer gently for 20 minutes. Add the long-grain rice, stir and recover. Cook gently for a further 20 minutes.

Meanwhile, rinse, trim and slice the mushrooms. Heat the butter in a frying pan, add the mushrooms and turn briefly in the hot butter to soften them.

When the rice grains are tender and the stock absorbed, add the mushrooms and any butter from the pan and mix through with a fork. Turn the mixture on to a hot serving dish and sprinkle with the chopped parsley.

Serve with any dish that has a sauce – where you would normally serve plain rice. Substitute toasted flaked almonds and raisins for the mushrooms, if you like.

Hot Gratin of Potatoes

SERVES 6

900 g (2 lb) potatoes

1 clove garlic

75 g (3 oz) butter

300 ml (½ pint) milk

300 ml (½ pint) double cream

salt and freshly milled pepper

grated nutmeg

Thinly sliced potatoes baked and served in the same dish are an excellent choice to serve with any roast – meat or game. They are sensible for a party occasion too because they need no supervision.

Peel the potatoes and cut into very thin slices – a mandoline slicer is useful here, as it slices the potatoes very quickly. Do not put the potato slices into water or you will rinse off the starch which is necessary to the dish.

Heat the oven to 160°C (325°F or gas no. 3). Select a large baking dish – the one you will serve the potatoes in. Peel and lightly press the garlic then, spearing it on a fork, rub round the inside of the dish. Generously butter the dish with about 25 g (1 oz) of the butter.

Put the milk, cream, remaining butter and a seasoning of salt and freshly milled pepper into a large saucepan. Add a little grated nutmeg. Bring to a simmer over the heat, then add all the potato slices and heat gently, bringing the contents back up to a simmer. Turn the contents of the pan into the prepared baking dish and spread the potato slices out evenly.

Set in the heated oven and bake for 1½ hours or until the potatoes are cooked and golden on the surface – test with a knife tip; they should feel quite tender.

RED CABBAGE WITH APPLE

SERVES 6

1 medium red cabbage

2 large cooking apples – Bramleys are best

1 medium onion

25 g (1 oz) butter

150 ml (¼ pint) boiling water

salt and freshly milled pepper

1 level tablespoon castor sugar

juice ½ lemon

P Can be prepared ahead: let cool completely, then cover and refrigerate for up to 24 hours. Return to the saucepan and reheat to a simmer before serving.

Red cabbage retains the most wonderful colour if you simmer it with sour cooking apples. Add a little sugar and lemon juice too, and the flavour comes out sweet-sharp. An excellent vegetable to serve with roasts of beef, pork or duckling or pot roast of venison, it can be made ahead – red cabbage reheats very well.

With a large kitchen knife, cut the red cabbage into quarters and slice away the white core. Press the cut surface of each quarter against a chopping board and shred the cabbage across the leaves. Peel, core and chop the apples coarsely, and peel and finely chop the onion.

Melt the butter in a large saucepan. Add the onion and soften over the heat for a few moments. Add the red cabbage shreds and the chopped apples and pack down in the saucepan – at first it will seem very full but the cabbage will soften and cook down. Pour in the boiling water – sufficient to cover the bottom of the saucepan. Add a seasoning of salt and pepper, the sugar and lemon juice. Stir the ingredients to mix, then cover the pan with a tight-fitting lid and leave to cook gently on low heat. Once the apple begins to soften, it will provide sufficient liquid for cooking the cabbage. Stir occasionally and only add more water if necessary to keep the cabbage moist.

Let the red cabbage simmer gently for 1½-2 hours – by the end of the cooking time there should be almost no liquid left and the cabbage will be tender and glazed. Check the flavour, adding more sugar or lemon juice to get the sweet-sharp taste that you like. **P**

WHITE CHOCOLATE MOUSSE IN DARK CHOCOLATE CASES

SERVES 6

100 g (4 oz) plain chocolate for the shells, or 6 dark chocolate shells bought ready-made

cocoa powder for dusting

For the mousse

100 g (4 oz) white chocolate

150 ml (¼ pint) soured cream

1 tablespoon rum

150 ml (¼ pint) double cream

An indulgent combination. White chocolate makes a particularly delicious mousse. The addition of soured cream may surprise you, but the acidity is the perfect foil for the sweet chocolate flavour.

To make the shells yourself (they taste much nicer than the bought ones), break the plain chocolate into a bowl and set over a saucepan of hot (not boiling) water until melted. Line 6 individual ramekin dishes closely with squares of foil – press the foil into the contours of the dishes. Put a good teaspoon of the melted chocolate in the bottom of each one. Spread over the bottom and around the sides up to the rim. Turn upside-down on a wax paper-lined tray and chill until set hard. Then remove from the ramekins and peel the foil away. Keep homemade (or bought ready-made shells) chilled while preparing the mousse filling.

Break the white chocolate into a bowl and set over a saucepan of hot (not boiling) water until melted. Remove the bowl from the heat. Stir in the soured cream and then the rum. In a separate bowl, whip the cream to soft peaks. Add to the chocolate mixture and fold in gently. Spoon the mousse into the chilled chocolate cases and return to the refrigerator. Cover and refrigerate for up to 6 hours so the texture firms up. **P**

Dust with cocoa powder before serving.

NESSELRODE ICED BOMBE

SERVES 8

4 eggs (size 2)

100 g (4 oz) castor sugar

300 ml (½ pint) double cream

½ recipe quantity nesselrode topping (see opposite)

Nesselrode topping is used for this stylish ice cream. If you don't want to bother with the moulded presentation, the mixture tastes just as wonderful scooped on to serving plates and served with crisp, thin petit four biscuits.

Thoroughly chill a 1.1 litre (2 pint) oven glass mixing bowl or mould. Separate the eggs, cracking the whites into a medium mixing bowl and the yolks into a second large bowl. Whisk the whites to stiff peaks and gradually whisk in two-thirds of the sugar to make a stiff glossy meringue. Add the remaining sugar to the egg yolks and beat to a soft, creamy blend.

Whip the cream to soft peaks and fold into the egg yolk

mixture. Next fold in the stiff, glossy meringue using the cutting edge of a metal tablespoon. Finally fold in the nesselrode topping and blend through. Turn the meringue into the chilled mould. Freeze until firm, then place greaseproof paper over the top and freeze overnight. **P**

About 1 hour before serving, dip the mould in lukewarm water for 5-10 seconds. Loosen the top edges with a spatula and unmould the bombe on to a wooden board or metal tray. Return to the freezer until serving time. Then, with the help of two wide spatulas or a fish slice, transfer the bombe to a chilled serving dish. Cut into eight wedges with a sharp knife dipped in warm water and serve.

NESSELRODE TOPPING

MAKES 6-8 SERVINGS

50 g (2 oz) red glacé cherries

50 g (2 oz) candied lemon peel

50 g (2 oz) candied citron peel

50 g (2 oz) candied orange peel

50 g (2 oz) glacé pineapple

100 g (4 oz) sultanas

150 ml (¼ pint) marsala wine

P Can be prepared ahead: will keep for 2-3 months.

This is a mouth-watering blend of chopped glacé fruits marinated in marsala wine that you can make ahead. A spoonful or two adds a classy touch to good vanilla or coffee ice cream, a trifle or glamorous dessert cake. The fruits tend to settle so stir well before using.

There is no need to wash the sugary coating from the glacé fruits – it will dissolve naturally during storage. Cut the glacé cherries in half. Cut the candied lemon and citron peel into small dice, and the candied orange peel and glacé pineapple into chunky dice.

Put all the fruits in a jar with a screwtop or polythene container with a lid. Add the marsala and mix. Cover and leave in a cool place for at least 2 weeks – nesselrode needs to marinate so the glacé fruits soften and absorb the flavours. **P**

To serve as an ice cream topping, turn the whole container into a pretty glass bowl and let guests help themselves.

CURD CHEESE AND SULTANA CRÊPES

SERVES 6

50 g (2 oz) sultanas

juice 1 orange

12 prepared crêpes (see page 104)

450 g (1 lb) curd cheese

50 g (2 oz) castor sugar

1 egg (size 2)

grated zest 1 lemon

150 ml (¼ pint) double cream

250 g (1 oz) flaked almonds, toasted (see page 210)

P Can be prepared ahead: cover and refrigerate for up to 24 hours. Let come to room temperature before baking, or allow extra baking time.

This dessert crêpe recipe has the kind of filling used for blinis. It couldn't be easier – put the prepared crêpes in to bake, timing it so you take them straight to the table. A hot pudding is unusual.

Soak the sultanas in the orange juice for 2-3 hours.

Have the crêpes prepared and stacked – there is no need to heat them at this stage. Set aside while preparing the filling.

Turn the curd cheese into a mixing bowl. Add the sugar, egg, grated lemon zest and sultanas along with any orange juice and mix well.

Heat the oven to 190°C (375°F or gas no. 5).

Put a dessertspoonful of the filling in the centre of each crêpe – on the paler, second cooked side. Fold the sides of the crêpe to the centre, then roll up to enclose the filling. Pack the filled crêpes neatly in a well buttered baking dish. **P**

Pour the double cream over the filled crêpes. Set in the heated oven and bake for 15-20 minutes or until bubbling. Sprinkle with the toasted flaked almonds and serve hot.

Hot Pineapple with Orange Shreds

SERVES 6

3 oranges

1 fresh pineapple

175 g (6 oz) granulated sugar

150 ml (¼ pint) water

juice ½ lemon

50 ml (2 fl oz) rum

300 ml (½ pint) double cream,
  for serving

The nice thing about serving hot fruit is that it emphasizes the fruit flavours. This pineapple recipe can be prepared completely in advance ready for reheating. Serve the hot fruit with chilled cream – the contrast is delicious.

Finely pare the zest from the oranges using a vegetable peeler. Squeeze the orange juice and set aside. Using a sharp knife, shred the best pieces of orange zest into very fine shreds. Put the shreds in a saucepan, cover with cold water and bring to the boil. Drain, then recover with fresh water and bring to the boil again. This time simmer for about 20 minutes or until the shreds are quite tender. Drain and reserve.

Turn the pineapple on its side and cut a slice from the top and base. Using a sharp kitchen knife (one with a long blade) and with the pineapple standing upright, cut down and around the sides of the fruit to slice away the outer skin. Then using a smaller knife cut out the 'eyes' diagonally round the fruit. Repeat following the same diagonal direction until all the stalky bits are removed. Lay the pineapple on its side again and slice the fruit across into six or eight slices. Arrange the slices in a heatproof serving dish.

Heat the oven to 180°C (350°F or gas no. 4).

Measure the sugar into a dry saucepan. Set over moderate heat and stir until the sugar has melted and turned to a golden caramel. Remove from the heat and add the water – cover your hand as the hot caramel will boil up furiously with the addition of a cold liquid. Replace the pan over the heat and stir until the caramel has dissolved and the syrup is clear. Add the orange shreds and simmer for about 10 minutes or until the shreds are glazed. Draw off the heat and add the reserved orange juice, lemon juice and rum. **P**

Pour the orange shred sauce over the pineapple slices, pushing them below the level of the sauce. Set in the heated oven and bake for 20 minutes or until the fruit is hot and beginning to bubble around the edges. Take straight to the table and serve with chilled pouring cream.

P Can be prepared ahead: cool, cover and refrigerate for up to 24 hours.

CHOCOLATE STEAMED PUDDING WITH CHOCOLATE SAUCE

SERVES 6

40 g (1½ oz) blanched almonds

50 g (2 oz) self-raising flour

100 g (4 oz) fresh white breadcrumbs

50 g (2 oz) plain chocolate

75 g (3 oz) butter, at room temperature

75 g (3 oz) castor sugar

1 egg (size 2)

½ teaspoon vanilla essence

4-5 tablespoons milk

For the chocolate sauce

50 g (2 oz) castor sugar

4 tablespoons water

100 g (4 oz) plain chocolate

½ teaspoon vanilla essence

15 g (½ oz) unsalted butter

25 g (1 oz) flaked almonds

Old-fashioned maybe, but there's nothing ordinary about this pudding – the recipe uses real chocolate and less flour with soft breadcrumbs for a light texture. A steamed pudding will keep hot perfectly in the bowl over gently simmering water – cooking times are never critical.

Select a 900 ml (1½ pint) pudding basin and butter it well. Chop the almonds, sprinkle into the basin and shake over the inside of the bowl. Chill while preparing the mixture.

Sift the flour on to a plate, add the breadcrumbs and mix lightly. Break the chocolate into a mixing bowl and set over a saucepan of hot (not boiling) water until melted. Meanwhile, in a mixing bowl, cream the butter with the sugar until soft and light. Separate the egg, cracking the white into a separate bowl and adding the yolk to the creamed mixture along with the melted chocolate and the vanilla essence. Beat well. Fold in the flour and breadcrumb mixture along with sufficient milk to make a soft consistency. Beat the egg white until stiff and fold into the mixture.

Spoon into the prepared pudding basin and spread level. Cover with a double thickness of greaseproof paper and kitchen foil and tie on securely. Steam briskly for 1½-2 hours.

Meanwhile, make the chocolate sauce. Measure the sugar and water into a small saucepan and set over moderate heat. Stir until the sugar has dissolved, then bring to a rolling boil. Draw off the heat and add the chocolate broken in pieces. Allow the chocolate to melt – the heat of the sugar syrup will be sufficient – and stir with a whisk until smooth. Add the vanilla essence and butter. While warm, this sauce is thin and shiny; as it cools it thickens, but this can easily be remedied by setting the jug of sauce in a saucepan of warm water for a few minutes.

Toast the flaked almonds (see page 210).

Unmould the hot pudding on to a serving plate. Add the almonds to the sauce, spoon a little of the sauce over the pudding and serve the remainder separately.

BARBECUES

Herbed cheese in radicchio cups

Tzatziki

Crunchy marinated vegetables

Filo triangles with garlic and herb filling

·

Butterfly lamb

Hamburgers

Pork chops in chinese-style marinade

Turkey fillet kebabs in honey mustard marinade

Swordfish or tuna steaks with fennel marinade

Glazed barbecue ribs

Pork satays with peanut sauce

Beef and pineapple kebabs

Chilli prawns

Lamb kofta with yogurt dip

·

Brown rice pilaff

Tabbouleh salad

Garlic baked tomatoes

Green and gold sweet pepper salad

Salad of new potatoes in a chive vinaigrette

Stewed courgettes with tomato and mint

·

Pumpkin bread

·

Frozen lemon yogurt cream

Hot bananas with rum and lime

Green fruits in a fresh mint syrup

Iced pineapple slices in ginger syrup

Geneva wafers

BARBECUES

A barbecue is fun, so let the workload be easy but the results spectacular. Straightforward fresh food, marinated in advance or skilfully seasoned on cooking, will have that wonderfully smoky taste, and all the extras by way of relishes, toppings and dipping sauces add to the enjoyment on this occasion.

Before you start, consider your barbecue and make sure the cooking area suits the requirements. It's a good idea to set up two tables – one for the food to be cooked along with bastes, oil, seasonings and serving plates required by you, the chef. The other table is for cutlery, salads, breads and desserts. Do remember to start the fire in good time – anything from 45 minutes to 1 hour ahead; don't be in too much of a hurry to cook over the barbecue fire – it's ready when the coals look ash grey. Never cook over flames. Have equipment to hand – you will need long oven gloves, long-handled tongs, a fish slice and a brush for basting; a water spray for dousing flames is useful too. Lay out the food for cooking on large platters – it looks good.

Prepare marinated meats early in the day or the night before – food needs several hours to absorb the flavours. In the refrigerator is the place to keep meats (marinated or otherwise) in hot weather. About ½ an hour before cooking, let them come up to room temperature – chilled meats take longer to cook and you just don't get as good a flavour. Make sure frozen foods are completely thawed.

Charcoal grilling is an uncompromising and fierce cooking method, so your choice of items must be good quality, tender and quick cooking: steaks of meat or fish, trimmed chicken joints, chops or cutlets of pork or lamb, or succulent links of cumberland sausage – the same foods as you would choose for grilling in the kitchen.

It takes time to cook over charcoal and space is limited, so tackle only the main items and supplement them with extras like garlic baked tomatoes, brown rice pilaff, crisp salads and hot breads prepared in the kitchen. Remember to take out all the condiments – salt and pepper mills, some delicious relish and a choice of gourmet mustards, in addition to your own prepared toppings and a flavoured butter or two. A bowl of cut lemons is a good idea – squeezed over cooked kebabs or grills they bring up the flavour.

Previous pages: Lamb kofta and tabbouleh salad

Stave off guests' hunger pangs with bowls of snippets – like crudités with dips, herbed cheese with hot bread or crunchy marinated vegetables – let people pick at things while the party gets going. And provide plenty of refreshments – beer, lager, light red or sparkling wine all suit this kind of food. Fruit juices are excellent too, as are jugs of a wine cup.

Round off the occasion with the freshest of fruit desserts or some delicious homemade ice cream – chilled pineapple slices, an exotic fruit salad or a delicious-tasting frozen yogurt cream. Add crisp thin wafer biscuits and your guests will be well content.

TANGY YOGURT DRESSINGS

Serve these fresh-tasting dressings over salad greens, sliced cucumber or tomatoes or mix into rice, potato or pasta salads. Use whole milk yogurt with a tablespoon or two of cream or olive oil to make them less sharp.

Basic yogurt dressing: 150 ml (¼ pint) natural yogurt, salt and freshly milled pepper, 1 tablespoon wine vinegar, 2 tablespoons olive oil and 1-2 tablespoons chopped fresh chives or parsley. Place all ingredients in a bowl and mix well. Or put in a screw-topped jar and shake to get a creamy emulsion. Use to dress green vegetable salads.

Spring onion and chive dressing: 1 bunch (6-8) spring onions, 150 ml (¼ pint) natural yogurt, salt and freshly milled pepper, 1 tablespoon wine vinegar, 2 tablespoons single cream and 2 tablespoons chopped fresh chives. Trim and chop the spring onions including all the white and some of the green stems. Place in a bowl along with the other ingredients and mix well. Or put in a screw-topped jar and shake to get a creamy emulsion. Use to dress potato salads.

Yogurt, mint and garlic dressing: 1-2 cloves garlic, salt and freshly milled pepper, 150 ml (¼ pint) natural yogurt, 1 tablespoon wine vinegar, 2 tablespoons single cream and 1 tablespoon chopped fresh (or 1 teaspoon dried) mint. Peel the garlic and mash to a purée with a little salt. Place in a bowl with freshly milled pepper and the remaining ingredients and mix well. Let stand for 2-3 hours before serving. Use to dress pasta or avocado salads.

Coleslaw dressing: 150 ml (¼ pint) natural yogurt, 2 tablespoons mayonnaise, 1 level teaspoon Dijon mustard, 1 tablespoon wine vinegar and a seasoning of salt and freshly milled pepper. Place all ingredients in a bowl and mix.

Yogurt mayonnaise: For a lighter less rich mixture, combine equal parts mayonnaise with natural yogurt. Use as for ordinary mayonnaise.

HOT BREADS

Give an extra appealing plus to cold meat, soups, snack or salad meals with hot breads. Take to the table in napkin-lined baskets.

Straight hot bread: Put crusty loaves in an oven heated to 200°C (400°F or gas no. 6) to bake for 5 minutes to crisp them up. Crusty rolls need only 2-3 minutes. Pitta bread can be heated under the grill for 2-3 minutes or popped in the toaster if they're small.

Hot garlic bread: Cut two Vienna loaves in 2.5 cm (1 inch) slices at an angle but not completely through – leave the bottom crust whole. Spread garlic and herb butter (see page 000) in between each bread slice. Wrap in kitchen foil. (Can be prepared ahead: chill for at least 1 hour or overnight.) Set in an oven heated to 200°C (400°F or gas no. 6) to bake for 20 minutes. For a crisp finish, open the foil and return to the oven for a few minutes.

Hot herb rolls: Make two cuts in single crusty rolls – to the bottom crust but not right through. Spread garlic and herb butter or browned onion butter (see page 00) into the cuts. Put the rolls on a baking tray and cover with foil. (Can be prepared ahead.) Set in an oven heated to 200°C (400°F or gas no. 6) to bake for 10 minutes. Individual hot rolls are easy to serve and it's nice for guests to have their own hot bread.

Garlic toasts: Slice French bread on the slant in 2.5 cm (1 inch) slices. Peel garlic and mash with olive oil to make a paste. Toast the bread slices on one side only under a hot grill. Spread the garlic paste on the untoasted sides. (Can be prepared ahead.) Set in an oven heated to 200°C (400°F or gas no. 6) and bake 3-4 minutes or until hot. Nice with pasta salads, cold meats and soups.

Flavoured bread slice rolls: Remove crusts from thinly sliced fresh bread. Flatten the slices with a rolling pin and spread with garlic and herb butter or mixed mustard butter (see page 000). Roll up each bread slice and pack close together in a buttered baking tin. (Can be prepared ahead.) Brush with extra melted butter and sprinkle with paprika. Set in an oven heated to 200°C (400°F or gas no. 6) to bake for 10-15 minutes or until browned. Serve with savoury mousses such as cucumber and chive or avocado.

Italian herb bread: This small homemade loaf is wonderful for summer lunches or barbecues. Using a bread mix gives you a head start. The quantity produced will be one small loaf about enough to serve four but it's easy to make more – most oven trays would hold two cob loaves.

Take a 1 × approx 300 g packet white bread mix and turn the contents into a bowl. According to packet directions, add the specified 200 ml (7 fl oz) hand hot water. Then add 3 tablespoons olive oil and 1 tablespoon chopped fresh sage or rosemary. Mix to a smooth dough and knead thoroughly for 5 minutes or until smooth. Shape into a neat round loaf and set on a greased baking tray. Cover and leave to rise in a warm place until doubled in size – about 30 minutes. Brush with salt water, slash the tops with a sharp knife and sprinkle with coarse salt, or poppy or sesame seeds. Set in an oven heated to 230°C (450°F or gas no. 7) and bake for 25-30 minutes. Serve warm and fresh.

FLAVOURED BUTTERS

Use flavoured butters with grills, sautées or hot breads. Made in reasonable quantities they will keep for 2-3 weeks in the refrigerator. Spoon into ramekin dishes and cover tightly. Each butter serves 12.

To make in a **food processor,** have the butter chilled and cut slices into the food processor bowl. Work in the machine to a light consistency, then add the remaining ingredients. Process until well mixed.

To make **by hand,** have the butter at room temperature and beat until soft. Beat in the remaining ingredients in the order given.

Garlic and herb butter: 225 g (8 oz) unsalted butter, 4 cloves garlic, peeled and crushed, 50 g (2 oz) chopped fresh parsley and freshly milled pepper. Use for hot breads, on top of baked potatoes, steak or hamburgers and to sauté mushrooms.

Mixed mustard butter: 225 g (8 oz) unsalted butter, 3 level tablespoons wholegrain mustard, 1 level tablespoon Dijon mustard and freshly milled pepper. Use to top grilled steak or hamburgers or to sauté pork steaks.

Blue cheese butter: 150 g (5 oz) unsalted butter, 150 g (5 oz) cream cheese, 100 g (4 oz) Roquefort or other blue cheese and freshly milled pepper. Use to top steaks or hamburgers and on baked potatoes.

Browned onion butter: 225 g (8 oz) unsalted butter, 1 medium onion, finely chopped and fried in 1 tablespoon oil until golden, 50 g (2 oz) chopped fresh parsley, 1 level tablespoon Dijon mustard and freshly milled pepper. Use to top steaks or hamburgers and baked potatoes or in hot breads.

WINE CUPS

For any hour of a summer's day or evening, serve wine cups with enough alcohol to stimulate the party spirit but keep them sufficiently diluted to be drunk in reasonable quantities.

- Use the best wine you can afford – medium dry whites, lighter reds or rosé wines. Chill wines well ahead – wine cups must be cool. Avoid putting ice cubes in jugs or glasses because ice waters down a wine cup and dilutes the taste.
- Some recipes include fruits to flavour the mixture – give these time to marinate. Any sparkling or soda water should be added at the last moment to keep the fizz.
- Sugar takes longer to dissolve in cold liquids; it's easier to sweeten to taste with a syrup that's already made. Dissolve 225 g (8 oz) granulated sugar in 150 ml (¼ pint) water and keep handy in a bottle.
- Wine cups look inviting in a big bowl with fruits floating, but they are easier to serve from tall jugs when you can circulate and top up glasses – guests rarely come forward to help themselves.
- Make wine cups pretty with leaves and fruits but keep both in the jug, not in the glasses. An alternative would be to slice a sliver of fruit into glasses, then pour in the wine cup.

Strawberry wine cup

This could be a 'pink' drink if you use rosé wine and it will look pretty if slices of fresh strawberry are dropped into each serving glass.

Chill 1 bottle each dry white or rosé wine and 1 bottle sparkling wine in advance. Slice 225 g (8 oz) strawberries into a tall jug and add 2 level tablespoons castor sugar, the juice of 1 orange and 2 tablespoons brandy. Let stand for 1 hour to macerate. Stir in the chilled white or rosé wine. Top up with the sparkling wine. Serves 12 glasses.

Badminton cup

Based on the old-fashioned claret cup, this is subtly-flavoured and light enough for drinking in quantity.

Chill 2 bottles red wine in advance. Measure 75 g (3 oz) castor sugar and 300 ml (½ pint) water into a saucepan. Thinly pare strips of zest (use a vegetable peeler) from 2 oranges and 1 lemon and add to the pan. Stir over low heat until the sugar has dissolved, then bring to a simmer and draw off the heat. Leave until cold. Add the squeezed juice from both oranges and the lemon. Strain into a tall jug. Add the wine and chill until serving time. Top up with 500 ml (18 fl oz) soda water, and add slices of orange and cucumber for decoration. Serves 20 glasses.

Charleston cup

A pretty white wine cup. Keep the additions to all green and yellow with cucumber and mint and a slice or two of lemon, if you like.

Chill 2 bottles dry white wine in advance. Measure 4 level tablespoons castor sugar into a bowl, then grate in the zest of 1 lemon using a very fine grater. With the back of a wooden spoon, crush the sugar with the grated zest until the sugar turns yellow with the absorbed lemon oils. Add the squeezed lemon juice and stir to dissolve the sugar. Stir in 150 ml (¼ pint) each dry sherry and brandy and pour into a tall jug. Add the wine and chill until serving time. Top up with 1 litre (1¾ pints) soda water. Add slices and strips of cucumber peel and sprigs of fresh mint for decoration. Serves 25 glasses.

Sparkling fruit cup

A 'softie' based on a lemon-flavoured syrup with fruit juice added. Include plenty of decoration so no one feels left out.

Pare the zest from 2 large lemons (use a vegetable peeler) and put into a mixing bowl. Squeeze the lemon juice and reserve. Add 100 g (4 oz) castor sugar to the lemon zest. Measure 600 ml (1 pint) water into a saucepan and bring to the boil. Pour over the lemon zest and sugar and stir to dissolve the sugar. Leave until cold.

Strain the syrup into a jug. Add the reserved lemon juice and 600 ml (1 pint) orange juice and chill until serving time. Top up with 600 ml (1 pint) ginger ale. Add slices of orange and mint for decoration. Serves 12 glasses.

HERBED CHEESE IN RADICCHIO CUPS

SERVES 6-8

100 g (4 oz) unsalted butter, at room temperature

450 g (1 lb) curd cheese

2-4 cloves garlic

salt and freshly milled pepper

juice ½ lemon

2-4 tablespoons single cream

2 tablespoons finely chopped fresh chives

2 tablespoons finely chopped fresh parsley

2 heads radicchio

6 radishes, to garnish

A simple delicious herbed cheese spread for slices of crusty French bread or hot toast. The radicchio cups are a snappy presentation idea – individual, portion-sized servings make it easier for guests to help themselves.

In a mixing bowl, cream the butter and curd cheese together until soft and smooth. Peel the garlic and mash to a purée with a little salt. Add to the cheese along with a seasoning of freshly milled pepper and lemon juice to taste. Then beat in sufficient cream to get a soft spreading consistency. Lastly mix in the chopped herbs. Cover and refrigerate for at least 2-3 hours for the flavour to develop. **P**

Separate out the leaves from the radicchio heads and select the best cup-shaped ones. Spoon the herbed cheese mixture into each one. Arrange on a serving platter, crowding them close together, and garnish with thin slices of radish. Pass warmed baguettes or dry toast slices (no butter) for serving.

TZATZIKI

SERVES 6-8

½ cucumber

salt and freshly milled pepper

1 clove garlic

450 g (1 lb) Greek-style yogurt

2 tablespoons olive oil

1 teaspoon white wine vinegar

2 teaspoons chopped fresh mint, or ½ level teaspoon dried mint

Cool and fresh-tasting, this is nice with thick slices of dry toast or warm pitta bread cut into strips. Be sure to use the thick, strained Greek yogurt for this and it will have the consistency of a spread.

Peel the cucumber, cut it in half lengthways and scoop out the inner seeds with a teaspoon. Cut the cucumber lengthways into thin strips and across into fine dice. Place the diced cucumber in a colandar and sprinkle with salt. Let stand for 1 hour, then rinse the cucumber in cold water and dry well by pressing in a clean cloth or absorbent kitchen paper to remove excess moisture.

Peel garlic and mash to a purée with a little salt. Turn the yogurt into a mixing bowl and add the garlic, diced cucumber, olive oil, wine vinegar, a seasoning of freshly milled pepper and the mint. Stir to blend, and check the seasoning.

Turn into a serving bowl. Cover and refrigerate for at least 1 hour so the flavours can blend. **P**

CRUNCHY MARINATED VEGETABLES

SERVES 6-8

450 g (1 lb) vegetables – one
  kind only or a blend of
  courgettes, button
  mushrooms, cauliflower
  florets and canned artichoke
  hearts

For the marinade

225 ml (8 fl oz) olive oil

75 ml (3 fl oz) white wine
  vinegar

½ level teaspoon salt

1 level teaspoon dried basil

6 whole peppercorns

½ level teaspoon coriander
  seeds

3 cloves garlic

My own favourite combination for these aromatic and spicy vegetables is courgettes with canned artichoke hearts. Let guests pick at the vegetables, and pass warmed French bread to use for mopping up the delicious dressing.

Prepare the vegetables according to kind: trim courgettes, do not peel but take strips off the skin to give them a striped effect, then cut in chunks; trim mushrooms, leaving them whole; break cauliflower into small florets; drain artichoke hearts from the liquid in the can. With the exception of the artichokes and mushrooms, bring prepared vegetables to the boil in water to cover and blanch for 2-3 minutes to tenderize them. Drain and let cool. Place the vegetables in a bowl.

Measure the olive oil, wine vinegar, salt, basil, peppercorns and lightly crushed coriander seeds in a saucepan. Peel the garlic, crush lightly and add to the pan. Bring the marinade to the boil, then pour over the vegetables. Cool, then cover and refrigerate for up to 4 hours for the flavours to develop. **P** Turn vegetables and marinade into a bowl for serving.

FILO TRIANGLES WITH GARLIC AND HERB FILLING

MAKES 24

8 sheets filo pastry

50 g (2 oz) butter, melted

1-2 tablespoons grapeseed or
  other mild oil

sesame seeds (optional)

For the filling

225 g (8 oz) curd cheese

1 clove garlic

salt and freshly milled pepper

2 tablespoons chopped fresh
  parsley or chives

Baked filo pastry is flaky and crisp, rather like puff pastry but not so rich. Any flavoured low-fat soft cheese can be used here – chive, prawn or mushroom, for instance. Make a variety and serve as finger food.

Start by preparing the filling. Turn the cheese into a mixing bowl. Peel the garlic and mash to a purée with a little salt. Add the mashed garlic to the cheese along with a good seasoning of freshly milled pepper – no extra salt will be required. Add the chopped herbs and mix well. Taste for flavour.

Keep the filo sheets in a stack covered with a damp cloth. Take one sheet at a time and brush with melted butter mixed with the oil. Then cut with a knife into 7.5 cm (3 inch) wide strips lengthways. Place a spoonful of the filling at one end of a strip and fold a corner of the pastry over the filling to make a triangle. Turn the triangle over and over (keeping the edges

P Can be prepared ahead: cover and refrigerate for up to 4 hours.

straight) to the end of the pastry strip. Repeat with the remaining filling and pastry. **P**

Heat the oven to 190°C (375°F or gas no. 5).

Arrange the filo triangles on greased baking trays with the sealed edges underneath. Brush with melted butter (a sprinkling of sesame seeds looks pretty on top). Set in the heated oven and bake for 10-12 minutes or until crisp and brown. Serve warm.

BUTTERFLY LAMB

SERVES 6

½ leg of lamb, fillet end

For the soy marinade

2 tablespoons dark soy sauce

2 level tablespoons light muscovado sugar

juice 1 lemon

1 tablespoon grapeseed or other mild oil

salt and freshly milled pepper

1 level teaspoon grated fresh root ginger

1 clove garlic

This is called butterfly because the lamb joint is boned and opened out flat. Putting both the marinade and meat in a freezer bag makes it easier to turn and flavour the joint all round. The taste is delicious – use this marinade for steaks and chicken joints too.

Open out the lamb so that the meat will lie flat. The best way to do this is to take a sharp knife and cut through the flesh to the bone, then scrape away the meat from around the bone until you can lift it away. Cut a few slashes on the skin side of the meat, then set aside while preparing the marinade.

Select a freezer bag big enough to take the piece of meat and open it out inside a medium mixing bowl. Into the bag measure the soy sauce, soft brown sugar, lemon juice, salad oil, a seasoning of salt and pepper, the grated root ginger and the peeled and chopped garlic. Add the piece of lamb, seal the bag closed and give the contents a few turns to mix the ingredients. Leave to marinate overnight, turning the bag several times. **P**

Lift the meat from the marinade and set on the grill bars over hot charcoal. Grill for 10-15 minutes on each side, turning the meat once. The outside should be crusty and well browned while the inside remains a little pink.

To carve, start at one end and cut across the grain in thin slices.

HAMBURGERS

MAKES 8

1.5 kg (3 lb) extra lean minced beef

salt and freshly milled pepper

dash soy sauce (optional)

sliced onion and tomato, crisp lettuce and mayonnaise, for serving

Homemade hamburgers are light in texture and deliciously juicy. Don't be tempted to add extra ingredients – it's the toppings (see below) that add the extra dimension.

Lightly toss the beef with the seasonings and a dash of soy sauce, if liked. Shape into patties, handling the mixture as little as possible. These quantities allow about 175 g (6 oz) meat per serving to make thick patties – don't make hamburgers too thin. **P**

Place the hamburgers directly on the grill bars over the hot charcoal. Cook, turning once, for 4-8 minutes, depending on how you like them cooked – rare or well done. Transfer to hot serving plates and serve with separate bowls of sliced onion, sliced tomato, crisp lettuce leaves and mayonnaise. Or top with a flavoured butter (see page 143). Alternatively, include a choice of soured cream toppings (see below) so guests can help themselves.

If hamburger buns are to be included, split them and brush with melted butter, then grill over the charcoal (open side down) for a few moments to toast them. Slide the hot hamburger between bun halves and let guests add their toppings.

● **Flavour plus:** Here are some easily mixed soured cream toppings for hamburgers, steaks or baked jacket potatoes.
Onion: peel and slice 2 medium onions and separate out the rings. Pour over boiling water to cover and leave to soak for 2 hours, then drain. Combine 150 ml (¼ pint) soured cream with a seasoning of salt and freshly milled pepper, a squeeze of lemon juice and the onion rings. Toss well and chill.
Mustard: combine 150 ml (¼ pint) soured cream with 2 level tablespoons Dijon mustard and a seasoning of salt and freshly milled pepper. Fold in 2 tbs finely chopped spring onions.
Horseradish: combine 150 ml (¼ pint) soured cream with 4 level tablespoons horseradish relish (not sauce), salt and freshly milled pepper and a dash Worcestershire sauce. Let stand for 30 minutes.
Blue cheese: in blender or food processor goblet, combine 150 ml (¼ pint) soured cream and 75 g (3 oz) Roquefort or other blue cheese and mix for a few seconds. Turn into a bowl and mix in 1 teaspoon chopped fresh herbs and a squeeze lemon juice. Let stand for 30 minutes.

P Can be prepared ahead: cover each hamburger with a square of greaseproof paper, or set on a tray and overwrap, to prevent the meat going brown, and refrigerate for up to 2-3 hours.

PORK CHOPS IN CHINESE-STYLE MARINADE

SERVES 6

6 boneless pork loin chops

Chinese-style marinade

1 tablespoon sesame seeds

225 ml (8 fl oz) grapeseed or other mild oil

2 cloves garlic

1 level teaspoon mild chilli powder

2 level tablespoons concentrated tomato purée

3 tablespoons red wine vinegar

2 tablespoons sesame oil

P Can be prepared ahead: marinate overnight. Let come to room temperature before grilling.

Make sure the pork chops are cut thick for barbecue cooking so they will be tender and succulent. The sesame flavour of this marinade comes through very nicely.

Place the pork chops in a shallow dish large enough to take them all in a single layer. Set aside.

In a frying pan, toast the sesame seeds in 2 tablespoons of the salad oil for 1-2 minutes or until golden. Add the peeled and chopped garlic and stir for 1 minute. Draw off the heat and cool to room temperature.

In a bowl, combine the sesame seed mixture, remaining salad oil, the chilli powder, tomato purée, vinegar and sesame oil. Pour over the pork chops. Cover and refrigerate for at least 4 hours. **P**

Lift the pork chops from the marinade and place directly on the grill bars over hot charcoal. Cook for 15-18 minutes, turning once or twice.

TURKEY FILLET KEBABS IN HONEY MUSTARD MARINADE

SERVES 6

4 turkey breast fillets

For the honey mustard marinade

3 tablespoons soy sauce

2 tablespoons grapeseed or other mild oil

2 tablespoons clear honey

1 level tablespoon wholegrain mustard

1 level teaspoon grated fresh root ginger

1 clove garlic

P Can be prepared ahead: marinate overnight. Let come to room temperature before grilling.

Instead of cutting turkey meat in chunks, try this idea where strips are pushed 'concertina' style on to skewers. It makes no difference to the taste, but they look very appetizing and exotic. Chicken breast fillets can be used in this way too, of course.

Cut the turkey breast fillets into thick slices lengthways. Arrange the slices in a shallow dish in a single layer.

Combine the soy sauce, salad oil, honey, mustard and grated root ginger in a bowl. Peel the garlic and chop finely, or push through a garlic press, and add. Pour the marinade over the turkey pieces. Cover and refrigerate for at least 2 hours. **P**

Thread the turkey pieces 'concertina' style on to six skewers – push two or more pieces on to each one. Set on the grill bars over hot charcoal and cook for 15-20 minutes, turning them once or twice. Push off the skewers for serving.

Swordfish or Tuna Steaks with Fennel Marinade

SERVES 6

6 swordfish or tuna steaks

For the fennel marinade

8 tablespoons grapeseed or
   other mild oil

2 lemons

2 level tablespoons fennel seeds

1 level teaspoon salt

4 tablespoons finely chopped
   fresh parsley

4 cloves garlic

P Can be prepared ahead:
marinate overnight. Let come to
room temperature before grilling.

Both these are meaty fish and the steak cuts are an excellent choice for a barbecue. There is no need to baste while they are cooking; the flesh stays moist and the aroma is delicious.

Arrange the fish steaks in a shallow dish in a single layer. Measure the oil into a mixing bowl. Add the grated zest of 1 lemon, the squeezed juice of both, the fennel seeds, salt and chopped parsley. Peel the garlic and chop finely, or push through a garlic press, and add. Mix the ingredients well and pour over the fish steaks. Cover and refrigerate for at least 4 hours. **P**

Lift the fish from the marinade and place directly on the grill bars over hot charcoal, or use a hinged grilling basket, and cook for 10 minutes on the first side. Turn and cook the second side for 8 minutes before serving.

Glazed Barbecue Ribs

SERVES 6

1.5 kg (3 lb) pork ribs

oil for brushing

For the barbecue marinade

4 tablespoons grapeseed or
   other mild oil

2 tablespoons light soy sauce

2 tablespoons clear honey

1 level teaspoon Dijon mustard

1 level tablespoon concentrated
   tomato purée

1 clove garlic

P Can be prepared ahead:
marinate overnight.

Brushed with a tangy barbecue marinade, these pork ribs are oven cooked first, then crisped off over the hot barbecue so they're quick and easy to produce.

Place the pork ribs in a shallow dish, large enough to take them all in a single layer. Combine the oil, soy sauce, honey, mustard and tomato purée in a bowl. Peel the garlic and chop finely, or push through a garlic press, and add. Mix the ingredients and pour over the pork ribs. Cover and refrigerate for at least 4 hours. **P**

Heat the oven to 200°C (400°F or gas no. 6).

Turn the pork ribs and marinade into a large roasting tin and spread them out. Set in the heated oven and roast for 40 minutes.

Transfer the ribs to a platter. Brush lightly with oil and set on the grill bars over hot charcoal to cook for 10-15 minutes or until crisp and brown.

PORK SATAYS WITH PEANUT SAUCE

SERVES 6

900 g (2 lb) lean pork fillet

2 tablespoons soy sauce

3 tablespoons grapeseed or other mild oil

1 tablespoon lemon juice

1 level tablespoon grated fresh root ginger

For the peanut sauce

1 small onion

2 cloves garlic

1 tablespoon grapeseed or other mild oil

1 level teaspoon mild chilli powder

2 heaped tablespoons crunchy peanut butter

225 ml (8 fl oz) water

1 tablespoon dark soy sauce

1 level teaspoon light muscovado sugar

1 tablespoon lemon juice

P Can be prepared ahead: marinate pork overnight. Let come to room temperature before grillng. Cool sauce, cover and refrigerate. Reheat sauce for serving.

Use the traditional bamboo satay sticks for these, and soak the sticks in cold water for several hours beforehand. Thread the marinated meat on each stick, leaving a little space between each piece of meat for even cooking.

Trim the pork fillet and cut out into bite-sized pieces. In a mixing bowl, combine the soy sauce, oil, lemon juice and grated root ginger. Add the meat pieces and turn in the marinade. Cover and refrigerate for up to 4 hours. **P**

Peel and finely chop the onion for the peanut sauce. Peel the garlic and chop finely. Heat the oil in a saucepan, add the onion and fry until soft. Add the garlic and chilli powder and fry for a few moments more. Add the peanut butter and water and stir until the mixture comes to a simmer. Cook gently for about 5 minutes. Stir in the soy sauce, brown sugar and lemon juice. **P**

Thread 4-5 pieces of pork on each of six soaked bamboo skewers. Set directly on the grill bars over the hot charcoal and cook for 8-10 minutes, turning once or twice. Serve with the warm peanut sauce.

BEEF AND PINEAPPLE KEBABS

SERVES 6

900 g (2 lb) beef rump steak

1 medium pineapple

3 tablespoons grapeseed or other mild oil

1 tablespoon clear honey

salt and freshly milled pepper

Fresh pineapple is a very effective meat tenderizer, and hot pineapple tastes wonderful. Here pieces of beef are marinated in pineapple purée, then grilled with pineapple pieces – a delicious combination.

Trim the steak and cut into bite-sized pieces. Put in a mixing bowl.

Take a slice from the top and base of the pineapple. Cut away the outer peel and then slice the pineapple first into

P Can be prepared ahead:
marinate for up to 1 hour.

wedges and then across into chunks. Select the nicest pineapple pieces for the skewers (allow 3-4 pieces for each one) and set them aside. Put the remaining pineapple in a blender or food processor. Add the oil, honey and a seasoning of salt and pepper and process to a purée.

Pour the pineapple purée over the steak pieces and mix through. Cover and refrigerate for at least 30 minutes. **P**

Thread the steak pieces and reserved pineapple chunks on each of six skewers. Set directly on the grill bars over hot charcoal and cook for 10-15 minutes, turning them once or twice. Push the steak and pineapple off the skewers for serving.

CHILLI PRAWNS

SERVES 6

900 g (2 lb) raw king prawns or 700 g (1½ lb) fresh monkfish

lemons, for serving

For the marinade

3 tablespoons grapeseed or other mild oil

1 tablespoon clear honey

1 tablespoon chilli sauce

1 tablespoon lemon juice

pinch five spice powder

1 tablespoon chopped fresh parsley

P Can be prepared ahead. Let come to room temperature before grilling.

King prawns look mouthwatering and taste deliciously firm and sweet but they are expensive. This marinade is well worth using with pieces of monkfish as an alternative.

Using forefingers and thumbs, pull open the prawn shells and peel them off, leaving the tails intact. Then with a knife, split along the back to remove the black vein. Cut the monkfish into chunky pieces.

Combine the oil, honey, chilli sauce, lemon juice and five spice powder in a mixing bowl. Add the prawns (or monkfish pieces) and the chopped parsley. Stir to mix the seafood with the marinade. Cover and refrigerate for up to 4 hours. **P**

Thread the prawns (or monkfish pieces) on to six skewers – push three or more on to each one. Baste with the marinade. Set on the grill bars over hot charcoal and cook for about 3 minutes (up to 6 minutes for monkfish) on each side. The flesh will turn pink (white) and firm when ready. Serve with lemon wedges for squeezing over.

LAMB KOFTA WITH YOGURT DIP

SERVES 6

900 g (2 lb) minced fresh lamb

2 medium onions

1 level teaspoon ground cumin

1 level teaspoon ground coriander

3 tablespoons chopped fresh parsley

These are tender little meatballs made using minced lamb and are mildly spiced. Cooked over charcoal, they are delicious – of course, you can grill them in the kitchen too. Especially good served with tabbouleh salad (see page 154) and warm pitta bread.

Put the minced lamb in a mixing bowl. Peel and finely grate the onions and add to the lamb along with the cumin,

salt and freshly milled pepper

grapeseed or other mild oil, for
  greasing

chopped parsley, to garnish

lemon wedges, for serving

For the dipping sauce

300 ml (½ pint) natural yogurt

2-3 tablespoons single cream

salt and freshly milled pepper

1 tablespoon chopped fresh
  mint, or 1 level teaspoon
  dried mint

P Can be prepared ahead: keep
refrigerated for up to 4 hours. Let
come to room temperature before
grilling.

coriander, chopped parsley and a seasoning of salt and freshly milled pepper. Mix very thoroughly to make a well-combined, smooth mixture. Alternatively, blend the ingredients in a food processor.

With oiled fingers (so the meat won't stick), shape tablespoons into meatballs – you should get about 24. Cover and refrigerate for at least 1 hour so the balls firm up. **P**

Meanwhile, make the dipping sauce. In a bowl, combine the yogurt, single cream and a seasoning of salt and pepper. Stir in the mint. Cover and refrigerate for at least 1 hour before serving.

Rub 6 skewers with a little oil, then push on the meatballs – about 3-4 on each skewer. Brush lightly with oil and grill over hot charcoal for 10 minutes, turning to cook both sides.

Serve hot, sprinkled with chopped parsley, with wedges of lemon to squeeze over – it sharpens up the taste – and the yogurt dip.

BROWN RICE PILAFF

SERVES 6

225 g (8 oz) long-grain brown
  rice

600 ml (1 pint) water

1 level teaspoon salt

½ level teaspoon turmeric

1 bunch (6-8) spring onions

225 g (8 oz) mange-touts

1 medium onion

1 red sweet pepper

1 clove garlic

50 g (2 oz) flaked almonds

2 tablespoons grapeseed or
  other mild oil

1 level teaspoon garam masala

50 g (2 oz) seedless raisins

Any kind of hot rice dish will team up well with barbecue foods. This pilaff is delicately spiced, mixed with colourful vegetables and sprinkled with crunchy almonds.

Measure the rice into a saucepan and add the water, salt and turmeric. Bring to the boil, stirring once or twice, then turn the heat to very low. Cover with the pan lid and let the rice cook gently, without disturbing it, for 45 minutes.

Meanwhile, trim the spring onions, then chop all the white and some of the green stems. Trim the mange-touts and blanch in boiling water for 2-3 minutes, then drain. Peel and chop the onion. Halve, deseed and chop the red sweet pepper. Peel and finely chop the garlic. Toast the almonds (see page 210).

Heat the oil in a frying pan, add the onion and red pepper and fry gently to soften – about 10 minutes. Stir in the garlic and garam masala and fry for a few moments more.

Add the contents of the frying pan to the saucepan of hot cooked rice. Add the chopped spring onions, mange-touts and raisins. Mix gently with a fork. Turn the hot rice pilaff on to a warmed serving platter and sprinkle with the toasted almonds.

TABBOULEH SALAD

SERVES 6

100 g (4 oz) bulgar wheat

1 bunch (6-8) spring onions

6 tomatoes

½ cucumber

4 tablespoons chopped fresh
  parsley

1 tablespoon chopped fresh
  mint

salt and freshly milled pepper

juice 1 lemon

2 tablespoons olive oil

cos lettuce leaves, for serving

P Can be prepared ahead: keep
refrigerated for up to 6 hours.

This salad is bursting with colour and flavour. The vegetable ingredients are diced very small so the effect is multi-coloured, and the dressing is mainly lemon juice so the taste is very fresh.

Soak the bulgar wheat in cold water to cover for 1 hour – it will soften and swell. Drain the soaked grains in a sieve and press well to squeeze out excess water, then spread on a clean teatowel to dry while preparing the salad ingredients.

Trim the spring onions, then finely chop all the white and some of the green stems. Scald the tomatoes in boiling water and peel away the skins. Halve and remove the seeds, then finely chop the tomato flesh. Halve the cucumber lengthways and remove the centre seeds using a teaspoon as a scoop. Then slice lengthways and across in small dice.

Put the bulgar wheat, spring onions, tomato and cucumber in a bowl. Add the chopped parsley and mint and fork all the ingredients together. Season with salt and pepper and add the lemon juice and just enough oil to make the ingredients glisten. Cover and refrigerate for at least 1 hour. **P**

To serve, turn into a salad bowl lined with the washed lettuce leaves.

GARLIC BAKED TOMATOES

SERVES 6-8

6-8 ripe tomatoes

50 g (2 oz) butter

2-3 cloves garlic

grated zest ½ lemon

1 tablespoon chopped fresh
  parsley

A bright splash of colour for serving with any grilled foods. You can do the same recipe with smaller cherry tomatoes – allow 3-4 per person and leave them whole.

Heat the oven to 180°C (350°F or gas no. 4).

Nick the skin on each tomato, then place them together in a mixing bowl. Pour over boiling water to cover. Let stand 1 minute, then drain off the water. Peel each tomato and place rounded side up in an ovenproof baking dish. Slash the tops.

Put the butter in a saucepan. Peel the garlic and chop finely, or press through a garlic crusher, and add. Add the grated lemon zest and chopped parsley. Set over medium heat until the butter is melted and bubbling hot, then pour over the tomatoes.

Set the dish in the heated oven and bake uncovered for 15-20 minutes – depending on the size of the tomatoes. Serve straight from the dish, piping hot.

GREEN AND GOLD SWEET PEPPER SALAD

SERVES 6

1 large onion – preferably mild
  Spanish

2 yellow sweet peppers

2 green sweet peppers

½ cucumber

juice 1 lemon

4 tablespoons olive oil

¼ level teaspoon dried oregano

salt and freshly milled pepper

P Can be prepared ahead: cover
and refrigerate for up to 24 hours.

This is a pretty combination so don't add other colours. You can shred all the vegetables with the food processor except the cucumber which looks prettiest cut in chunks.

Peel, halve and finely slice the onion. Halve, deseed and shred the yellow and green sweet peppers. Peel the cucumber, cut in half lengthways and scoop out the seeds using a teaspoon. Slice lengthways and then across into chunky pieces. Combine the onion, peppers and cucumber in a bowl. **P**

Combine the lemon juice, oil, oregano and a seasoning of salt and pepper in a bowl. Pour over the salad and toss before serving.

SALAD OF NEW POTATOES IN A CHIVE VINAIGRETTE

SERVES 6

900 g (2 lb) new potatoes

1 bunch (6-8) spring onions

salt and freshly milled pepper

2 tablespoons wine vinegar

1 level teaspoon wholegrain
  mustard

4 tablespoons olive oil

3 tablespoons chopped fresh
  chives

P Can be prepared ahead:
marinate for up to 4 hours.

New potatoes look and taste best with their skins on. For this salad, cook and then toss them in the chive dressing while still warm, and you will find that it improves the flavour considerably.

Scrub or rinse the new potatoes and add whole to a saucepan of boiling salted water. Reboil and simmer for 6-8 minutes or until just tender. Drain in a colander. Leave until cool enough to handle, then slice thickly into a salad bowl.

Wash and trim the spring onions, then shred all the white and some of the green stems. Add to the sliced potatoes.

In a bowl, combine a seasoning of salt and pepper, then wine vinegar and mustard. Add the oil in a stream, whisking to get an emulsion. Stir in the chopped chives. Pour the dressing over the warm potatoes and leave to marinate for at least 1 hour before serving. **P**

STEWED COURGETTES WITH TOMATOES AND MINT

SERVES 6

700 g (1½ lb) courgettes

salt

1 clove garlic

1 medium onion

2 tablespoons olive oil

900 g (2 lb) ripe tomatoes

1 level tablespoon concentrated
  tomato purée

1 level teaspoon light
  muscovado sugar

1 tablespoon red wine vinegar

2 tablespoons chopped fresh
  mint

P Can be prepared ahead (for
serving cold).

*Sliced courgettes gently fried with tomato and onion make a
simple ragoût that's not unlike ratatouille. Served hot or cold, it
makes a delicious accompaniment to grilled foods.*

Rinse the courgettes, trim and cut into rounds about 10 mm
(½ inch) thick. Put the slices in a colander, sprinkle with salt
and leave for 30 minutes to draw out excess moisture. Rinse,
then shake dry.

Peel and crush the garlic to a purée, and peel and slice the
onion. Heat the oil in a frying pan, add the onion and fry gently
to soften – about 5 minutes. Add the garlic and give the
mixture a stir, then add the courgettes and cover the pan with a
lid. Simmer for 10-15 minutes, stirring occasionally until the
courgettes are soft.

Meanwhile, scald the tomatoes in boiling water and peel
away the skins. Halve and remove the seeds, then chop the
tomato flesh coarsely.

Add the tomatoes, concentrated tomato purée, sugar,
vinegar and a seasoning of freshly milled pepper to the
courgettes. Stir and continue cooking, uncovered, until the
tomatoes have softened and the mixture is thick but still juicy.
Check the seasoning and stir in the chopped mint.

Serve hot or cold. **P**

PUMPKIN BREAD

MAKES 2 LOAVES

700 g (1½ lb) self-raising flour

1 level tablespoon baking
  powder

1 level teaspoon salt

50 g (2 oz) butter

1 × approx 400 g can pumpkin
  purée, or 300 ml (½ pint)
  freshly cooked pumpkin
  purée (see below)

1 level teaspoon wholegrain
  mustard

*An unusual hot bread, this is moist and golden in colour. It is
nice cut in thick slices – no need for butter. You can make it
with canned or freshly cooked pumpkin purée, and it works
with carrot purée too. Sometimes I add a small handful of
chopped walnuts to the mixture.*

Heat the oven to 200°C (400°F or gas no. 6). Grease two
baking trays with butter.

Sift the flour, baking powder and salt into a large mixing
bowl. Add the butter and rub in with fingertips. Turn the
pumpkin purée into a smaller bowl, add the mustard, eggs and
milk and mix together. Pour this into the dry ingredients and

2 eggs (size 2)

300 ml (½ pint) milk

mix quickly to a soft dough using a table knife.

Turn the dough on to a floured work surface and divide in half. Knead each piece two or three times to smooth the underside, and turn on to a buttered tray. Flatten slightly with floured fingers and then cut a deep cross in each one with a kitchen knife.

Dust the tops with flour. Set in the heated oven and bake for 30-35 minutes. Slide on to wire cooling trays and serve warm.

● **Fresh pumpkin purée:** take 900 g (2 lb) fresh pumpkin, peel and cut the flesh to make 450 g (1 lb). Place in a saucepan with 25 g (1 oz) butter (no water) and cover with the pan lid. Simmer to a soft purée. Remove the pan lid towards the end of the cooking time so excess moisture can evaporate and the purée is fairly dry. Let cool.

FROZEN LEMON YOGURT CREAM

SERVES 4-6

450 g (1 lb) Greek-style yogurt

150 ml (¼ pint) double cream

100 g (4 oz) castor sugar

juice 2 lemons

This creamy, smooth yogurt ice cream is the nicest I've come across. The quantities here are just right for a home ice cream making machine. If preparing this for a crowd, I'd make one batch of lemon and one of orange (see end of recipe).

Turn the chilled yogurt into a mixing bowl and add the cream and castor sugar. Stir with a whisk to dissolve the sugar. Add the lemon juice and mix.

Freeze the mixture in an ice cream freezer machine according to manufacturer's instructions. Or turn into a suitable container and freeze in a domestic freezer until almost frozen but still mushy. With a fork, turn the sides into the centre and mix until smooth, then continue to freeze until firm. Cover with a container lid for storage. **P**

Frozen orange yogurt cream: follow the instruction above substituting 1 × 190 g carton frozen concentrated unsweetened orange juice, thawed, for the lemon juice.

HOT BANANAS WITH RUM AND LIME

SERVES 6-8

6-8 firm but ripe bananas

grated zest and juice 1 lime

75 g (3 oz) light muscovado
  sugar

¼ level teaspoon ground
  cinnamon

¼ level teaspoon grated
  nutmeg

pinch ground cloves

25 g (1 oz) butter

2-3 tablespoons rum

Is there ever a more popular barbecue dessert than hot bananas? Note these are grilled on the barbecue or baked instead of fried which makes them easier to handle. Serve straight from the foil or cooking dish with all the delicious juices.

Choose bananas that are all yellow or slightly green tipped at the stalk end, which means the bananas will be firm enough to cook (cooking ripens bananas immediately and brings out a delicious flavour). Cut out 6-8 pieces of heavy-duty foil, each large enough to enclose a banana comfortably. Alternatively, select a large baking dish. Butter the foil or dish well. Peel the bananas and cut in half lengthways. Place two halves on each piece of foil, or arrange close together in the baking dish in a single layer. Finely grate the lime zest directly over the bananas and then add the juice.

In a small bowl, combine muscovado sugar, cinnamon, nutmeg and cloves. Sprinkle evenly over the bananas. Top with the butter cut in flakes.

Wrap the foil around the bananas to seal, then place on the barbecue grid over hot coals, seam up. Cook for 15 minutes.

To bake indoors, heat the oven to 190°C (375°F or gas no. 5). Bake the bananas for 10-15 minutes or until they are tender and easily pierced with a fork.

Warm the rum, flame and pour over the hot fruit in the opened foil parcels or baking dish. Nice with chilled cream.

GREEN FRUITS IN A FRESH MINT SYRUP

SERVES 6

100 g (4 oz) castor sugar

150 ml (¼ pint) water

grated zest and juice 1 lime

2 tablespoons chopped fresh mint

2 ripe ogen melons

225 g (8 oz) green grapes

3 kiwi fruits

Traditionally the colours in a fruit salad were always mixed, but now there are so many fruits to choose from, it's fashionable to go for single shades and very effective it is too. You have a choice here of green or yellow.

Start with the sugar syrup which will provide the juice for the mixture. Measure the sugar and water into a small saucepan. Grate the zest of the lime directly into the pan (so you catch all the flavour) and stir over low heat to dissolve the sugar. Bring to the boil and simmer for 1 minute, then draw off the heat. Add the squeezed lime juice and chopped mint and pour into a serving bowl.

Halve the melons and remove the seeds. Slice the melon into quarters and cut the flesh from the skin. Slice then dice the melon flesh and add to the syrup. Split and deseed the grapes and add to the melon. Finally, using a small sharp knife, pare away the brown skin from the kiwi fruits to reveal the pretty green flesh underneath. Slice and add to the fruit bowl. Cover and let the fruit marinate for at least 4 hours. **P**

For a yellow fruit salad: prepare a syrup as above using a lemon instead of lime to sharpen the flavour and 2-3 coriander seeds or crushed cardamom pods for flavour. Strain into a serving bowl and add fruits such as diced pineapple, papaya or mango, sliced nectarine or peaches, bananas or star fruit and a garnish of passion fruit seeds, if you like.

P Can be prepared ahead: marinate overnight.

159

ICED PINEAPPLE SLICES IN GINGER SYRUP

SERVES 6

1 fresh pineapple

75 g (3 oz) granulated sugar

2 tablespoons water

50 g (2 oz) stem ginger

2 tablespoons stem ginger
  syrup

juice 1 lemon

Fresh juicy pineapple and ginger have very compatible flavours. Prepare the pineapple as directed – there should be absolutely no stalky bits and the resulting fluted edges on each slice adds to the simple prettiness.

Turn the pineapple on its side and cut a slice from the top to remove the crown and from the base. Using a sharp knife (one with a long blade) and with the pineapple standing upright, cut down and around the fruit to slice away the outer rind close to the surface. Then using a small vegetable knife, cut out the 'eyes' diagonally around the pineapple. Repeat, following the same diagonal direction, until all the brown bits are removed and the fruit has an attractive 'corkscrew' swirl. Lay the pineapple on its side and slice the fruit across. Arrange the slices in a serving dish.

Measure the sugar and water into a saucepan and stir over low heat to dissolve the sugar. Bring to a simmer and draw off the heat. Slice the stem ginger in bold pieces and add to the syrup along with the ginger syrup from the jar. Add lemon juice to sharpen the flavour. Spoon over the pineapple slices.

Cover and refrigerate for several hours – the syrup draws juice from the pineapple. Serve chilled. **P**

GENEVA WAFERS

MAKES 36

75 g (3 oz) butter, at room
  temperature

75 g (3 oz) castor sugar

few drops vanilla essence

2 egg whites (size 2)

75 g (3 oz) plain flour

These are fragile, thin biscuits for serving with sorbets, cream ices or with fresh fruit salads. Keep them crisp by storing, as soon as they are cold, in a biscuit tin, tightly sealed.

Heat the oven to 200°C (400°F or gas no. 6). Grease at least two baking sheets with white cooking fat.

In a mixing bowl, cream the butter with the sugar until soft and light. Mix in the vanilla essence. Beat in the lightly mixed egg whites in three parts, adding a little of the flour after each addition. Fold in the remaining flour.

Drop teaspoons of the mixture on to the prepared baking sheets, leaving space to spread. Set in the heated oven and bake for 6-7 minutes or until the edges of the wafers are golden. Transfer the wafers to a wire cooling tray. Repeat until the mixture is used up.

Let cool completely, then store in an airtight container. **P**

P Can be prepared ahead: will keep for up to 1 week.

PICNICS

Tarragon mayonnaise dip with cucumber sticks

Hot tomato and tarragon soup

.

Prosciutto with pears in a mint vinaigrette

Chicken liver and cognac pâté

Glazed avocado mousse

Picnic tortilla

Teriyaki steak slices

Chicken salad with a yogurt, mint and garlic dressing

Pasta and salami salad with pesto dressing

Tuna, white bean and spring onion salad

Smoked mackerel and new potatoes in a mustard dressing

Chicken mostarda

.

Marinated mushrooms

Curried rice and raisin salad

Spiced green lentil and cherry tomato salad

Orange and tomato vinaigrette

.

Blueberry cupcakes

Chocolate frosted brownies

Eccles cakes

PICNICS

The perfect picnic is a planned cold meal, prepared in your kitchen, packed and carried to some idyllic place where it is laid out elegantly. For the grand occasion, there is nothing nicer than china plates, silver cutlery, proper napkins and glasses for the wine. Go for big dinner plates, remembering that at a picnic everything goes on one plate, and don't stint on the size of the napkins. Choose large ones – they look stylish and keep pretty dresses clean.

Check over your picnic kit, making sure you have included the basic necessities – a corkscrew, bottle opener, salt and pepper mills, serving spoons, a jug for the Pimm's. Go over the dishes in your picnic menu, considering all requirements or special serving spoons. Pack these separately so heavy plates and cutlery don't squash food – a strong butcher's basket with a big handle for carrying is ideal. Set plates and cutlery in first with tablecloth and rugs last, so everything comes out in the right order to set out the picnic proper. Alongside, put something waterproof to go under the rugs. Include small fold-up chairs for those who don't like lolling around on the grass and as many cushions as you can for those that do.

At a picnic you tend to set everything out and let guests help themselves. Lavishness is the essential feature – at least half a dozen dishes spread on the cloth with a brimming salad bowl, a basket of fruit and some cheese (chèvre is the perfect picnic cheese; it's so spreadable and not thirst-making.) Aim for foods that combine well – a choice of main dish with a selection of interesting salads of rice, grains or new young vegetables. For dessert consider some delicious finger-sized portions of luscious cake – frosted brownies or blueberry cup cakes. Apart from anything else, this relieves you of carrying yet more bowls and plates.

For foods that are cold, the answer is a cool box or insulated bag with ice packs (store ice packs permanently in the freezer so they are always frozen). Conversely, hot items like soup (a welcome surprise if there's a nip in the air) can be carried in wide-mouthed thermos flasks. Let salad greens crisp up in the refrigerator until the last minute, then carry in a serving bowl sealed over with clear film. Take the dressings separately in a

Previous pages: Chicken mostarda and tarragon mayonnaise dip with cucumber sticks

screw-topped jar – always toss leafy salads on the spot otherwise they may wilt on the journey. Mousses (like salad) can be carried in the serving bowl or tarts in the baking tin for slicing and serving. Use rigid boxes with flexible leakproof lids that seal for other foods.

Freeze fruit juices solid in the cartons and use them as cool packs for other foods – they will thaw on the way. Don't forget scissors to cut open the tops. Be generous with the liquid refreshments – there's nothing like a glass of sparkling wine or a jug of Pimm's to get the picnic going. Fruit juices, topped up with sparkling mineral water, are very refreshing and, of course, fruit juice combines perfectly with champagne – try peach, mango or lychee juice. A wide-mouthed thermos flask can be used to carry ice cubes for dropping into tumblers of iced coffee, and a vacuum flask of boiling water to infuse tea – Earl Grey tea bags are a good choice (it's best to choose a tea that doesn't need milk).

Make your final offering small hand towels, previously damped with scented water, rolled up and popped in the freezer; carry to the picnic in a polythene bag. These are cool and refreshing after finger foods.

PACK AND CARRY SANDWICHES

Simple brown bread and butter sandwiches filled with a lettuce leaf or two are delicious taken on a picnic with home-cooked ham or rare roast beef, very thinly sliced.

You can replace the lettuce with chopped fresh herbs like chives, tarragon or dill to make herb sandwiches, and serve with gravadlax, cooked quail's eggs or egg mayonnaise. A little lemon added to the butter makes them extra good with smoked salmon.

Trim crusts, then cut lettuce sandwiches in halves and herb sandwiches – into quarters.

ORANGE AID

Perk up straight orange juice in one of the following ways . . .
● Top up with sparkling mineral water to give it a fizz.
● Mix with equal quantities canned tomato juice – great for a starter.
● Mix with equal quantities of pineapple juice – the flavour is delicious.
● Mix with equal quantities apple juice – good for brunch.
● Add a squeeze of lemon juice and slices of fresh orange.
● Top up with sparkling wine or, best of all, champagne.

TARRAGON MAYONNAISE DIP WITH CUCUMBER STICKS

SERVES 6-8

1 egg (size 2)

1 egg yolk (size 2)

1 level teaspoon castor sugar

½ level teaspoon Dijon mustard

2 tablespoons tarragon wine vinegar

salt and freshly milled pepper

300 ml (½ pint) grapeseed or other mild oil

3-4 tablespoons coarsely chopped fresh tarragon

2 tablespoons soured cream

½ cucumber, for serving

A delicately flavoured herb dip with the lightest texture. This is perfect for your guests to dip into while they sip a glass of wine. It can also double as a dressing for cold salmon.

Put the whole egg, egg yolk, sugar, mustard and 1 tablespoon of the wine vinegar into a food processor or blender goblet. Season with salt and pepper, cover and blend for a few seconds. Measure the oil into a jug.

Remove the centre cap from the machine lid and slowly pour in half the oil while the machine is running – the mayonnaise will begin to thicken when the blades are covered. Add the remaining vinegar, then pour in the rest of the oil in a steady stream. Add the tarragon and run the machine until the leaves are finely minced. Spoon into a container and stir in the soured cream. Cover and refrigerate. **P**

Trim the cucumber, cut it in half lengthways and scoop out the centre seeds using a teaspoon. Cut the cucumber across in 4 cm (1½ inch) chunks, then lengthways into small sticks. Serve the tarragon mayonnaise in a bowl, surrounded with the cucumber sticks for dipping.

● Carry the dip in a suitable container; keep the cucumber sticks chilled and sealed in a polythene bag.

HOT TOMATO AND TARRAGON SOUP

SERVES 6

900 g (2 lb) ripe tomatoes

1 medium onion

3 carrots

25 g (1 oz) butter

salt and freshly milled pepper

1 level teaspoon castor sugar

2 tablespoons chopped fresh tarragon leaves

750 ml (1¼ pints) vegetable stock

A mug of hot soup is a nice idea if the weather looks variable. This fresh tomato and tarragon soup is very summery, and homemade it has a delicious astringency that you never get in the canned versions.

Nick the skin on each tomato and put them all together in a mixing bowl. Pour in boiling water to cover, let stand 1 minute, then drain them. Peel away the skins. Halve the tomatoes and squeeze the seeds and juice into a small bowl. Cut up the tomato flesh coarsely. Peel and chop the onion, and pare and dice the carrots.

Heat the butter in a saucepan, add the onion and cook gently

1 level tablespoon concentrated tomato purée

P Can be made ahead: cool, cover and refrigerate for up to 24 hours. Reheat for serving.

to soften – about 5 minutes. Add the diced carrots and cut up tomatoes. Strain in the juice from the tomato seeds. Add a seasoning of salt and pepper, the sugar and chopped tarragon. Cover and cook gently for about 15 minutes to soften and draw juices from the tomatoes.

Add the stock and concentrated tomato purée. Recover and simmer the soup for 40 minutes by which time all the vegetables should be quite soft – check the carrots since they will take the longest time to cook. Draw off the heat. Purée the soup in a food processor or blender, then reheat if necessary. Check the seasoning before serving. **P**

● Carry the hot soup in a vacuum jug or flask; remember to take along mugs for serving.

PROSCIUTTO WITH PEARS IN A MINT VINAIGRETTE

SERVES 6

2 tablespoons chopped fresh mint

1 level teaspoon castor sugar

salt and freshly milled pepper

2 tablespoons raspberry wine vinegar

4 tablespoons grapeseed or other mild oil

2 tablespoons olive oil

4-6 ripe dessert pears, depending on size

12 slices prosciutto (dry cured ham)

P Can be prepared ahead: marinate overnight.

To serve fruits with cured ham is popular. Here an unusual dressing speckles the pear slices prettily with flecks of green. You can use melon if you prefer, or instead of the cured ham you can substitute the thinnest slices of smoked venison.

In a mixing bowl, pound the chopped mint with the sugar (use a wooden spoon) to draw out the flavouring oils. Add a seasoning of salt and pepper and the raspberry vinegar and stir to dissolve the sugar. Stir in the grapeseed and olive oils and blend thoroughly. Taste for flavour – the dressing should be sweet-sharp.

Peel and core the pears and cut in thin slices, adding them to the dressing as they are prepared to keep their colour. Turn the pears in the dressing, then cover and leave to marinate for several hours. **P**

Crinkle slices of prosciutto on individual serving plates, and add the pears and a spoonful of the dressing. Or arrange on a single platter with prosciutto down one side and pears opposite.

● Carry the pears and dressing in a sealed container; pack the prosciutto separately.

CHICKEN LIVER AND COGNAC PÂTÉ

SERVES 6

450 g (1 lb) chicken livers

1 small onion

1 clove garlic

50 g (2 oz) butter

4 tablespoons chicken stock

salt and freshly milled pepper

150 ml (¼ pint) double cream

2 eggs (size 2)

1 level tablespoon cornflour

2-3 tablespoons cognac

25 g (1 oz) melted butter, for the top

P Can be prepared ahead: will keep for 2-3 days.

Pâté is ideal for making ahead because it actually tastes better after a day or so. This is a soft spreading mixture and the protective layer of butter that seals the top will keep the mixture fresh. It looks pretty if you set a bay leaf or a few green peppercorns in the melted butter before it sets.

Separate and trim the chicken livers. Peel and finely chop the onion and the garlic. Melt the butter in a saucepan, add the onion and fry gently for a few minutes to soften. Add the garlic and stir for a moment, then add the chicken livers, the stock and a good seasoning of salt and freshly milled pepper. Cover with the pan lid and simmer gently for about 10 minutes to partly cook the livers.

Heat the oven to 170°C (325°F or gas no. 3). Well butter a 1.1 litre (2 pint) baking dish or terrine (the pâté is served from the dish).

Turn the contents of the saucepan into the bowl of a food processor. Cover and blend to a purée. Add the cream, eggs and combined cornflour and cognac. Blend for a moment more. Pour the mixture (it is quite soft) into the prepared dish. Cover with a lid or foil.

Place the dish in a larger roasting tin and add boiling water to come 2.5 cm (1 inch) up the sides. Set in the heated oven and bake for 1-1½ hours or until the pâté feels firm when pressed in the centre. Let cool to room temperature.

Pour the melted butter over the surface to seal, and refrigerate overnight. **P**

Serve scooped from the dish with crusty bread and onion marmalade (see page 58).

● Carry the pâté in the baking dish, covered with clear film, and the onion marmalade in a suitable sealed container; slip the bread (baguettes) into the picnic basket.

GLAZED AVOCADO MOUSSE

SERVES 6

150 ml (¼ pint) chicken stock

15 g (½ oz) powdered gelatine

3 ripe avocados

juice 2 lemons

salt and freshly milled pepper

1 teaspoon onion juice (see recipe)

150 ml (¼ pint) mayonnaise

150 ml (¼ pint) double cream

1 recipe quantity lemon aspic jelly (see page 170)

fresh coriander leaves, to garnish

P Can be prepared ahead: keep refrigerated overnight.

Prepared this way, avocado mousse can be transported in the serving bowl, but to preserve the green colour the glaze of lemon aspic on top is essential. Use the opportunity to add a pretty garnish – coriander leaves and thin segments of orange look pretty. A mixed leaf salad tossed on the spot with a herb dressing would be a lovely addition.

Measure the chicken stock into a saucepan. Sprinkle in the gelatine and let soak for 5 minutes. Then set the pan over low heat and stir to dissolve the gelatine – do not boil. Draw off the heat.

Halve the avocados and remove the stones. With a dessertspoon, scoop out the flesh into a food processor bowl, making sure you get all the green flesh close to the skin. Add the lemon juice and purée the mixture until smooth. Transfer to a large mixing bowl. Add a good seasoning of salt and pepper, the onion juice (twist an onion half on a lemon squeezer) and the mayonnaise. Add the dissolved gelatine and blend through. Whip the cream to soft peaks and fold in.

Turn the mixture into a 900 ml (1½ pint) serving dish and spread level. Spoon a little of the lemon aspic jelly over the surface and chill until set. Dip a few coriander leaves in the remaining jelly and arrange decoratively on the surface. Chill to fix the garnish in position. Use the remaining aspic jelly to cover and seal the mousse – it will retain the green colour. Cover and refrigerate for at least 4 hours. **P**

● Carry the mousse in its serving dish, covered with clear film, and transport in a cool box.

LEMON ASPIC JELLY

MAKES 175 ML (6 FL OZ)

150 ml (¼ pint) cold water

2 level teaspoons powdered
  gelatine

juice ½ lemon

1 level teaspoon castor sugar

pinch salt

1 teaspoon tarragon wine
  vinegar

*Use this lemon-flavoured jelly glaze to seal the surface of any
savoury mousse and fix a pretty garnish too. Aspic prevents the
surface from drying out which is important where dishes are
prepared ahead and chilled.*

Measure the water into a saucepan and sprinkle in the
gelatine. Let soak for 5 minutes. Add the lemon juice, sugar
and salt. Stir over low heat to dissolve the gelatine – do not
boil. Draw off the heat and add the tarragon vinegar.

Allow the mixture to cool until it begins to thicken and
shows signs of setting. When it takes on the consistency of
unbeaten egg whites it is ready to use. You can speed up the
setting by putting the base of the pan in a bowl of cold water
with ice cubes.

Be sure to have the item for glazing close at hand. Quickly
spoon sufficient jelly over to cover the surface, and chill to set.
If a garnish is included, start by setting a thin layer of aspic jelly
first. Then add the garnish (dipped in a little of the aspic) and
chill to fix in position. Finally, spoon more aspic jelly over the
top to give an even shine.

PICNIC TORTILLA

SERVES 4-6

450 g (1 lb) new potatoes

2 medium onions

1-2 cloves garlic

3 tablespoons olive oil

6 eggs (size 2)

2 tablespoons water

salt and freshly milled pepper

2 tablespoons chopped fresh
  chives

*A thick, firm omelette, packed with vegetables, this is cut in
slices to serve with a salad – very moist and pleasant to eat. I
like a combination of new summer potatoes, onion and chives,
but there's nothing to stop you increasing the variety of cooked
vegetables to include sliced courgettes, asparagus tips or garden
peas, for instance.*

Scrape the new potatoes and boil in salted water until just
tender, then drain and cool. Cut in thick slices. Peel and finely
chop the onions, and peel and chop the garlic.

Heat the oil in a 25 cm (10 inch) frying pan (preferably
non-stick), add the onions and cook gently to soften – about 5
minutes. Add the garlic and stir through for a moment, then
draw the pan off the heat. With a perforated spoon, transfer
the onions from the pan to a plate, leaving the oil behind.

Crack the eggs into a mixing bowl, add the water, a
seasoning of salt and pepper and the chopped chives and mix

well. Add the sliced potatoes and the onion mixture.

Replace the frying pan over the heat. When hot, pour in the omelette mixture and spread out evenly. Cover with the pan lid and cook gently for 5-6 minutes or until the omelette is just set. Remove the lid and pass the omelette under a hot grill to brown the top. Let stand for 10 minutes, then loosen the sides and turn on to a serving plate. Leave until cold. Serve cut in wedges. **P**

● Carry on the plate, covered with clear film.

TERIYAKI STEAK SLICES

SERVES 6

1 × 900 g (2 lb) piece thick cut rump steak
2 tablespoons soy sauce
2 level tablespoons light muscovado
juice 1 lemon
1 tablespoon grapeseed or other mild oil
salt and freshly milled pepper
1 clove garlic
1 level teaspoon grated fresh root ginger

Marinated in soy sauce, then grilled in one piece and sliced for serving, this is an excellent way to put together a cold beef salad. Aim for pink, rare-cooked steak. Let it cool completely before slicing, and the meat will be moist and tender.

Trim the steak and place in a shallow dish. In a bowl combine the soy sauce, soft brown sugar, lemon juice, salad oil and seasoning of salt and freshly milled pepper. Peel the garlic and chop finely or press through a garlic crusher. Add along with the grated root ginger. Pour this mixture over the steak and leave to marinate for several hours, turning the meat several times. **P**

Heat the grill to hot. Place the steak on the grill rack, reserving the marinade in the dish. Set the grill rack about 7.5 cm (3 inches) from the heat source and grill for 8-10 minutes for medium rare, turning once; the steak should be brown on the outside and pink in the middle. Baste with the marinade during cooking.

Let cool completely, then cut the steak in thin diagonal slices. Arrange on a serving platter and add extras such as cooked green beans, new potatoes and cherry tomatoes.

● Carry steak slices in a suitable container; keep beans, potatoes and cherry tomatoes chilled and sealed in a polythene bag. Carry oil and vinegar dressing (see page 00), mayonnaise and mustard in jars along with crisp bread (baguettes) slipped into the picnic basket.

CHICKEN SALAD WITH A YOGURT, MINT AND GARLIC DRESSING

SERVES 6

1 × 2 kg (4 lb) oven ready chicken

50 g (2 oz) butter

4 cloves garlic

½ cucumber

250 g (8 fl oz) natural yogurt

3 level tablespoons mayonnaise

1 tablespoon tarragon wine vinegar

freshly milled pepper

2 tablespoons chopped fresh mint, or 1 teaspoon dried mint

paprika, to garnish

A summery, garlic-flavoured dressing coats these chicken pieces, but don't be alarmed – the garlic is baked in the oven which turns the flavour sweet and mild.

Heat the oven to 190°C (375°F or gas no. 5).

Remove the chicken giblets from the body cavity and place a knob of butter inside. Spread the remaining butter over the chicken skin and set the bird in a roasting tin. Put in the heated oven and roast for 1¼ hours. Wrap the garlic in a loose foil parcel and set on the oven shelf below the chicken for the last 30 minutes cooking time. The garlic cloves will feel soft when gently pressed once the cooking time is complete. Let the garlic and chicken cool.

Take one third of the cucumber and slice it thinly for garnish; set aside. Peel the remaining cucumber, halve it lengthways and remove the centre seeds using a teaspoon. Cut the cucumber lengthways and across into neat dice. Place in a colander, sprinkle with salt and let stand for 1 hour to draw out the juices, then rinse under cold water and press the cucumber dry on absorbent kitchen paper.

Lift the chicken meat from the bones, discarding the skin, and cut into bite-sized pieces.

Peel the softened garlic cloves and turn them into a mixing bowl. Mash the garlic to a purée with a fork. Add the yogurt, mayonnaise and wine vinegar and blend well. **P**

Add the chicken pieces, diced cucumber and chopped fresh or dried mint to the dressing. Turn to combine the ingredients well. Arrange the slices of cucumber around the border of a serving bowl and turn the salad into the centre. Garnish with a sprinkling of paprika.

● Carry chicken pieces and dressing in a suitable container; keep cucumber slices chilled and sealed in a polythene bag. Include a jar of paprika with a shaker top in the picnic basket.

P Can be prepared ahead: cover and refrigerate for up to 24 hours.

172

PASTA AND SALAMI SALAD WITH PESTO DRESSING

SERVES 6

225 g (8 oz) green spiral (fusilli)
  pasta

2 tablespoons olive oil

1 bunch (6-8) spring onions

225 g (8 oz) cherry tomatoes

100 g (4 oz) feta cheese

8-10 black olives

2 tablespoons chopped fresh
  parsley

100 g (4 oz) thinly sliced Italian
  salami

fresh basil or lamb's lettuce
  leaves, to garnish

For the pesto dressing

salt and freshly milled pepper

1 level teaspoon wholegrain
  mustard

1 tablespoon wine vinegar

3 tablespoons olive oil

2 level teaspoons prepared
  pesto sauce

Pasta is neutral which makes it the perfect foil for strong flavours, like the basil taste of this green-flecked dressing. This is a salad with everything in it – vegetables, cheese and meat with herb overtones – a personal favourite.

Bring a large pan of salted water to the boil. Add the pasta, stir until reboiling and cook for 6-8 minutes or until just tender, then drain. Turn the pasta into a large mixing bowl, add the oil and mix through. Let cool for about 10 minutes.

Trim the spring onions then chop all the white and some of the green stems. Cut the cherry tomatoes in half, and break the feta cheese into pieces. Add the spring onions, tomatoes, cheese and olives to the pasta.

For the dressing, put a seasoning of salt and pepper, the wholegrain mustard and vinegar into a small bowl. Mix to blend, then stir in the olive oil and the pesto sauce. Taste for flavour. Add the dressing to the salad along with the chopped parsley and toss to mix the ingredients.

Arrange the salami slices around the edge of a serving bowl. Turn the salad into the centre and sprinkle the basil or lamb's lettuce leaves over the top.

● Carry salad and dressing in a suitable container; pack salami slices and lamb's lettuce separately.

TUNA, WHITE BEAN AND SPRING ONION SALAD

SERVES 6

225 g (8 oz) dried white haricot
  beans, soaked overnight

salt and freshly milled pepper

2 tablespoons lemon juice

1 level teaspoon Dijon mustard

6 tablespoons olive oil

1 bunch (6-8) spring onions

1 stalk celery

An alternative serving idea here would be to spoon this tuna and bean salad into scooped-out beefsteak tomatoes to make a summery main dish, with other salad accompaniments.

Drain the soaked beans, rinse and put in a saucepan with fresh, unsalted water to cover. Bring to a simmer and cook gently for 1 hour, or until the beans are tender, stirring occasionally. Drain and turn into a mixing bowl.

Combine a seasoning of salt and freshly milled pepper, the lemon juice, mustard and oil and pour over the warm beans.

2 tablespoons chopped fresh
parsley

2 × approx 200 g cans tuna in
oil

P Can be prepared ahead: cover
and refrigerate for up to 24 hours.

Stir and leave to marinate for at least 1 hour – this way the beans absorb the flavour of the dressing.

Trim the spring onions, then chop all the white and some of the green stems. Scrub and string the celery, then shred the stalks finely. Add the spring onions, celery and 1 tablespoon of the chopped parsley to the beans. Mix, and check the seasoning with salt and pepper. **P**

Pile the salad into a serving bowl. Drain the tuna and break into chunky pieces. Arrange on top of the beans. Sprinkle with the remaining chopped parsley.

● Carry assembled salad in a suitable container.

SMOKED MACKEREL AND NEW POTATOES IN A MUSTARD DRESSING

SERVES 6

3 smoked mackerel fillets

450 g (1 lb) new potatoes

1 medium onion

3 stalks celery

150 ml (¼ pint) soured cream

1 level teaspoon Dijon mustard

1 tablespoon tarragon wine
vinegar

3 tablespoons grapeseed or
other mild oil

salt and freshly milled pepper

crisp lettuce, for serving

2 tablespoons chopped fresh
chives

Deliciously moist and succulent, flakes of smoked mackerel are excellent in salads. This combination, with sliced new potatoes, onion and crunchy celery, makes a perfect picnic lunch.

Pull away the skin from the mackerel fillets and flake the flesh into chunky pieces. Scrub the potatoes, leaving on the skins (or just wash well in cold water), and add to a saucepan of boiling salted water. Bring back to a simmer, cover and cook until just tender – about 10 minutes. Drain, then shake the potatoes in the pan over the heat to dry them for a moment. When cool, cut them in thick slices.

Peel and slice the onion, then separate into rings. Cover the onion rings with boiling water, let stand 10 minutes, then drain and chill them. Scrub and string the celery and shred finely.

In a medium mixing bowl combine the soured cream mustard, tarragon wine vinegar and salad oil. Season with salt and freshly milled pepper. Add the potatoes, onion rings, flaked mackerel and shredded celery. Toss the salad until the ingredients are combined well. Leave to marinate for 1 hour or longer. **P**

Turn into a serving bowl lined with crisp lettuce leaves and sprinkle with the chopped chives.

● Carry marinated salad in a suitable container, keep lettuce leaves and chives chilled and sealed in polythene bags.

CHICKEN MOSTARDA

SERVES 6

100 g (4 oz) tenderized dried
  apricots

juice 1 orange

225 g (8 oz) curd cheese

salt and freshly milled pepper

6 chicken breast fillets, with
  skins on

2 tablespoons sherry wine
  vinegar

1 level tablespoon light
  muscovado sugar

2 level tablespoons wholegrain
  mustard

100 ml (4 fl oz) grapeseed or
  other mild oil

2-3 tablespoons lemon juice

Tender chicken fillets stuffed with apricot cheese, then cooked and served cold in a mustard marinade – these are cut into nice slices for serving.

Cut the apricots quite small and soak for 2 hours in the orange juice to soften.

Turn the curd cheese into a food processor bowl. Add the apricots and any orange juice along with a seasoning of salt and freshly milled pepper. Cover and blend the ingredients.

Partially loosen the skin on each chicken breast fillet with fingertips to form a pocket. Take dessertspoons of the apricot mixture and spoon into each pocket, spreading it under the chicken skin. Place the prepared fillets in a baking dish.

In a bowl, combine the sherry vinegar, sugar and wholegrain mustard. Stir in the oil. Pour over the chicken pieces. Cover and marinate for several hours or overnight in the refrigerator.

Heat the oven to 180°C (350°F or gas no. 4).

Baste the chicken pieces with the marinade in the dish, then set in the heated oven and bake for 30-35 minutes or until a rich golden brown.

Transfer the chicken to a serving dish. Pour the marinade into a saucepan, add lemon juice to taste and bring to a simmer. Spoon over the chicken and leave until quite cold. **P** Serve cut in slices with the marinade as a dressing.

● Carry in a suitable container; take your choice of crisp chilled salad greens and vinaigrette separately.

MARINATED MUSHROOMS

700 g (1½ lb) button
  mushrooms

1 medium onion

3 cloves garlic

salt

4 tablespoons olive oil

6 coriander seeds

8 black peppercorns

6 sun-dried tomatoes (optional)

1 level tablespoon concentrated
  tomato purée

1 level teaspoon dried mixed
  herbs

75 ml (3 fl oz) water

175 ml (6 fl oz) dry white wine

2 tablespoons red wine vinegar

2 tablespoons chopped fresh
  parsley

These mushrooms are cooked and then marinated in a spicy tomato dressing. Prepared this way, mushrooms stand up well and actually improve in flavour. Take care to choose 'buttons': open mushroom juices will darken the dressing.

Trim the mushroom stalks level with the caps, then wipe the mushrooms with a damp cloth, or shake them in a sieve under running cold water and press gently in absorbent kitchen paper to dry them. Peel and finely chop the onion. Peel the garlic and crush to a purée with a little salt.

Heat the oil in a large saucepan, add the onion and soften over gentle heat. Add the garlic and stir for a moment. Lightly crush the coriander seeds and black peppercorns with the end of a rolling pin (for a more aromatic flavour) and add to the pan along with the sun-dried tomatoes, tomato purée, dried mixed herbs, water, wine and wine vinegar. Bring to a simmer for 2 minutes, then add the mushrooms. Cover with the pan lid and cook gently for 8-10 minutes.

With a perforated spoon transfer the mushrooms to a serving bowl.

Replace the pan of dressing over the heat and boil fast for 5 minutes to reduce and concentrate the flavour. Cool, then pour over the mushrooms. Leave to marinate overnight. **P**

Check the seasoning and serve at room temperature, sprinkled with the parsley.

● Carry in a suitable container.

CURRIED RICE AND RAISIN SALAD

SERVES 6

225 g (8 oz) long-grain rice

salt and freshly milled pepper

½ level teaspoon curry powder

2 tablespoons lemon juice

2 level tablespoons mango
  chutney

3 tablespoons grapeseed or
  other mild oil

The trick with any rice salad is to mix the dressing with the hot freshly cooked rice so that the grains will absorb the flavour as the rice cools. Here the salad takes a golden colour and the flavour is mildly spicy – nice with cold sliced meats or chicken.

Add the rice to a saucepan of boiling salted water, stir until the water reboils and then cook for 6-8 minutes or until the rice is tender – test by pressing a grain between the forefinger and thumb; there should be no hard core. Drain and turn the hot rice into a mixing bowl.

*2 level tablespoons seedless
raisins*

1 red sweet pepper

Combine a seasoning of salt and pepper, the curry powder, lemon juice, mango chutney (chop up any large pieces) and oil in a bowl. Add this dressing to the hot rice and fork through. At first the mixture may seem rather moist, but the hot rice will absorb the dressing as it cools.

Meanwhile, cover the seedless raisins with hot water from the kettle and let stand 5 minutes to plump them up. Halve, deseed and finely chop the red sweet pepper. When the rice is cold, add the drained raisins and chopped pepper. **P**

P Can be prepared ahead: cover and refrigerate for up to 24 hours.

● Carry in a suitable container.

SPICED GREEN LENTIL AND CHERRY TOMATO SALAD

SERVES 6

225 g (8 oz) green lentils

salt and freshly milled pepper

1 medium onion

*5 tablespoons grapeseed or
other mild oil*

1 level teaspoon ground cumin

*1 level teaspoon ground
coriander*

3 tablespoons red wine vinegar

225 g (8 oz) cherry tomatoes

Green lentils are unusual – when cooked they remain whole and prettily shaped. Add a spicy dressing and something colourful like cherry tomatoes and you have a really nice mixture that's easy to eat with a fork.

Rinse and drain the green lentils (no need to soak), then place in a saucepan with cold salted water to cover generously. Bring to the boil, then reduce heat and simmer, covered, for 10-15 minutes or until the lentils are tender. Drain and turn into a mixing bowl.

Peel the onion and slice thinly in rings. Heat 1 tablespoon of the oil in a frying pan. Add the onion and cook gently until softened. Stir in the ground cumin and coriander and cook for a moment longer, then draw off the heat. Stir in the remaining oil and the vinegar. Add a seasoning of salt and pepper. Bring back to a simmer, then pour the hot dressing over the lentils. Leave to cool, then cover and refrigerate for at least 1 hour. **P**

Nick the skins on the cherry tomatoes and put them in a colander. Pour through boiling water from the kettle to loosen the skins. Peel the tomatoes and slice them in half. Add to the salad and turn the ingredients to mix. Turn into a shallow bowl or salad platter for serving.

P Can be prepared ahead: cool, cover and refrigerate for up to 24 hours.

● Carry in a suitable container.

ORANGE AND TOMATO VINAIGRETTE

SERVES 6

3 oranges

450 g (1 lb) ripe tomatoes

1 medium onion

6-8 black olives

For the orange vinaigrette

salt and freshly milled pepper

1 level teaspoon Dijon mustard

1 tablespoon lemon juice

3 tablespoons orange juice

1 level teaspoon grated orange
zest

2 tablespoons chopped fresh
parsley

4 tablespoons grapeseed or
other mild oil

2 tablespoons olive oil

P Can be prepared ahead: keep
refrigerated for up to 6 hours.

Salads with fruit in them do not taste at all sweet because the flavours balance out perfectly with tangy dressings. Orange slices combine marvellously with tomatoes – the flavours are compatible and the contrasting colours quite brilliant.

Cut a slice from the top and base of each orange, then cut around to remove the peel and pith from the fruits. Slice the orange horizontally and discard any pips.

Scald the tomatoes in boiling water and peel away the skins. Slice the tomatoes across.

Peel the onion and slice into rings. If you prefer a mild onion flavour, pour boiling water over the onion rings and let stand for 10-15 minutes, then drain.

Arrange orange and tomato slices, onion rings and olives on a salad platter. In a bowl combine a seasoning of salt and pepper, the mustard, lemon juice, orange juice and zest and chopped parsley. Add the oils in a stream and mix to an emulsion. Pour over the salad ingredients. Cover and refrigerate for at least 1 hour before serving. **P**

● Carry in a suitable container.

BLUEBERRY CUPCAKES

MAKES 12

150 g (5 oz) plain flour

1 level teaspoon baking powder

¼ level teaspoon salt

1 level teaspoon ground
cinnamon

100 g (4 oz) butter, at room
temperature

100 g (4 oz) castor sugar

2 eggs (size 2)

2 tablespoons milk

100 g (4 oz) fresh blueberries or
blackcurrants

For the glaze

100 g (2 oz) icing sugar

Pretty little cakes baked with fresh berries, these make an attractive mouthful. The taste is quite tangy when blackcurrants are used.

Heat the oven to 190°C (375°F or gas no. 5). Place 12 paper baking cases in a tray of deep bun tins. Sift the flour, baking powder, salt and cinnamon on to a plate and set aside.

Cream the butter with the sugar until soft and light. Lightly mix the eggs and add to the creamed mixture a little at a time, beating well after each addition and adding a little of the flour along with the last addition of egg. Gently fold half the remaining flour into the mixture, then add the rest of the flour and the milk and mix until just combined. Fold in the berries.

Put tablespoons of the mixture into the paper cases. Place in the heated oven and bake for 18-20 minutes. Transfer to a rack and let them cool.

2 tablespoons lemon juice

½ level teaspoon grated lemon zest

Combine the icing sugar and lemon juice and zest to make the glaze. Spread 1 teaspoon glaze over each cupcake. Let the cupcakes stand until the glaze is set. **P**

● Carry in a suitable container, separating the layers of cupcakes with sheets of greaseproof paper.

CHOCOLATE FROSTED BROWNIES

MAKES 9

75 g (3 oz) self-raising flour

½ oz cocoa powder

pinch salt

50 g (2 oz) butter

175 g (6 oz) light muscovado sugar

1 tablespoon water

100 g (4 oz) plain chocolate, chopped in pieces

½ teaspoon vanilla essence

2 eggs (size 2)

25 g (1 oz) shelled walnuts

For the frosting

100 g (4 oz) plain chocolate

150 ml (¼ pint) soured cream

Luscious squares of pure indulgence, these frosted brownies are the perfect finger food to top off a picnic menu. Or, consider them a greedy nibble that would team up wonderfully with a tall, cool glass of iced coffee.

Heat the oven to 160°C (325°F or gas no. 3).

Butter a 20 cm (8 inch) square baking tin. Sift the flour, cocoa powder and salt on to a plate.

Put the butter, sugar and water into a medium saucepan and stir over low heat to melt the butter – do not boil. Draw off the heat and add the chocolate pieces and vanilla essence. Stir as the chocolate melts – the heat of the pan should be sufficient to do this. Beat in the eggs, one at a time. Then add the sifted dry ingredients and beat to a smooth shiny mixture. Finally, chop and stir in the walnuts.

Pour the mixture into the prepared tin. Set in the heated oven and bake for 20 minutes. Let the brownies cool in the tin.

To make the frosting, break the chocolate into a mixing bowl and set over a saucepan of hot (not boiling) water until melted. Stir until smooth, then remove from the heat. Stir in the soured cream and beat until evenly blended. Spoon the frosting over the brownies and swirl attractively, Leave in a cool place to set. **P** Cut into squares and serve from the baking tin.

● Carry in the baking container. Protect the layers of brownies with sheets of greaseproof paper; keep cool.

ECCLES CAKES

MAKES 12

1 recipe quantity flaky pastry (see page 85)

25 g (1 oz) butter

25 g (1 oz) light muscovado sugar

25 g (1 oz) chopped candied peel

100 g (4 oz) currants

½ level teaspoon mixed spice

milk and granulated sugar, for the tops

A crisp, sugary 'bite' with a spicy, dried fruit filling, these are extra special when you bake them yourself.

Roll out the pastry thinly on a cool, lightly floured surface to about 30 × 50 cm (12 × 16 inches). Cover and rest for 20 minutes. Meanwhile, melt the butter in a saucepan and draw off the heat. Stir in the sugar, peel, currants and spice and mix well.

Using a 9-10 cm (3½-4 inch) cutter, stamp out rounds of the pastry. Or use a saucer as a guide, cutting round the rim with the tip of a knife. Place teaspoons of the spiced filling in the centre of each pastry round. Brush the pastry borders with water. With fingers, draw the pastry edges up over the filling and pinch them together to form small pouches. Turn them over (with sealed edge underneath), flatten with the hand and then roll out each one to a round about 7.5 cm (3 inches) diameter – the dried fruit will begin to show through. Cover and refrigerate for at least 10 minutes.

Heat the oven to 220°C (425°F or gas no. 7).

Make three slashes across each 'cake' with a sharp knife and place the cakes on ungreased baking trays. Brush with milk and sprinkle with granulated sugar. Set in the heated oven and bake for 15-20 minutes or until they are crisp and brown. Let cool completely on a wire cooling tray. **P**

● Carry in a suitable container or sealed polythene bag.

THE SPREAD THAT PLEASES
BUFFETS

Oriental beef with pineapple

Swedish meatballs in a soured cream sauce

Vegetable lasagne with ricotta cheese

Pork paprika with soured cream

Chicken braised in beer with prunes

Basmati rice with onion and spices

.

Spiced chicken satays

Chicken in a sweet curried dressing

Chicken tarragon salad with toasted pine nuts

Boned duck roll

Sugar baked gammon with pickled fruits

Whole poached salmon

Seafood terrine

.

Coleslaw with pineapple, grapes and dates

Wholewheat and chick pea salad

Golden rice salad with apricots and almonds

Wilted cucumber salad

.

Chocolate cheesecake

Brown sugar meringues with a caramel and lime sauce

Pineapple dacquoise

Apple strudels in a lemon syrup

BUFFETS

A buffet is one of the easiest ways to entertain your guests to a meal since it is the one occasion when everything can be cooked in advance. Normally the number of invited guests will be 12 or more and limited only by the amount of space at your disposal, but do take into consideration the fact that most people hate eating standing up.

Buffet food needs to be eaten with a fork only, otherwise little tables should be set up so plates can be put down. Don't feel obliged to offer an enormous choice of food – plenty of a few dishes is often more appealing. Too much choice confuses guests and they tend to heap everything on one plate. Select dishes that are complementary – a hot dish that has a gravy or sauce with rice or pasta, cold foods with salads that suit. Take into account the contrasts of colour, flavour and texture of the dishes you are putting together – little things like the fact that cold sliced meats taste best with moist salads while a dish with a thin dressing needs something to absorb it. Avoid leafy greens; they are difficult to eat with a fork. Instead go for prepared mixtures that stand up well and keep looking good such as vegetable, bean or pasta salads.

You can't have enough good-sized serving platters for buffet foods – space rather than depth means food can be set out attractively and makes it easier for guests to help themselves. When possible arrange foods in suitable serving portions so it is easier to control how much guests will take – cold meats carved, a quiche or tart cut in portions and a pâté or terrine sliced. You have less control when guests help themselves – dipping into a casserole, for instance. In this case it's advisable to slightly overestimate the amount of food required. Buffets need to be maintained because food gets picked over and looks messy so be prepared to sneak dishes back to the kitchen to tidy them up or transfer to another plate where necessary.

Offer a choice of desserts and don't overlook something very simple like a bowl of strawberries in orange juice for anyone who might prefer to avoid sweet foods. Delicate dessert cakes or tarts should be cut into serving portions beforehand – use a kitchen knife dipped into hot water and wiped clean between each cut and you won't drag up the crumbs.

Setting up the buffet

The situation for your buffet table depends on the number of guests and the layout of your room. Extend the dining room table and cover with a sheet or cloth – it will be covered with dishes so a plain colour is best. The table can be pushed against the wall in a small room or left central if there's more space. Remember that the service is faster if guests can move on both sides.

Set the buffet up in a logical serving order so guests can move along easily; they should pick up plates, food, then cutlery (wrapped in a napkin) and a drink. For a crowd duplicate the service at either end of the buffet with two stacks of dinner plates – when there are two lines of guests everything will move more quickly.

Make sure every dish is within easy reach and that each one has its own serving silver, in or beside it – otherwise guests will move spoons from one dish to another. Leave enough room around the edge of the buffet table so guests don't have to perform balancing acts and can put their plates down to serve themselves. It's a good idea to have someone serving the main dish – it speeds things up.

Set dessert on a side table from which guests can help themselves – place dessert plates and cutlery alongside. Have the drinks on a cleared sideboard – make a kind of bar with corkscrew and bottle openers and enlist a friend to pour. Include a choice of red or white wines and have mineral water available. A fresh-tasting fruit cup in jugs would be nice in summer. Set coffee cups on trays in the kitchen and set on a cleared section of the buffet at a suitable time. Have the coffee in jugs so that guests can pour their own and remember to include sugar, milk and cream. If coffee is brewed ahead, at least two vacuum jugs would be a real help.

MULLED WINES

Hot spiced wine is a deliciously reviving drink for cold midwinter. Offer a glass before Sunday lunch, or to welcome guests for a reception or buffet.
● Use reasonable red wines, the best you can afford. The extras provide the kick – sugar, whole spices like cinnamon, cloves or nutmeg with brandy, rum or fortified wines.
● Avoid over-spicing mulls and add sliced citrus fruits like orange and lemon (more orange than lemon or the flavour is too sharp); a clove-studded orange floating in the cooking pot looks good and adds flavour.
● Use a big saucepan, preserving pan or casserole for heating – let mulls heat thoroughly until hot but hold them below boiling point; mixtures quickly cool down once you start to serve them.
● Ladle mulls into warmed jugs for serving; this is more convenient than attempting to ladle the mixture directly into glasses from a punch bowl. Guests rarely help themselves so it's better to have jugs of the mixture circulating.
● Any glasses are fine, including stemmed ones; take the chill off them, if you like, but putting a mull in a jug takes the initial heat out and glasses will rarely crack. A mull should be pleasantly hot for sipping slowly.

MULLED WINE RECIPES

The best mulled wines are made by dissolving sugar in water to make a syrup and infusing it with the spices. Then wine is added and the whole warmed through for serving.

Measure 175 g (6 oz) light muscovado sugar and 300 ml (½ pint) water into a big saucepan or preserving pan and stir over low heat to dissolve the sugar. Add 1 lemon and 2 oranges sliced thinly. Stud a third orange with 6 cloves and add to the pan with a 5 cm (2 inch) stick cinnamon. Infuse gently for 10 minutes. Pour in 3 bottles red wine, ½ bottle ruby port (non-vintage) and 100 ml (4 fl oz) brandy or rum and heat slowly until almost boiling. Remove from the heat and ladle into warmed jugs for serving – leave the fruit in the pan. Makes 25 glasses.

Dr Johnson's choice

A classic mulled wine with all the right flavours – plenty of body, a touch of spice and delicious fruit flavours.

Measure 1.1 litres (2 pints) water and 100-175 g (4-6 oz) castor sugar into a large saucepan or preserving pan and stir over low heat to dissolve the sugar. Add a 5 cm (2 inch) cinnamon stick and 6 cloves and infuse for 10 minutes. Strain and return the syrup to the pan. Add 3 bottles red wine and 2 oranges cut in thin slices and heat slowly until almost boiling. Add 100 ml (4 fl oz) each orange curaçao and brandy, then grate a little nutmeg over the top. Remove from the heat and ladle into warmed jugs for serving – leave the fruit in the pan. Serves 25 glasses.

Vin chaud

A delightful 'hot' wine that's only mildly spiced. It's easy to make in small quantities and nice for serving spontaneously, although you can quickly adapt the recipe for larger amounts.

Put 1 bottle red wine, 300 ml (½ pint) water and 100 g (4 oz) castor sugar in a saucepan. Add a 5 cm (2 inch) stick cinnamon and the pared zest (use a vegetable peeler) of 1 lemon. Set over low heat and bring slowly to a simmer. Draw off the heat, cover the pan with a lid and leave to infuse for 10 minutes. Remove the cinnamon and lemon zest. Cut away the peel from 2 more lemons, slice the fruit thinly and place one lemon slice in each serving glass. Pour the warmed wine directly into the glasses. Carry the vin chaud through to guests on a tray. Serves 8 glasses.

DRESSED-UP DRESSINGS

It takes a lot of trying and tasting to become really adept at mixing salad dressings – such a simple mixture but with so many possible combinations. Green salads rely on good dressings, the more individual the better, and, while it's handy to have a quantity ready made in a jar just to shake and use (see below), the serious cook will mix them as the occasion requires.

• Olive oil and wine vinegar are the basis (malt vinegar is too strong and sharp-flavoured) and the usual proportions are three parts oil to one part vinegar. I measure in table-spoons which works out just about right for an average-sized mixture – never drown salad greens in dressing; there should be just enough to shine the leaves and no more.

Olive oil has a dominating flavour and if you're not sure whether you like it or not you can either use it half and half with a lighter grapeseed oil or go right to the top end of the scale and use Extra Virgin Olive Oil (a first cold pressing of selected olives) which is green and fruity but deliciously light-tasting.

There's an assortment of vinegars available, all different in flavour – white or red wine vinegars, sherry vinegar, fruit-flavoured ones like raspberry, and herb vinegars of which I use tarragon wine vinegar the most. All these are wine-based while cider vinegar, very popular in the States, is made from soured cider.

Red wine or sherry vinegar with fruity olive oils are deli-cious in gutsy garlic dressing – especially over salads with a Mediterranean theme that in-clude olives, sweet peppers or aubergines. The combination is also good over the mildly bitter leaves of curly endive and radicchio – these greens can take stronger dressing. For delicate salad leaves use white or tarragon wine vinegar, or lemon juice which has a clean, sparkling flavour, and extra virgin olive oil. Fruit vinegars really do taste of the fruit, especially raspberry which I use in dressings for mixing the likes of pears or apples with, sur-prisingly, cold chicken.

Flavoured oils can be mixed to good effect. Walnut and hazelnut oils have a subtle flavour and can be blended with olive oil or used alone. Start by substituting 1 table-spoon olive oil for a nut oil – I'm particularly fond of hazel-nut oil. A nice idea is to toss toasted chopped walnuts (see page 210) into a salad with a walnut oil dressing. Sesame oil is best used in combination – just 1 teaspoon in a dressing adds a toasty, warm flavour and is delicious when mixed with sliced mushrooms or avocado.

• Start a dressing with freshly milled sea salt and black pep-percorns (grind straight into the salad bowl if you like). Extras are up to you – ½ level teaspoon of Dijon mustard adds a tangy taste although I've graduated on to coarsegrain mustard because it not only adds flavour but makes the dressing look pretty. Add some garlic, fresh peeled and pressed through a garlic crusher, if you like it. Then add the vinegar and stir to dissolve the season-ings. Now add the oil, whisking the mixture with a fork to get an emulsion. Fresh herbs I add last, snipped chives or tarragon, chopped chervil or coriander or torn basil leaves. Fresh herbs look lovely in a dressing and add more flavour.

Oil and vinegar dressing

Make up a quantity of your own basic oil and vinegar dres-sing – it keeps well in a screw-topped jar and all you need to do is shake the jar before using.

Measure a good seasoning of salt and freshly milled pepper into a screw-topped jar. Add 2 level teaspoons wholegrain or Dijon mustard and 75 ml (3 fl oz) tarragon wine vinegar. Cover and shake to dissolve the seasonings. Add 225 ml (8 fl oz) grapeseed or other mild oil and 50 ml (2 fl oz) good olive oil and shake again. If the dressing is made in a food processor or blender it will hold the emulsion. Put seasonings and vinegar in the processor bowl, switch on for a few seconds, then with the machine running pour in the oil of your choice. Store the dressing in the refrigerator. Any extras are best added fresh, just before using. Makes 300 ml (½ pint).

ORIENTAL BEEF WITH PINEAPPLE

SERVES 12

2 kg (4 lb) lean braising steak

3 medium onions

6 stalks celery

3 tablespoons grapeseed or
  other mild oil

2 × approx 350 g cans
  pineapple chunks in natural
  juice

900 ml (1½ pints) beef stock

salt and freshly milled pepper

4 level tablespoons cornflour

2 tablespoons soy sauce

50 g (2 oz) light muscovado
  sugar

4 tablespoons wine vinegar

P Can be prepared ahead: cool,
cover and refrigerate for up to 24
hours. Reheat to simmering before
adding cornflour mixture.

A combination of soy sauce, brown sugar and vinegar provides a pleasant sweet-sharp flavour for those beef pieces. This definitely has an oriental feel about it, so make hot rice the accompaniment.

Heat the oven to 160°C (325°F or gas no. 3).

Trim the steak and cut into bite-sized pieces. Place the meat pieces in two casserole dishes. Peel and chop the onions. Scrub, string and shred the celery. Put the oil in a frying pan and when hot add the onions and fry gently for 20 minutes until softened and golden. Add onion and celery to the meat. Drain the juice from the cans of pineapple chunks and reserve the pineapple. Combine the pineapple juice, beef stock and a seasoning of salt and pepper and, dividing the mixture equally, add to the contents of both casseroles. Cover and set in the oven to cook for 3 hours or until the meat is tender. **P**

In a bowl, combine the cornflour, soy sauce, soft brown sugar and vinegar. Stir to blend, then add half the mixture to the hot contents of each casserole and stir through. Add the reserved pineapple. Recover and return to the oven to cook for a further 40 minutes.

SWEDISH MEATBALLS IN A SOURED CREAM SAUCE

SERVES 12

3 slices white bread

6 tablespoons milk

1 large onion

1.5 kg (3 lb) extra lean minced
  beef

salt and freshly milled pepper

grated nutmeg

3 eggs (size 2)

seasoned flour

75 g (3 oz) butter

1.1 litres (2 pints) beef stock

4 level tablespoons
  concentrated tomato purée

Carefully made meatballs are delicious: these are mildly spiced and slow simmered. It takes a little time and a large frying pan to make and brown them all, but it's worth the effort and once in the oven there is little more to do.

Trim the crusts from the bread slices and crumble the white part into a mixing bowl. Add the milk to moisten and mix with a fork to break up the crumb. Peel and chop the onion. Add the minced beef, onion, a seasoning of salt, pepper and nutmeg and the eggs to the bowl. Mix the ingredients very thoroughly. With wetted fingers, shape the mixture into about 60 small meatballs. Chill for 2 hours to firm them up.

Roll the meatballs in seasoned flour. Melt 25 g (1 oz) of the butter in a good-sized frying pan. When frothing and hot, add a batch of meatballs. Cook until brown on all sides, shaking the

2 level tablespoons wholegrain mustard

1 tablespoon wine vinegar

600 ml (1 pint) soured cream or natural yogurt

3 level tablespoons cornflour

P Can be prepared ahead: cool, cover and refrigerate, keeping meatballs and stock mixture separate, for up to 24 hours. Let meatballs come to room temperature, and bring stock mixture to the boil before continuing with recipe.

pan to keep them moving. Using a perforated spoon, transfer the meatballs to a large roasting tin. Brown the remaining meatballs, adding more butter to the pan as required.

Heat the oven to 180°C (350°F or gas no. 4).

Combine the stock, tomato purée, wholegrain mustard and vinegar and add about one third to the hot frying pan. Stir to pick up the flavouring bits in the pan and bring to the boil. Combine with remaining stock. **P**

Pour the stock mixture over the meatballs. Cover the roasting tin with kitchen foil and set in the oven to cook for 40 minutes.

Combine the soured cream or yogurt and cornflour and stir into the meatballs. Return to the oven to cook for a further 20-30 minutes or until bubbling hot. Serve with basmati rice with onion and spices.

VEGETABLE LASAGNE WITH RICOTTA CHEESE

SERVES 12

5 medium onions

4 cloves garlic

900 g (2 lb) courgettes

6 tablespoons grapeseed or other mild oil

4 × approx 400 g cans chopped tomatoes

3 level tablespoons concentrated tomato purée

2 tablespoons red wine vinegar

2 level teaspoons dried oregano

2 level teaspoons castor sugar

salt and freshly milled pepper

900 g (2 lb) ricotta or curd cheese

2 bunches (6-8 each) spring onions

4 eggs (size 2)

1.1 litre (2 pints) milk

100 g (4 oz) butter

Use lasagne sheets straight from the packet: there is no need to precook them as long as you keep the sauces used moist and thin. Let the prepared dish stand overnight before cooking so the lasagne sheets have time to absorb the liquid and soften.

Start with the vegetable sauce: peel and finely chop four of the onions. Peel the garlic and chop finely. Trim and slice the courgettes. Heat the oil in a large saucepan, add the onions and cook gently to soften and take just a little colour. Add the garlic and cook for a moment longer, then add the courgettes. Cover with the pan lid and stew the courgettes for about 10 minutes, then stir in the contents of the cans of tomatoes, the tomato purée, red wine vinegar, oregano, sugar and a seasoning of salt and pepper. Cover and cook for 15-20 minutes or until you have a delicious vegetable ragoût. Draw off the heat.

Turn the ricotta or curd cheese into a mixing bowl. Trim the spring onions, then finely chop all the white part and some of the green stems. Add the chopped spring onions, the eggs and a seasoning of salt and pepper to the cheese and mix well – the texture should be soft and easy to spread. Set aside while preparing the bechamel sauce.

Pour the milk into a saucepan and add the remaining onion,

100 g (4 oz) plain flour

8-16 sheets lasagne, regular or
 spinach-flavoured

100 g (4 oz) grated Parmesan
 cheese

P Can be prepared ahead: cover
and refrigerate for up to 24 hours.
Let come to room temperature
before baking or allow extra
baking time.

peeled and cut in half. Bring to a simmer, then draw off the heat and let the milk infuse for about 15 minutes. Remove the onion. Melt the butter in saucepan over low heat. Stir in the flour and cook gently for 1 minute, then gradually stir in the hot milk, beating well all the time, to get a smooth sauce. Let the sauce simmer gently for 10 minutes.

Heat the oven to 180°C (350°F or gas no. 4).

Well butter two 1.7 litre (3 pint) square or rectangular baking dishes with deep sides. Cover the base of each with a quarter of the vegetable sauce. Arrange a layer of the lasagne sheets on top. Add the remaining vegetable sauce. Arrange a second layer of lasagne sheets. Spoon over the cheese mixture and spread evenly. Top with the remaining lasagne sheets and pour over the bechamel sauce. Finally sprinkle with the grated parmesan cheese. **P**

Place the prepared lasagne in the heated oven and bake for 1½ hours. Let the mixture settle for 5 minutes, then cut in portions with a wet knife and lift out with a serving slice.

PORK PAPRIKA WITH SOURED CREAM

SERVES 12

2 kg (4 lb) lean pork fillet

900 g (2 lb) onions

2-4 cloves garlic

2 level tablespoons caraway
 seeds

3 tablespoons grapeseed or
 other mild oil

4 level tablespoons paprika

salt and freshly milled pepper

3 level tablespoons
 concentrated tomato purée

900 ml (1½ pints) vegetable
 stock

150 ml (¼ pint) soured cream

2 tablespoons chopped fresh
 parsley

The initial slow simmering of pork, garlic, onions and paprika (with no extra liquid) brings out lots of flavour in this recipe; then the ingredients are transferred to the oven and require no more supervision. Paprika provides a lovely colour and the caraway seeds are a must as they add to the mild spiciness of the sauce.

Trim the meat and cut in bite-sized pieces. Peel and thinly slice the onions. Peel the garlic and mash to a purée with the caraway seeds. Heat the oil in a large saucepan, add the onion and cook gently until soft – about 10 minutes. Add the pork pieces and turn in the hot onions. Add the garlic and caraway seeds, the paprika and a seasoning of salt and pepper. Stir well, cover with the pan lid and turn the heat to its lowest setting. Leave the meat and onions to cook gently for 1 hour. Stir occasionally but add no extra liquid; sufficient will come from the onions and meat as they simmer together. **P**

Heat the oven to 180°C (350°F or gas no. 4).

Combine the tomato purée and stock and stir into the pork mixture. Bring to a simmer, then transfer the contents of the saucepan equally to two casseroles. Cover the casseroles, place

P Can be prepared ahead: cool, cover and refrigerate up to 24 hours. Let come to room temperature before baking.

in the heated oven and cook gently for a further 1½ hours or until the meat is tender.

Check the seasoning. Stir in the 2-3 tablespoons soured cream into each casserole, leaving it a little streaked rather than stirring right through. Sprinkle with chopped parsley before serving.

CHICKEN BRAISED IN BEER WITH PRUNES

MAKES 12

10 skinned chicken breast fillets

4 medium onions

50 g (2 oz) butter

300 ml (½ pint) light ale

900 ml (1½ pints) chicken stock

3 level tablespoons light muscovado sugar

2 tablespoons wholegrain mustard

1 level tablespoon concentrated tomato purée

salt and freshly milled pepper

4 bay leaves

24 tenderized prunes, stoned

3 level tablespoons cornflour

1 tablespoon wine vinegar

6 tablespoons cold water

This is an unusual combination but one that really works well. Use light ale or lager and you will find it gives the gravy a rich flavour – helped of course by onion, mustard, brown sugar and a dash of vinegar. The chicken breasts are sliced to ensure it's fork food.

Heat the oven to 180°C (350°F or gas no. 4).

Trim the chicken breast fillets and cut diagonally in thick slices. Place the chicken pieces in two casserole dishes. Peel and thinly slice the onions. Heat the butter in a large frying pan, add the onions and cook gently to soften, then raise the heat and let them brown – this takes about 15 minutes. Draw the pan off the heat. Add the light ale and stir well to pick up all the flavouring bits, then pour over the chicken pieces.

Combine the chicken stock, sugar, wholegrain mustard and tomato purée. Mix and pour equally over the chicken pieces. Add a seasoning of salt and freshly milled pepper to each casserole along with the bay leaves and prunes. Cover the casseroles, set in the heated oven and cook for 1½ hours.

In a bowl, combine the cornflour, vinegar and water. About 20 minutes before the end of the cooking time, stir up the cornflour blend and mix half into the hot contents of each casserole. Recover and complete the cooking time.

BASMATI RICE WITH ONION AND SPICES

SERVES 12

700 g (1½ lbs) basmati rice
2 medium onions
50 g (2 oz) butter
2 level tablespoons fennel seeds
2 level teaspoons whole mustard seeds
1.7 litres (3 pints) boiling water
1 level tablespoon salt
10 whole black peppercorns
3 bay leaves

Oven cooking is an easy way to prepare rice for a crowd – it needs very little supervision and there's no need to drain the rice because all the liquid is absorbed.

Heat the oven to 160°C (325°F or gas no. 3).

Wash the rice grains thoroughly and drain well. Peel and finely chop the onions. Melt the butter in a large saucepan, add the chopped onions and fry for a few minutes to soften. Add the fennel seeds and whole mustard seeds and fry for a few moments longer, then add the rice and mix into the butter, onion and spices. Transfer the hot rice mixture to a large casserole.

Stir in the boiling water and add the salt, lightly crushed peppercorns and the bay leaves. Cover with a lid, place in the heated oven and cook undisturbed for 45-50 minutes. When ready the rice will have absorbed all the liquid and the grains will be tender. Fluff up the grains with a fork, or turn the rice into hot dishes for serving.

SPICED CHICKEN SATAYS

SERVES 12

12 skinned chicken breast fillets
4 lemons, for serving
For the marinade
300 ml (½ pint) natural yogurt
1 level teaspoon mild chilli powder
½ level teaspoon ground cumin
½ level teaspoon ground coriander
½ level teaspoon ground ginger
2 level teaspoons garam masala
1 level tablespoon concentrated tomato purée
grated zest and juice 2 lemons
2 cloves garlic
salt and freshly milled pepper

Serve these cold but not chilled. The yogurt marinade tenderizes the chicken and the satays are grilled to cook so they have a crusty, golden appearance. The wooden satay sticks are essential: not only do they look good but they make it easier for guests to pick up the individual servings.

Trim the chicken fillets and cut each one into three slices lengthways. Arrange in a large shallow dish. Combine the yogurt, chilli powder, cumin, coriander, ginger and garam masala in a mixing bowl. Add the concentrated tomato purée, grated lemon zest and lemon juice. Peel the garlic and crush to a purée with a little salt. Add to the marinade along with a good seasoning of freshly milled pepper. Pour over the chicken pieces and mix well. Cover and leave to marinate for at least 4 hours or overnight in the refrigerator.

Heat the grill to moderately hot. Line the grill pan with foil, lightly grease the grill rack and set about 7.5 cm (3 inches) below the heat source. Lift the chicken pieces from the marinade and thread the pieces 'concertina' style on to each of

P Can be prepared ahead: cover and refrigerate for up to 3 hours.

the 12 soaked wooden satay sticks – push two or more pieces on to each one. Set under the heated grill (in batches) and cook for 10-15 minutes, turning them once or twice. Let cool completely. **P** Serve with lemon wedges for squeezing over.

CHICKEN IN A SWEET CURRIED DRESSING

SERVES 12

2 × 2 kg (4 lb) oven ready chickens

75 g (3 oz) butter

75 g (3 oz) flaked almonds

fresh coriander, to garnish

For the dressing

1 medium onion

2 tablespoons grapeseed or other mild oil

2 level tablespoons curry paste

2 level tablespoons concentrated tomato purée

225 ml (8 fl oz) red wine

2 tablespoon wine vinegar

4 level tablespoons mango chutney

900 g (2 lb) fromage frais

P Can be prepared ahead: cover and refrigerate for up to 6 hours.

A popular flavour but quite different from the usual recipe, this sauce is made using fromage frais and the result is tangy and fresh-tasting. Serve with a garnish of exotic fruit such as mango or papaya cut in chunks.

Heat the oven to 200°C (400°F or gas no. 4).

Remove the chicken giblets and place a knob of butter in each body cavity. Spread the remaining butter all over the chickens and place together in a large roasting tin. Set in the heated oven and roast for 1½ hours. Allow to cool completely.

Peel and finely chop the onion. Heat the oil in a saucepan, add the onion and fry gently to soften. Stir in the curry paste, tomato purée, red wine and wine vinegar. Bring to a simmer and cook gently for about 10 minutes to make a thick spicy sauce. Draw off the heat and add the mango chutney. Allow to cool, then purée the mixture in a food processor. For a very smooth sauce, press the mixture through a sieve.

Turn the fromage frais into a large mixing bowl and stir in the curried dressing. Joint the cold chickens. Discard the skin and lift the meat from the bones. Cut the meat into bite-sized pieces and add to the dressing. **P**

Toast the flaked almonds (see page 210).

Turn the chicken and dressing on to serving platters. Sprinkle with the toasted flaked almonds and add a garnish of fresh coriander leaves.

Chicken Tarragon Salad with Toasted Pine Nuts

SERVES 12

2 × 2 kg (4 lb) oven ready chickens
75 g (3 oz) butter
6 stalks celery
2 bunches (6-8 each) spring onions
300 ml (½ pint) mayonnaise
300 ml (½ pint) natural yogurt
2 level teaspoons Dijon mustard
1 tablespoon tarragon wine vinegar
salt and freshly milled pepper
75 g (3 oz) pine nuts
chopped fresh tarragon, to garnish

P Can be prepared ahead: cover and refrigerate for up to 24 hours.

Carefully prepared chicken salad is a useful buffet dish and invariably popular. Here's a version using a tangy tarragon-flavoured dressing. Toasted flaked almonds or chopped pecans are alternatives for garnish, but do try pine nuts if you can get them – they look so unusual.

Heat the oven to 200°C (400°F or gas no. 6).

Remove the chicken giblets and place a knob of butter in each body cavity. Spread the remaining butter all over the chickens and place together in a large roasting tin. Set in the heated oven and roast for 1½ hours. Allow to cool completely.

Scrub and string the celery stalks, then shred finely. Trim the spring onions, then finely chop all the white and some of the green stems. Measure the mayonnaise, yogurt, mustard, tarragon wine vinegar and a seasoning of salt and pepper into a large mixing bowl.

Joint the cold chickens, discard skin and lift the meat from the bones. Cut the chicken meat into bite-sized pieces. Add the chicken, celery and spring onions to the dressing. **P**

Toast the pine nuts (see page 210).

Turn the chicken salad on to serving platters. Sprinkle with the pine nuts and chopped tarragon to garnish.

Boned Duck Roll

SERVES 8-10

1 × 2.2 kg (5 lb) fresh duck, oven ready
For the stuffing
4 skinned chicken breast fillets
1 medium onion
1 clove garlic
50 g (2 oz) butter
100 g (4 oz) fresh white breadcrumbs
1 egg (size 2)
salt and freshly milled pepper
12 tenderized prunes, stoned

A boned bird makes serving easier – just slice this duck right across – and it goes a long way. The dark prune garnish shows up attractively against the white chicken meat stuffing.

Boning a duck is simply a matter of taking a sharp knife around the carcass and removing it, then cutting out the wing and thigh joints. It takes time but it's not difficult. The important thing is not to cut through the skin of the bird.

Put the duck on a board, breast down and make a cut with a sharp knife along the backbone. Starting on one side of the bird, scrape the meat away from the carcass, holding the knife blade flat against the side of the carcass to avoid slashing the skin. Break the socket joint at the wing and thigh and cut through the meat around them. Take special care when you get

P Can be prepared ahead: cover and refrigerate for up to 24 hours.

to the breast bone as you will be cutting close to the skin. Lift the carcass away and then take each wing and leg in turn, first cutting through the meat to the bone and then scraping the meat away from around it. Lay the boned duck out flat on a chopping board.

To make the stuffing, pass the chicken breasts through the coarse blade of a mincer or chop them in a food processor. Peel and finely chop the onion. Peel the garlic and chop finely. Melt the butter in a saucepan, add the onion and cook gently until softened – about 5 minutes. Add the garlic and cook for a moment more. Turn the onion mixture into the breadcrumbs and stir with a fork. Add the chicken, the egg and a good seasoning of salt and freshly milled pepper. Mix very thoroughly by hand or with a wooden spoon.

Press half the stuffing mixture down the centre of the boned duck. Then add the prunes in pairs, running the length of the duck on top of the stuffing. Cover with the remaining stuffing. Draw the sides of the boned duck up over the stuffing to enclose it. With trussing needle and string, sew the duck closed. Turn the bird over so the breast faces upwards and press into a neat shape. Tie with string at intervals like a joint of meat.

Heat the oven to 180°C (350°F or gas no. 4).

Place the duck roll on a rack in a roasting tin. Set in the heated oven and roast for 1½ hours – there is no need to baste. Allow to cool completely. **P**

Serve cut in slices with pickled fruits (see page 194).

SUGAR BAKED GAMMON WITH PICKLED FRUITS

SERVES 24

1 whole gammon on the bone, about 6.4 kg (14 lb)

3 level tablespoons French mustard

3-4 level tablespoons demerara sugar

A whole gammon is very economical for a large buffet and when it's cooked on the bone the flavour is superb. Soak the joint very thoroughly, then you can oven roast, and, if you put the whole thing inside a roasting bag it will cook beautifully.

Let the gammon soak in cold water to cover for two days, changing the water for fresh at least once – this will eliminate most of the salt. Drain well.

Heat the oven to 160°C (325°F or gas no. 3).

Wrap the gammon in a large sheet of kitchen foil or place inside a large roasting bag. Set skin side up in the biggest roasting tin you have. Set the gammon in the oven centre and roast, allowing 20 minutes per 450 g (1 lb) – in this case about 4½ hours. Slow roasting is best for a really large joint on the bone.

About 15-20 minutes before the end of the cooking time, remove the gammon from the oven and raise the oven temperature to 220°C (425°F or gas no. 7). Open up the foil (or cut open the roasting bag) and take care to let the juices run into the roasting tin. Then using a sharp knife, carefully strip the rind from the joint and slash the fat in a 'criss-cross' diagonal pattern. Smear the fat with the mustard, then sprinkle with demerara sugar, pressing it on to the surface.

Replace the gammon in the oven and after 15-20 minutes it should be beautifully glazed and golden. Let the joint cool slowly overnight. **P**

Serve cold thinly carved, with tangy pickled fruits (see below).

● Smaller gammon joints vary from between 1.5 kg (3 lb) to 4 kg (8 lb) and they can be oven cooked in the same way. My favourites are corner gammon 1.5 kg (3 lb) for serving along with other cold meats and middle gammon 2 kg (4 lb) – 4.9 kg (6 lb) for a buffet. Let your joint soak for 24 hours. Then oven roast (as above) allowing 30 minutes per 450 g (1 lb) for joints up to 1.5 kg (3 lb) at 190° C (375° F or gas no. 5); reduce cooking time to 25 minutes per 450 g (1 lb) for joints up to 4.9 kg (6 lb) at 180° C (350° F or gas no. 4); and for joints over 4.9 kg (6 lb) allow only 20 minutes per 450 g (1 lb) at 160° C (325°F or gas no. 3). Any joint can be glazed and served as above.

PICKLED FRUITS

MAKES SUFFICIENT FOR ABOUT 25 SERVINGS

2 large onions

2 large lemons

600 ml (1 pint) cold water

300 ml (½ pint) sherry vinegar

450 g (1 lb) light muscovado sugar

This sweet-sharp pickle is made with dried apricots and prunes, the tenderized ones that are ready to eat straight from the packet. These taste best after 24 hours.

Peel the onions and slice into fine rings. Slice the lemons very thinly and discard the pips. Measure the water into a saucepan, add the onions and bring to the boil. Add the lemon slices, sherry vinegar, soft brown sugar, whole apricots and prunes. Bring back to the boil, stirring once or twice to dissolve the

225 g (8 oz) tenderized whole
dried apricots

225 g (8 oz) tenderized prunes,
stoned

sugar. Reduce the heat to a gentle simmer, cover with the pan lid and cook gently for 20-25 minutes or until the fruits are plump and soft.

Draw off the heat and leave until quite cold. Then transfer the fruit to a storage container and refrigerate. **P**

To serve, turn the fruits and some of the syrup into serving bowls and let guests fork out pieces. Or spoon into orange serving shells (see below) and arrange round the edge of each serving platter.

● **To make orange shells** Cut about 6 oranges in half across the equator, then loosen the segments and discard along with the white pith. Blanch the shells by simmering in boiling water to cover for about 20 minutes, then drain and separate out to cool.

P Can be prepared ahead: will keep up to 1 month.

WHOLE POACHED SALMON

SERVES 12

1 whole salmon, about 2-2.2 kg (4-5 lb)

salt

1 tablespoon vinegar (optional)

1 cucumber

chopped fresh parsley (optional)

A whole poached salmon makes a wonderful buffet party centrepiece and it's not difficult to prepare, but you will need a fish kettle. Check with your fishmonger – quite often they will lend a kettle to a customer buying a whole fish.

The fishmonger will gut the salmon for you but leave the head on. If you like, take the head off *after* cooking – otherwise you will loose precious juices during the cooking.

Set the fish on the rack and put the rack in the fish kettle. Add cold water to cover the fish and lift the fish out (on the rack). Add salt to the water – about 2 teaspoons – and a tablespoon of vinegar if you like. Set the kettle over the heat and bring the water to the boil. Lower the fish (on the rack) back into the simmering water, let it come back to the boil and cook for 2 minutes only. Draw off the heat, cover the kettle with the lid and leave the salmon overnight – it will continue to cook in the reducing heat of the water and will be perfectly done the next day. If it is possible to lift the kettle to a cool place (such as a pantry), it is better but the weight will require two people to lift the pan.

Next day, lift it out of the poaching water on the rack and slide off on to a sheet of greaseproof paper. Peel the skin from one side, then roll the salmon over and remove the skin from the second side. Remove the fins and scrape away any creamy brown curd that lies along the surface. Using the greaseproof

P Can be prepared ahead: cover and keep in a cool place for up to 24 hours.

paper, lift and roll the salmon on to a serving plate.

If you remove the bone from the fish it will be easier to serve. Do it this way – run a knife along the length of the fish to divide the upper fillet in two. Using a spatula, carefully lift these fillets off. With scissors, snip through the backbone at the neck and tail end and lift the bone away. Replace the top fillets to reshape the fish.

To keep the flesh moist, decorate the entire fish with cucumber slices cut very thinly (use a mandoline cutter): really thin slices take the curve of the fish and show the pink flesh through from underneath. Lay the slices from head to tail so they resemble fish scales. If you don't like the look of the head, cover it with chopped parsley. **P**

Serve with homemade plain or tarragon mayonnaise (see page 166).

SEAFOOD TERRINE

SERVES 8

900 g (2 lb) fresh, skinned
  whiting, haddock or sole
  fillets

350 g (12 oz) fresh salmon or
  pink trout fillets

1 bunch fresh watercress,
  or 3 tablespoons chopped
  fresh chives

4 egg whites (size 2)

salt and freshly milled pepper

grated nutmeg

300 ml (½ pint) double cream,
  chilled

For the tomato vinaigrette

2 ripe tomatoes

50 ml (2 fl oz) red wine vinegar

100 ml (4 fl oz) olive oil

salt and freshly milled pepper

1 tablespoon chopped fresh
  tarragon leaves

Decorate the top of this terrine with shapely fresh coriander or dark watercress leaves before serving, then slice with a very sharp knife – you'll find it helps if you dip the blade in hot water between each slice.

Cut the white fish fillets into small pieces. Remove any skin from the salmon or pink trout fillets and cut into 2.5 cm (1 inch) wide strips. Pick the leafy tops from the watercress and place in a colander. Pour through boiling water from the kettle to blanch, then drain well, pressing out excess moisture. Reserve the watercress leaves. Lightly mix the egg whites.

Heat the oven to 160°C (325°F or gas no. 3). Lightly oil a 1.4 litre (2½ pint) terrine and line the base with a strip of oiled greaseproof paper.

Place the white fish in the bowl of a food processor. Using the on/off switch, chop the fish coarsely. Add the egg whites in about three lots, buzzing each addition with the on/off switch to purée but without over-mixing. Add the blanched watercress (or chives), a seasoning of salt and pepper and a little grated nutmeg and blend again for a moment. Turn the mixture into a chilled mixing bowl. With a wooden spoon, gradually beat in the chilled double cream. Taste for seasoning.

Turn half the mixture into the prepared terrine and spread level. Cover with a layer of the salmon or pink trout strips. Add the remaining white fish mixture. Cover the top of the mixture with a strip of lightly oiled greaseproof paper and then overwrap the tin with a covering of kitchen foil. Place the terrine in a larger roasting tin and add boiling water from the kettle to the tin to come 2.5 cm (1 inch) up the sides of the terrine. Set in the heated oven and bake for 1-1¼ hours. To test if the terrine is cooked, push a skewer into the centre of the mixture and leave for 1 minute; then hold the skewer against your wrist – it should feel hot. Let the terrine cool, then remove the foil covering. Cover the terrine with a plate or piece of card and a weight and refrigerate overnight. **P**

To make the vinaigrette, scald the tomatoes in boiling water and peel away the skins. Deseed the tomatoes and cut the flesh in small dice. In a mixing bowl, combine the red wine vinegar, oil and a seasoning of salt and freshly milled pepper. Stir in the chopped tomato and the tarragon leaves.

Remove the weight and covering from the terrine and unmould it on to a chopping board. Peel off the base paper and cut the terrine in 1 cm (½ inch) thick slices. Arrange on a large serving platter and pass the tomato vinaigrette separately.

COLESLAW WITH PINEAPPLE, GRAPES AND DATES

SERVES 2

1 white cabbage, about 900 g (2 lb)

350 g (12 oz) green grapes

2 × approx 225 g cans pineapple slices in natural juice

450 g (1 lb) fresh dates

300 ml (½ pint) natural yogurt

300 ml (½ pint) mayonnaise

1 level tablespoon Dijon mustard

2 tablespoons wine vinegar

salt and freshly milled pepper

P Can be prepared ahead: cover and refrigerate for no longer than overnight.

Coleslaw is a good buffet salad. It stands up well and actually improves in flavour when made ahead. Here unusual fruits make the mixture suitably party-style.

Discard any outer bruised leaves from the cabbage, then cut first in half and then in quarters. Slice away the hard stalk, then shred the cabbage finely across the leaves – a mandoline slicer is invaluable here for really fine coleslaw shreds. Rinse the shredded cabbage in salt water and drain in a colander. Turn into a large bowl.

Wash, halve and deseed the grapes. Drain the pineapple slices and cut in neat dice. Nick the dates at the stalk end, then squeeze them out of the skins. Remove the date stones and chop the dates coarsely. Add the fruit to the cabbage shreds.

Combine the natural yogurt, mayonnaise, mustard and vinegar. Add to the salad and turn to mix the ingredients. Season to taste with salt and freshly milled pepper. **P**

Give the coleslaw a good mix (the dressing tends to drop to the bottom) and turn into a serving bowl.

Overleaf: Seafood terrine and tomato vinaigrette

WHOLEWHEAT AND CHICK PEA SALAD

SERVES 12

350 g (12 oz) wholewheat

2 × approx 400 g cans chick peas

2 medium onions

2 red sweet peppers

4 cloves garlic

150 ml (¼ pint) grapeseed or other mild oil

2 level teaspoons ground cumin

2 level teaspoons ground coriander

4 tablespoons red wine vinegar

2 level teaspoons wholegrain mustard

P Can be prepared ahead: cover and refrigerate for no longer than overnight.

I've done my best to look for unusual salads and this is one that I particularly like. Wholewheat (from a health food store) and chick peas have lots of texture and they are marinated in a spicy cooked dressing. Remember that bean salads need lots of extra flavour.

Soak the wholewheat overnight in water to cover.

Drain the soaked wholewheat and place in a saucepan. Add fresh cold water to cover and bring to a simmer. Cook gently for 20-25 minutes or until tender – test a grain; it should be pleasantly chewy. Drain and turn into a mixing bowl.

Drain the chick peas, rinse under cold water and add to the wholewheat. Set aside while preparing the dressing.

Peel and finely chop the onions. Halve, deseed and thinly slice the red peppers. Peel and finely chop the garlic. Heat 3 tablespoons of the oil in a frying pan. Add the onions and cook gently until softened. Add the red peppers and the chopped garlic and fry for a further few minutes to soften the peppers. Add the cumin and coriander and stir well. Cook for a moment to draw out the flavourings.

Stir in the rest of the oil, the vinegar and the mustard. Bring to a simmer and pour over the wholewheat and chick peas. Toss and leave the salad to marinate for at least 4 hours in a cool place. **P**

GOLDEN RICE SALAD WITH APRICOTS AND ALMONDS

SERVES 12

225 g (8 oz) dried apricots

juice 3 oranges

450 g (1 lb) long-grain rice

1 medium onion

3 tablespoons grapeseed or other mild oil

1 level teaspoon turmeric

1 level teaspoon ground coriander

900 ml (1½ pints) water

This pretty rice salad won't get left out because it looks very appetizing. It is yellow in colour from the addition of turmeric, with sweet apricots and the crunch of toasted flaked almonds added at the last moment.

Rinse the apricots, then cut in slivers. Soak in the squeezed orange juice for several hours (or overnight).

Wash the rice grains and drain well. Peel and finely chop the onion. Heat the oil in a large saucepan, add the onion and fry gently to soften. Add the turmeric and coriander and stir for a moment over the heat, then add the rice grains and turn in the onion and spices. Stir in the water, add the salt and bring

1 level teaspoon salt
150 ml (¼ pint) oil and vinegar dressing (see page 185)
2 bunches (6-8 each) spring onions
75 g (3 oz) flaked almonds

P Can be prepared ahead: cover and refrigerate for up to 24 hours.

to a simmer, stirring until the water reboils. Cover with the pan lid and cook over low heat for 20 minutes or until rice is just tender and liquid is absorbed. Draw off the heat and leave undisturbed for a further 10 minutes.

Measure the dressing into a mixing bowl. Turn the hot rice into the dressing and mix to coat the rice grains thoroughly. Let cool. **P**

Trim the spring onions, then chop all the white part and some of the green stems. Add the spring onions and soaked apricots with any orange juice to the rice and fork through.

Just before serving, toast the almonds (see page 00) and fork through the salad.

WILTED CUCUMBER SALAD

SERVES 12

2 medium cucumbers
salt
50 g (2 oz) castor sugar
4 tablespoons boiling water
6 tablespoons white wine vinegar
freshly milled pepper
3 tablespoons chopped fresh chives

P Can be prepared ahead: keep refrigerated for up to 8 hours.

The Scandinavians have a way of serving cucumber that is quite different – the dressing is sweet-sour and very fresh. This dressing softens the cucumber slices so they are wilted rather than crunchy. It goes especially well with cold meats or chicken and with a fish mousse.

Rinse the cucumbers and dry, then slice thinly without removing the skin – a mandoline slicer is excellent for this. Layer the slices in a colander, sprinkling them with salt, and leave to drain for about 1 hour to draw out the excess moisture. Rinse under the cold tap and then press cucumber dry in absorbent kitchen paper.

Measure the sugar into a mixing bowl, add the boiling water and stir to dissolve the sugar. Add the wine vinegar and the cucumber slices. Season with freshly milled pepper. Cover and refrigerate for at least 1 hour. **P**

Turn into serving dishes, sprinkle with chopped chives and serve with a fork to scoop out the slices.

CHOCOLATE CHEESECAKE

SERVES 12

75 g (3 oz) shelled hazelnuts
50 g (2 oz) butter
200 g (7 oz) shortbread biscuits
350 g (12 oz) plain chocolate
700 g (1½ lb) curd cheese

Very luscious and rich-tasting. Don't worry if a split appears on the surface during baking – cheesecakes nearly always crack just a little bit. Prepare this one ahead, so it really does have a chance to chill and firm up for serving.

Heat the oven to 160°C (325°F or gas no. 3).

Skin and toast the hazelnuts (see page 210). Melt the butter in

175 g (6 oz) light muscovado
  sugar

3 eggs (size 2)

225 g (8 oz) fromage frais

150 ml (¼ pint) double cream

cocoa powder, to decorate

P Can be prepared ahead: keep
refrigerated for up to 24 hours.

a saucepan over low heat. Break the shortbread biscuits into the bowl of a food processor, add 50 g (2 oz) of the hazelnuts and process both to fine crumbs. Stir in the melted butter.

Turn the crumb mixture into a 22.5cm (9 inch) spring clip tin and press over the bottom and up the sides. Set in the heated oven and bake for 15 minutes.

Meanwhile, break the chocolate into a medium mixing bowl and set over a saucepan of hot (not boiling) water to melt. Turn the curd cheese into a large mixing bowl, add the soft brown sugar and beat until smooth and creamy. Beat in the eggs one at a time. Add the melted chocolate and the fromage frais and mix through.

Pour into the crumb-lined tin and spread level. Return to the heated oven and bake for 50 minutes or until the cheesecake is firm. Let cool completely, then cover and refrigerate for at least 24 hours. **P**

Loosen the sides and remove the cheesecake from the tin. Whip the cream to soft peaks and spoon or pipe around the cheesecake border. Decorate with the remaining toasted hazelnuts and a dusting of cocoa powder and chill.

Brown Sugar Meringues with a Caramel and Lime Sauce

MAKES 12

50 g (2 oz) walnut pieces

175 g (6 oz) light muscovado
  sugar

3 egg whites (size 2)

½ teaspoon white wine vinegar
  or lemon juice

300 ml (½ pint) double cream

**For the caramel and lime
  sauce**

225 g (8 oz) granulated sugar

175 ml (6 fl oz) water

juice 1 lime

2 tablespoons rum

Soft brown sugar gives these meringues the most wonderful flavour and golden colour. Do dry the sugar in the oven before starting the recipe; it's the trick that makes these successful and it only takes a few moments while the oven is heating up.

Toast the walnuts in a dry frying pan over medium heat to bring up the flavour, then chop or buzz them in a food processor to medium fine pieces.

Heat the oven to 150°C (300°F or gas no. 2). Put the sugar on a baking tray and slip into the oven (as it is heating up) for about 15 minutes to dry. Then crush the sugar with a rolling pin to make it fine and powdery – this is easy if you tip the sugar into a polythene bag and then roll the bag. Cut two sheets of non-stick baking parchment to fit two baking sheets and fix the paper in position with a smear of fat on the baking sheet at each corner.

In a large mixing bowl, whisk the egg whites to stiff peaks. Add half the sugar, one tablespoon at a time, while whisking

P Can be prepared ahead: store meringues in an airtight tin or polythene bag. Cover sauce and keep in a cool place.

well. Whisk in the vinegar or lemon juice. Sprinkle in the remaining sugar along with 2 tablespoons of the chopped nuts and fold in gently using the cutting edge of a tablespoon.

Scoop dessertspoons of the mixture on to the lined baking sheets – you should get 24 shells. Sprinkle each shell with the remaining chopped walnuts. Set in the heated oven and immediately lower the oven heat to 110°C (225°F or Gas ¼). The shells will take about 2 hours to firm up. Slip a palette knife under each one and turn them on their sides. Turn the oven heat right down to lowest setting and leave the shells to dry out for a further 1 hour. Allow to cool completely. **P**

Measure the granulated sugar for the sauce into a dry saucepan. Set over medium heat and stir – as the sugar heats it will begin to melt, first in lumps and then to a golden caramel. Draw off the heat and add the measured water – cover your hand with a cloth since the hot caramel will boil up furiously with the addition of a cold liquid. Replace the pan over the heat and stir until the mixture forms a clear caramel syrup. Pour into a bowl, add the lime juice (it's a good idea to cut a lime slice for decoration before squeezing the fruit) and the rum and leave until cold. **P**

About 2 hours before serving, sandwich the meringue shells with the whipped double cream. Refrigerate for at least 2 hours so meringues soften. Serve with the caramel and lime sauce – with one slice of lime floating.

PINEAPPLE DACQUOISE

SERVES 6 (MAKE 2 FOR 12 SERVINGS)

3 egg whites (size 2)

175 g (6 oz) castor sugar

1 teaspoon vinegar or lemon juice

50 g (2 oz) ground almonds

For the filling

½ fresh pineapple

300 ml (½ pint) double cream

icing sugar, for the top

Almond-flavoured meringue layers filled with whipped cream and slices of fresh pineapple gives a happy contrast of sweet and sharp. Segments of orange or sliced kiwi fruits are nice too.

Heat the oven to 150°C (300°F or gas no. 2).

Select two baking sheets and cut a sheet of non-stick baking parchment to fit each one. On each sheet mark a 20 cm (8 inch) circle with pencil (use a plate as a guide). Turn the papers over (so the pencilled outline is underneath) and fix on to the baking sheets with a smear of fat at each corner (the paper will remain in position when you spoon and spread the meringue).

Whisk the egg whites to stiff peaks. Add half the sugar, one tablespoon at a time, whisking well after each addition of sugar. Continue whisking until the meringue is thick and glossy, then whisk in the vinegar or lemon juice. Fold in the remaining sugar and the ground almonds using a tablespoon to cut

P Can be prepared ahead: keep in a tightly lidded tin or polythene bag for up to 3 days.

through the mixture gently.

Divide the meringue between the two prepared baking sheets. Use a spoon to push the mixture out to a round, keeping within the pencilled outline. Set in the heated oven and bake for 40 minutes – the layers will be light golden and crisp when ready. Cool completely. **P**

Cut away the stalk and base from the pineapple, then cut into wedges lengthways. Trim away the peel from each wedge and cut across into thin slices. Whip the cream to soft peaks and spoon over one meringue layer. Arrange the pineapple pieces over the cream and top with the second meringue layer. Refrigerate for at least 2 hours. Dust with icing sugar and cut in slices for serving.

APPLE STRUDELS IN A LEMON SYRUP

MAKES 12

12 sheets filo pastry, thawed
50 g (2 oz) butter
450 g (1 lb) dessert apples
50 g (2 oz) shelled walnuts
50 g (2 oz) sultanas
50 g (2 oz) light muscovado sugar
50 g (2 oz) fresh white breadcrumbs
½ level teaspoon ground cinnamon
For the lemon syrup
100 g (4 oz) castor sugar
2 lemons

P Can be prepared ahead: cover and refrigerate for up to 6 hours. Return strudels, in the baking dish, to a heated 160°C (325°F or gas no. 3) oven for 15-20 minutes to warm through before serving.

Using paper-thin prepared sheets of filo pastry takes all the hard work out of making apple strudels. These are prepared as individual ones which makes them perfect for a buffet. The lemon syrup adds a tangy flavour.

Lay the filo sheets out flat (in a stack) and cover with a damp cloth to prevent them drying out. Melt the butter and set aside. Peel core and *finely* chop the apples into a mixing bowl. Finely chop the walnuts and add to the apples along with the sultanas, soft brown sugar, breadcrumbs and cinnamon and mix well.

Work with one sheet of filo at a time. Brush all over with melted butter, then fold the sheet in half lengthways and brush with butter again. Place a spoonful of the apple filling 2.5 cm (1 inch) in from the top end and fold the sides of the filo sheet in over the filling to meet right along the length of the pastry. Fold the top 2.5 cm (1 inch) in over the filling and roll to the end of the pastry to completely enclose the apple mixture. Place in a large buttered baking dish with the ends of the pastry underneath. Repeat with the remaining filling and filo sheets to make 12 individual strudels. **P**

Heat the oven to 190°C (375°F or gas no. 5).

Brush each filled strudel with melted butter. Set in the heated oven and bake for 30-35 minutes or until golden brown.

Meanwhile, measure the sugar for the syrup into a saucepan. Add the finely grated rind of 1 lemon and the squeezed juice of both. Stir over low heat until the sugar has dissolved and a syrup is formed. Pour the hot syrup over the baked strudels, turning, to coat them in the syrup. Serve warm. **P**

DRINKS PARTIES

Blue cheese dip with sweet pepper strips

Guacamole dip with tortilla chips

·

Smokie mousse on pumpernickle

Houmous with black olives on melba toast

Celery stuffed with Stilton pâté

Smoked mackerel croûtes

Taramosalata croûtes

Aubergine and mushroom croûtes

Smoked salmon and cucumber canapés

·

Pizza bites

Goat's cheese toasts

Ginger chicken satays

Smoked salmon rolls

Hot bacon roll-ups

Sesame prawn fingers

Salted and spiced nuts

DRINKS
PARTIES

People have to stand for drinks parties so don't let them drag on. Be specific about the arrival and departure time; it makes things much easier and puts everybody in the picture. A drinks party can be intimidating if you don't know anybody, so this is an occasion when the hostess should look after guests with extra care.

The kind of snack you serve with drinks is not meant to provide a meal. Foods to eat on an occasion such as this should be bite-sized and pretty. Avoid those fearful bouchées as well as anything made from puff pastry, which will flake and crumble all over the carpet, and anything fried and greasy unless it's speared on a cocktail stick. Hot snacks are nice but have only one on the menu or you'll be in the kitchen all the time as they need to be heated in relays to keep them on the go.

Because foods are cut small you'll find recipes go quite a long way. When working out the quantities you'll need to reckon on about six to eight items per person. That's usually enough. There is no need for too many different items – three or four eats will look surprisingly busy when you get them together.

Clear the kitchen before you start on the preparation because you will need lots of space. Small items like these have to be laid out; it's difficult to stack or store them. For ease and speed, go for recipes that you can bake as a whole and then cut up, or decorate in strips and then slice into small pieces – decorating numerous small items is hard work. Collect together your prettiest pastry cutters and remember that a nylon piping bag, fitted with a plain nozzle, makes it quicker to squeeze on toppings than spooning each one. And, if you don't want to bother with bits of pastry, slices of cucumber, celery stalks, chicory leaves, mushroom caps or bits of red sweet pepper make good containers.

Pretty arrangements make good impressions. You should have plenty of small offerings – cocktail snacks look wonderful on black trays and large meat platters are useful too. Have a mixture of items together but arrange them in orderly rows rather than a

Pages 206-207: clockwise, Filo triangles with garlic and herb filling (p. 146), salted and spiced nuts, pear slices with parma ham, houmous with black olives on melba toast, smokie mousse on pumpernickel and crunchy marinated vegetables (p. 146)

jumble and they will look very professional. Add a discreet garnish but choose one that won't wilt – no lettuce leaves or watercress that will droop in a warm room. Frilled celery or spring onion pieces, made by trimming stalks into 5 cm (2 inch) pieces, slashing the ends and then soaking in iced water until the fringes curl back, are my favourites. Cover prepared eats with clear film and they will keep fresh for up to 4 hours in a cool place.

People like to circulate at drinks parties and it's better for the party if they do. Make it easier by clearing smaller pieces of furniture out of the way. And encourage guests to pick up a tray of eats and circulate with it – it's a good opportunity to meet and talk to people – a colleague of mine met her husband that way. Depending on the occasion, offer red and white wine, and have mineral water, fruit juices and a non-alcoholic fruit cup to hand. For a winter party, mulled wine served from jugs is fun.

MIDDAY DRINKS

Cool, subtle, sparkling or non-alcoholic, there are plenty of alternatives.

- Chilled white wine – a good Chablis or Sancerre served cool and fresh – or a light fragrant vermouth such as Chamberey.
- Champagne is the most delicious midday drink – an expensive bottle is best appreciated on its own. Less expensive champagne or sparkling wine gets a lift if mixed with orange, mango, peach or lychee juice – in half and half proportions or as strong as you would like.
- White wine with crème de cassis (blackcurrant), mûre (blackberry) or framboise (raspberry) – a teaspoonful in a glass topped up with the chilled wine makes the wine lightly coloured and subtly flavoured. Experiment and use sparkling wine or champagne, if you like.
- A spritzer is wine made a bit longer with soda water – pleasant and very light. Use about one-third white wine to two-thirds soda water. Add a slice of lemon or fruit to make it look pretty, but no ice.
- Pure apple juice is fresh-tasting with ice or a slice of fruit and a bit of fresh mint in tall glasses.
- Pimms – a wonderful gin-based mix which should be served in tall glasses and topped up with good quality lemonade (follow directions on the bottle). Serve with ice, cucumber, a twist of lemon peel and sprig of fresh borage – all summer in a glass.
- Any fruit juice topped up with sparkling mineral water – something fizzy makes fruit juice more interesting. Add slices of any fruit to the glass that is appropriate.
- A fruit syrup such as Elderflower cordial served well chilled with ice and a dash of water is quite delicious. Elderflower has the most stunning, perfumed flavour.

Almonds have brown skins which are easily removed by blanching. Cover nuts in a bowl with boiling water and let stand 2 minutes, then drain. While nuts are still warm, slip off the skins by pressing each nut between thumb and forefinger. Then dry on absorbent paper. Newly blanched almonds are warm and supple – it's the best time to sliver, flake or chop them for decorations. To toast, spread the almonds (whole or sliced) in a shallow baking tray. Then bake at 180°C (350°F or gas no. 4) for 6-8 minutes – stirring now and then so they brown evenly. Or, set under a hot grill for a few minutes – watch them though, they will scorch easily.

Brazil nuts look pretty when slivered or sliced. Take off shaving with a vegetable peeler for decoration. Or, put brazils in a saucepan, cover with cold water and bring to a simmer for 3 minutes, then drain. Now they'll slice easily. While nuts are warm, use a sharp knife to cut slices or slivers. Set prepared brazil nuts under the grill for a few moments to toast them. The shavings will cut up and tinge with brown – use as decoration, they look and taste delicious.

Hazelnuts have feathery brown skins. To remove, spread hazelnuts on a shallow baking tray and set under a hot grill for a few minutes. Then tip nuts into a tea towel, rub them together and the skins will flake off. A further few moments under the heat to toast the nuts, will give them a more pronounced flavour. Hazelnuts are too hard to chop with a knife – put them in a food processor and chop using the on/off switch. Or grind finely in a Mouli grater.

Walnuts can be chopped with a knife but it's easier to snip them with a pair of scissors. For decoration buy whole walnut halves but for general purposes walnut pieces are less expensive. For finely grated walnuts a Mouli grater is the quickest. Crisp up walnuts in the oven to emphasize the walnut flavour – spread whole walnuts or walnut pieces on a shallow baking tray and bake at 180°C (350°F or gas no. 4) for 5-6 minutes, stirring often.

Pine nuts are tiny with a delicate flavour and a soft texture. To toast them it's easier to put the quantity required in a dry frying pan and shake over a moderate heat, stirring so nuts colour evenly. Then tip pine nuts on to a plate and let them cool.

Sesame seeds are also best toasted in a dry frying pan over moderate heat. Shake them continuously and when coloured evenly turn on to a plate and let them cool. Toasted sesame seeds taste and look much prettier when used in recipes.

BLUE CHEESE DIP WITH SWEET PEPPER STRIPS

SERVES 12

100 g (4 oz) Danish blue cheese

250 g (9 oz) Greek-style yogurt

2 tablespoons mayonnaise

4-6 sweet peppers – a mixture of red and yellow

Thick Greek-style yogurt has the perfect dipping consistency, soft and easy to scoop. I have been specific about the choice of cheese here because it makes all the difference to the flavour – this dip is tangy.

Break the blue cheese into a mixing bowl. Add 2 tablespoons of the yogurt and mash with a fork to get a smooth blend. Stir in the remaining yogurt and the mayonnaise and taste for seasoning (personally, I don't think any is necessary). Cover and refrigerate. **P**

Quarter the sweet peppers lengthways and remove the inner seeds. Then slice the quarters into lengthways strips – not too thin or they will bend and break when used. Enclose the pepper strips in a polythene bag and refrigerate until serving time. **P**

Turn the blue cheese dip into a serving bowl, set on a plate and surround with the pepper strips for dipping – it looks pretty if you group the colours.

GUACAMOLE DIP WITH TORTILLA CHIPS

SERVES 12

½ small onion

2 ripe tomatoes

2 tablespoons lemon juice

1 tablespoon olive oil

salt and freshly milled pepper

2 ripe avocados

3 × approx 100 g packets tortilla chips, for serving

A bright green colour is the result if you purée this mixture in the food processor at the last minute. It is all easily done if you have the marinade of vegetables ready.

Peel and finely slice the onion. Scald the tomatoes in boiling water and peel away the skins. Halve, then remove the seeds and cut up the tomato flesh. Put the tomatoes and onion slices in a small bowl. Add the lemon juice, olive oil and a seasoning of salt and pepper. Leave to marinate for several hours to draw out the juices. **P**

Halve the avocados and remove the stones. Using a tablespoon, scoop the avocado flesh into the bowl of a food processor – take care to scoop out all the very green flesh close to the skins. Cover and blend to a purée. Add the marinade of tomato, onion and lemon juice, cover and blend for a further few seconds using the on/off switch – leaving the vegetables finely chopped in preference to a smooth purée.

Turn the guacamole dip into a serving bowl, set on a plate and surround with the tortilla chips for dipping.

SMOKIE MOUSSE ON PUMPERNICKLE

MAKES 40

1 pair of smokies

300 ml (½ pint) double cream

juice of 1 lemon

2 level teaspoons horseradish
relish

freshly milled pepper

2 × approx 250 g packets
pumpernickle bread

P Can be prepared ahead: cover
and refrigerate for up to 6 hours.

Smokie mousse also makes a very good first course served with slices of dry wholemeal toast. Keep this mixture well chilled, especially when the weather is warm.

Place the smokies in a small roasting tin or baking dish and cover with boiling water from the kettle. Let stand for 2-3 minutes to loosen the skins, then drain. Peel away the skins and carefully lift the flesh from the bones.

Chop the smokie flesh in a food processor for a few seconds until fine. Turn the cream into a mixing bowl, add the lemon juice and whip to soft peaks. Add the smokie flesh, the horseradish relish and a good seasoning of freshly milled pepper and fold together wtih a tablespoon. Taste for flavour, adding salt only if necessary. **P**

Spread the smokie mousse on each pumpernickle bread slice. Then with a sharp kitchen knife, cut each slice lengthways and across into six bite-sized pieces. Top each with a little extra freshly milled pepper and arrange on serving trays.

HOUMOUS WITH BLACK OLIVES ON MELBA TOAST

MAKES 30

1 × approx 400 g can chick
peas

1 clove garlic

salt and freshly milled black
pepper

2 level tablespoons tahini
(sesame seed paste)

2 tablespoons olive oil

2 tablespoons lemon juice

4-5 bread slices from a
sandwich loaf

8 stoned black olives

Houmous is a purée of chick peas with garlic, lemon and the sesame seed paste called tahini (the latter is available from a delicatessen or health food stores). Mash the ingredients with a fork if you like a coarse texture or purée in a food processor for a smooth mixture. Keep the consistency fairly thick for spooning – a thinner consistency is nice as a dip.

Drain the can of chick peas and mash them with a fork to make a thick purée. Peel the garlic, then crush to a paste with a little salt. Add the garlic, tahini, olive oil, lemon juice and a seasoning of pepper to the chick peas and mix together. Or turn all ingredients into a food processor bowl and purée until smooth. Taste for flavour. **P**

Prepare small triangles of melba toast as follows: toast the bread slices on both sides under the grill (not in the toaster). With a sharp kitchen knife, trim off the crusts and then cut each toast slice through the middle to split it into two thin

P Can be prepared ahead: cover houmous and refrigerate for up to 6 hours. Keep melba toast in an airtight tin or polythene bag.

sheets. Cut each of these crossways into four triangles. Slip the toast triangles back under the grill (with untoasted sides towards the heat) until browned and the tips curl up. Let cool completely. **P**

Cut the black olives into thin slivers and mix into the houmous. Spoon the mixture on to the toast triangles for serving.

CELERY STUFFED WITH STILTON PÂTÉ

MAKES 40

175-225 g (6-8 oz) blue Stilton cheese

3 tablespoons single cream

225 g (8 oz) cream cheese

50 g (2 oz) shelled walnuts

8-10 stalks celery

paprika or chopped celery leaves, to garnish

P Can be prepared ahead: cover and refrigerate for up to 6 hours.

Celery stalks make useful troughs for a variety of mixtures. Alternatives here could be taramosalata (see page 214) or smoked mackerel pâté (see below).

Trim away the rind and break the Stilton into a mixing bowl. Mash very thoroughly with a fork, adding the single cream to make a smooth purée. Add the cream cheese and mix well. Or put all the ingredients in the bowl of a food processor and blend until smooth. Chop the walnuts and mix in by hand.

Separate the celery stalks (reserve any inner green leaves for garnish), scrub well and, with a sharp knife, pull away the celery strings. Spread the Stilton cheese pâté along each stalk to fill the hollow. **P**

Sprinkle the celery stalks with paprika or with finely chopped celery leaves. With a sharp knife, cut each across in 2.5 cm (1 inch) pieces. Arrange on a serving platter.

SMOKED MACKEREL CROÛTES

MAKES 40

225 g (8 oz) smoked mackerel – about 2 medium fillets

50 g (2 oz) butter, at room temperature

100 g (4 oz) cream cheese, at room temperature

juice ½ lemon

2 level teaspoons horseradish relish

salt and freshly milled pepper

This smoked mackerel pâté has proved very popular – the addition of horseradish relish complements the rich flavour of the smoked fish. Try serving this with hot French bread or dry toast slices for a menu starter.

Pull away the skin from each smoked mackerel fillet and flake the flesh on to a plate. In a mixing bowl, cream the butter until soft, then beat in the cream cheese. Add the flaked fish, lemon juice, horseradish relish, a seasoning of salt and pepper and the cream and beat to a smooth mixture. Or place all ingredients in a food processor bowl and blend to a smooth purée. **P**

Spread or spoon the smoked mackerel pâté on each toast

4 tablespoons single cream

40 toast croûtes (see below)

P Can be prepared ahead: cover and refrigerate overnight.

croûte. Arrange on serving trays and cover. Will stand for 1-2 hours before serving.

● **Toast croûtes:** Slice one long baguette across into 5 mm (¼ inch) thick slices – you should get about 40 from one stick. Spread out in a roasting tin or on baking trays and dry out in an oven heated to 160°C (325°F or gas no. 3) for 20-30 minutes or until the slices are crisp and pale golden. Let cool completely, then store in a tightly lidded tin or in a sealed polythene bag. Will keep for several days.

TARAMOSALATA CROÛTES

MAKES 40

225 g (8 oz) smoked cod's roe

150 ml (¼ pint) olive oil

1 thick slice white bread

2 tablespoons water

1 clove garlic or thin slice of onion

2 tablespoons lemon juice

freshly milled pepper

40 toast croûtes (see above)

chopped fresh chives or spring onions to garnish

P Can be prepared ahead: cover and refrigerate overnight.

Taramosalata is something I would never buy – the homemade version is so much nicer. If you get in the smoked roe a day or so ahead, keep it refrigerated and well covered to contain the flavour.

Put the piece of smoked cod's roe in a mixing bowl, pour over boiling water from the kettle to cover and let stand for 2-3 minutes to loosen the skin. Drain and peel off as much of the skin as possible – lightly smoked roe will peel more easily. Cut the roe in pieces, put in a bowl with 2 tablespoons of the olive oil and leave to soften for 15 minutes.

Meanwhile, trim the crusts from the bread slice and soak the bread in the water for a few minutes. Squeeze the bread dry – it should be soft and pulpy. Peel the garlic and chop finely. Press the cod's roe and oil through a sieve (to remove any traces of skin) and place in a food processor bowl. Add the soaked bread, lemon juice and garlic (or onion). Cover and blend to a purée. With the machine still running, pour in the rest of the oil through the feed tube until the mixture is thick and light. Taste and season with freshly milled pepper. **P**

Spread or spoon the taramosalata on to each toast croûte. Sprinkle with chopped chives or spring onion. Arrange on serving trays and cover. Will stand for 1-2 hours before serving.

AUBERGINE AND MUSHROOM CROÛTES

MAKES 40

2 medium aubergines, about
  450 g (1 lb)

1 bunch (6-8) spring onions

225 g (8 oz) cream cheese

2 tablespoons lemon juice

salt and freshly milled pepper

40 toast croûtes (see below)

100 g (4 oz) button
  mushrooms, to garnish

Most cooks slice and fry aubergines, but there are more interesting things to do if you start with a purée. It's easy to bake aubergines in the oven until they are black and soft, then you can use the flesh to make this delicious spread.

Heat the oven to 180°C (350°F or gas no. 4).

Remove the green leaves at the stalk ends and prick the aubergines all over with a fork. Set them in the heated oven, on the oven shelf, and bake for 45 minutes or until the skins are wrinkly and the aubergines feel quite soft. Let them cool for 10 minutes, then peel off the skins and squeeze the aubergines to get rid of the bitter juices. Chop the flesh coarsely.

Trim the spring onions, then chop all the white and some of the green stems. In a mixing bowl, soften the cream cheese by beating with a spoon, then add the aubergine flesh, spring onions, lemon juice and a good seasoning of salt and pepper and mix to a smooth soft purée. Or put all the ingredients in a food processor bowl and blend to a smooth purée. **P**

Spoon or spread the aubergine mixture on each of the toast croûtes.

Brush or wipe (don't wash) the button mushrooms. Trim the stalks level with the caps, then slice the mushrooms thinly. Take the best mushroom slices and press one on top of each aubergine croûte. Arrange on serving trays and cover. Will stand for 1-2 hours before serving.

P Can be prepared ahead: cover and refrigerate overnight.

SMOKED SALMON AND CUCUMBER CANAPÉS

MAKES 30

225 g (8 oz) smoked salmon –
  slices or off-cuts

50 g (2 oz) unsalted butter

1 tablespoon grapeseed or
  other mild oil

2 tablespoons lemon juice

freshly milled pepper

4 tablespoons double cream

1 medium cucumber

paprika or sprigs fresh dill, to
  garnish

Smoked salmon pâté is expensive to make even if you use off-cuts, but the flavour is delicious. Cucumber slices make novel canapé bases, but this is just one more mixture that would also taste very good on toast croûtes (see page 214).

Put the smoked salmon pieces in a food processor bowl and add the butter, oil and lemon juice. Cover and blend to a purée. Add a good seasoning of freshly milled pepper and the cream. Cover and blend again to get a smooth pink pâté. **P**

Trim the cucumber – slices will look pretty if you use a canelle knife to remove strips of peel from the sides. Peel the cucumber if you prefer. Slice the cucumber across in 5 mm (¼ inch) thick slices – not too thin or they will be difficult to

P Can be prepared ahead: cover and refrigerate overnight.

pick up. Cover and refrigerate the slices until nearer serving time

Spoon or pipe the smoked salmon pâté on each cucumber slice. Top with a dusting of paprika or sprigs of dill. Arrange on platters not more than 1 hour before serving.

PIZZA BITES

MAKES 24

3 medium onions

2 tablespoons olive oil

2 level tablespoons concentrated tomato purée

2 tablespoons water

1 tablespoon red wine vinegar

1 teaspoon light muscovado sugar

salt and freshly milled pepper

1 level teaspoon dried mixed herbs

2 × approx 50 g (2oz) cans anchovy fillets

8 stoned black olives

For the pizza crust

350 g (12 oz) self-raising flour

¼ level teaspoon salt

1 level tablespoon baking powder

75 g (3 oz) butter

25 g (1 oz) grated Parmesan cheese

200 ml (7 fl oz) mixed equal parts milk and water

1 tablespoon olive oil

P Can be prepared ahead: replace pizza bites on the baking tray and completely cover with kitchen foil. Warm through in a heated 180°C (350°F or gas no. 4) oven for 10 minutes.

This can be baked as one sheet, then cut into bite-sized pieces for serving. There is no yeast dough to make, just a simple scone mixture with a quick onion, tomato and herb topping.

Peel and finely chop the onions. Heat the oil in a frying pan, add the onions and cook gently for about 10 minutes to soften. Stir in the tomato purée, water, red wine vinegar and sugar and mix well. Draw off the heat. Season with salt and freshly milled pepper and let the mixture cool.

To make the pizza crust, sift the flour, salt and baking powder into a medium mixing bowl. Add the butter cut in pieces and rub in with fingertips. Add the cheese and mix. Stir in the mixed milk and water and mix to a rough dough in the bowl. Turn on to a floured surface and knead for a moment just to smooth the surface. Cover with the upturned mixing bowl and let rest for 10 minutes.

Heat the oven to 200°C (400°F or gas no. 6).

Roll out the prepared dough and press over a buttered 32.5 × 22.5 cm (13 × 9 inch) biscuit tray (with a rim) or baking sheet. Prick all over with a fork and brush lightly with the olive oil.

Spread the tomato mixture over the surface and sprinkle with the mixed herbs. Drain the anchovy fillets and chop coarsely. Sliver the olives. Scatter both over the pizza crust. Set in the heated oven and bake for 20 minutes or until golden. Trim the crusts and slice the pizza lengthways and crossways into serving portions. **P**

GOAT'S CHEESE TOASTS

MAKES 30

1 baguette or French stick

2 × approx 200 g (7 oz)
  log-shaped goat's cheeses –
  about 2.5-4 cm (1-1½ inches)
  in diameter

2-3 tablespoons walnut oil

paprika, to garnish

P Can be prepared ahead: cover
with clear film but do not
refrigerate.

*Just a fashionable version of toasted cheese, but I must admit,
when heated through, goat's cheese takes on a mouthwatering
soft texture and is very good to eat.*

Heat the oven to 180°C (350°F or gas no. 4).

Slice the baguette across in 5 mm (¼ inch) thick slices. Heat
the grill to hot and arrange the bread slices on the grill rack.
Toast the bread slices on one side only.

Unwrap the goat's cheese and slice in rounds of about the
same thickness as the bread slices or just a little more – you
should get about 15 slices from each cheese. It helps to use a
sharp kitchen knife and to dip the blade in a jug of hot water
between each slice.

Set a slice of goat's cheese on the untoasted side of each
bread slice. **P**

Brush the cheese slices with walnut oil and sprinkle lightly
with paprika. Arrange the slices close together on one or more
baking trays. Set in the heated oven and bake for 7-8 minutes
or until the cheese is warm and beginning to soften. Transfer to
a platter and serve at once.

GINGER CHICKEN SATAYS

MAKES 40

4 skinned chicken breast fillets

150 ml (¼ pint) natural yogurt

1 level teaspoon garam masala

½ level teaspoon turmeric

1 level teaspoon grated fresh
  root ginger, or ¼ level
  teaspoon ground ginger

2 tablespoons lemon juice

1 tablespoon olive oil

salt and freshly milled pepper

P Can be prepared ahead: keep in
a cool place for up to 3-4 hours.

*Satays are pretty served on cocktail sticks – with a couple of
bite-sized pieces on each one. Try the spiced chicken satay (see
page 190) for an alternative version.*

Trim the chicken fillets and cut each one into bite-sized pieces
– this is easiest if you slice the breasts lengthways and then
crossways. In a mixing bowl, combine the yogurt, garam
masala, turmeric and ginger. Add the lemon juice, oil and a
seasoning of salt and pepper. Mix well, then add the chicken
pieces and stir to coat them all over. Cover and marinate for at
least 4 hours or overnight in the refrigerator.

Heat the grill to moderately hot and set the grill rack about
7.5 cm (3 inches) from the heat source. Lift the chicken pieces
from the marinade using a perforated spoon and place in a
shallow baking dish. Set directly under the heated grill and
cook for 10-12 minutes. Stir up chicken pieces as they cook.

Spear two pieces of chicken on each of about 40 cocktail
sticks. Let cool completely. **P**

SMOKED SALMON ROLLS

MAKES 40

1 large unsliced wheatmeal or
brown loaf

100 g (4 oz) unsalted butter, at
room temperature

450 g (1 lb) smoked salmon,
thinly sliced

freshly milled pepper

lemon juice

2-3 lemons, to garnish

Straight smoked salmon sandwiches take a lot of beating when they are cut small to be served with drinks, but these rolls do look pretty and are worth the extra trouble. Once sliced and arranged, keep well covered until the moment of serving – you know how quickly bread dries and we don't want any curled-up edges!

Using a long sharp knife, cut away all the crusts from the loaf except the bottom one. Then put the unsliced loaf in the freezer for about 1 hour, so the bread texture firms up and it's easier to cut. Holding the bottom crust, cut the loaf in thin slices lengthways – you should get about 8 slices; the bread slices will thaw again very quickly, in about 10 minutes.

Butter each bread slice to the very edge. Arrange the trimmed smoked salmon slices to cover. Season with a little freshly milled pepper and squeeze over just a little lemon juice. Starting at one short end, roll up each bread slice tightly. Wrap individually in clear film or kitchen foil and refrigerate for several hours. **P**

Cut the chilled rolls across in 5-10 mm (¼-½ inch) thick slices and you will get a pretty pinwheel effect. Arrange on a serving tray with cut lemon wedges for garnish. Keep covered with clear film until ready to serve.

P Can be prepared ahead: keep
refrigerated overnight.

HOT BACON ROLL-UPS

MAKES 24

12 rashers streaky bacon

24 tenderized stoned prunes or smoked oysters, or 1 × approx 350 g can pineapple chunks

There's an easy way to cook these bacon rolls – by threading them on long kebab skewers. Then you can grill and turn them all at once using the whole of the grill pan. It would be easy to make double the amount with a choice of fillings.

Trim rinds from the bacon rashers and stretch the rashers by pressing them flat with a knife blade along the surface of a chopping board. Cut each rasher in half. Roll a prune, smoked oyster or pineapple chunk in each piece of bacon. Thread the 'roll-ups' close together, on long kebab skewers. **P**

Heat the grill to hot and set the grill rack about 7.5 cm (3 inches) from the heat source. Set the skewers under the heat and cook for 3-5 minutes, turning the skewers to cook both sides – the bacon should be crisp.

Push the roll-ups off the skewers with a fork. Spike each one with a cocktail stick and transfer to a serving platter. Serve hot.

Angels on horseback: If you want to do the real thing – you'll need 2 dozen fresh oysters opened on the half shell so they retain their juices. Poach the oysters in their own liquor (juices) very gently for 2 minutes only. Drain. Dust lightly with freshly milled pepper and sprinkle with a few drops of lemon juice. Wrap each one in bacon and grill as above.

P Can be prepared ahead: cover and refrigerate for up to 4 hours.

SESAME PRAWN FINGERS

MAKES 24

225 g (8 oz) peeled, cooked prawns

1 egg white (size 2)

¼ level teaspoon salt

1 level tablespoon chopped spring onion

1 level teaspoon grated fresh root ginger

1 level tablespoon cornflour

6 thin slices white bread

2-3 tablespoons sesame seeds

oil for frying

These are crunchy and have a definite prawn taste. Make sure you drain them well on absorbent kitchen paper.

Put the prawns in a food processor bowl. Add the egg white, salt, spring onion, fresh root ginger and cornflour. Cover and blend to a smooth paste. Alternatively, chop the prawns with a kitchen knife and mix in the other ingredients with a wooden spoon. Cover and refrigerate for 30 minutes.

Spread the bread slices thickly with the prawn paste. Trim the crusts and cut the slices in half. Spread the sesame seeds on a plate and dip the bread slices (prawn side down) in the sesame seeds. Press firmly, coating them evenly. Cover and refrigerate for at least 1 hour. **P**

Pour sufficient oil into a frying pan to cover the bottom to a

P Can be prepared ahead: keep refrigerated for up to 4 hours.

depth of 5 mm (¼ inch). Set over moderate heat and when hot, slide in the bread pieces, sesame seed side down. Fry until golden, turning to brown both sides. (You will have to fry these in batches.) Drain the slices on absorbent kitchen paper, then divide slices into fingers and arrange on a plate for serving.

SALTED AND SPICED NUTS

SERVES 12

Salted Brazil nut chips

350 g (12 oz) shelled Brazil
  nuts

15 g (½ oz) butter

sea salt

Spiced mixed nuts

350 g (12 oz) mixed shelled
  nuts – Brazils, cashews and
  walnuts – or just one kind

½ level teaspoon mild chilli
  powder

¼ level teaspoon ground
  coriander

¼ level teaspoon ground cumin

1 level teaspoon garam masala

15 g (½ oz) butterz

P Can be prepared ahead: will keep for 1 week or more.

Brazil nut chips are made by shaving slices; spiced mixed nuts are left whole. Both look interesting and will go down well.

Heat the oven to 180°C (350°F or gas no. 4).

Salted Brazil nut chips: Put the Brazil nuts in a saucepan, cover with cold water and bring to the boil (it is best to do half at a time). Simmer for 3 minutes, then drain. With a sharp kitchen knife, cut the warm nuts lengthways in slivers. Spread in a baking dish or baking tray. Add the butter in flakes and sprinkle with sea salt from a mill. Set in the heated oven and bake for 15 minutes or until toasted, stirring occasionally.

Spiced mixed nuts: Spread the nuts in a baking dish or baking tray. Sprinkle over the chilli powder, coriander, cumin and garam masala. Add the butter in flakes. Set in the heated oven and bake for 15 minutes or until toasted, stirring occasionally.

Transfer the hot salted or spiced mixed nuts on to absorbent kitchen paper. Let cool completely, then tip into a bowl for serving. **P**

INDEX

ACKNOWLEDGEMENTS

Photographs reproduced by kind permission of
IPC SouthBank Publishing Group.
Mike Botha: pp. 11, 138-39
Martin Brigdale: pp. 10, 14, 15, 198-99
Simon de Courcey Wheeler: pp. 54-5, 66-7, 70, 94-5
Laurie Evans: front cover, back cover, title page, pp. 6, 206-7
Peter Myers: pp. 114-15
Alan Newnham: pp. 18-19
Andy Seymour: pp. 162-63

All illustrations by Mike Allport.

Thanks to my editor at Pavilion, **Maria Leach** and to my copy-editor
Norma MacMillan for all their valuable help.

My thanks also to the following colleagues at *Woman's Journal*:

Editor: **Deirdre Vine**
Deputy Art Editor: **Cherry Ramseyer**
Secretary: **Debbie Wells**
Home Economist: **Caroline Young**

And to **Laurie Purden** MBE, ex-Editor of *Woman's Journal*, with whom I
worked for many years.